Movie Medievalism

Movie Medievalism

The Imaginary Middle Ages

Nickolas Haydock

McFarland & Company, Inc., Publishers
Jefferson, North Carolina, and London

Chapter 3 originally appeared in different form in
Studies in Medievalism 12, "Film and Fiction: Reviewing in
the Middle Ages."

Chapter 4 originally appeared in different form in
Exemplaria 19.2 (Summer 2007).

Chapter 6 is an extended version of a chapter that will appear in
the *Blackwell Companion to Arthurian Literature* to be published
in 2008.

LIBRARY OF CONGRESS CATALOGUING-IN-PUBLICATION DATA

Haydock, Nickolas.
    Movie medievalism : the imaginary Middle Ages /
Nickolas Haydock.
        p.   cm.
    Includes bibliographical references and index.

    ISBN 978-0-7864-3443-5
    softcover : 50# alkaline paper ∞

    1. Middle Ages in motion pictures.   I. Title.
PN1995.9.M52H39   2008
791.43'658401— dc22   2008005531

British Library cataloguing data are available

Cover photograph: *The Messenger: The Story of Joan of Arc*, 1999,
France (Sony Pictures Entertainment/Photofest)

Manufactured in the United States of America

McFarland & Company, Inc., Publishers
  Box 611, Jefferson, North Carolina 28640
    www.mcfarlandpub.com

For my dear mother, Margaret,
and my sweet wife, Socorro

Acknowledgments

My debts to family and friends, colleagues and students, institutions and administrators in the completion of this book are all too real. Pride of place goes to three exceptional teachers at the University of Iowa who became mentors and continue as dear friends: Gertrud Champe, Stavros Deligiorgis, and Roger Hornsby. I could never begin to recount, much less repay, the kindness and patience of these different people in their different ways; I can only renew my commitment to pay it forward. Tom Shippey first encouraged my halting steps into the world of movie medievalism and keeps on setting standards for erudition and generosity that both daunt and inspire us mere mortals. Richard Burt kindly invited me to give a plenary at the University of Florida for the conference "Getting Medieval on the Movies" and later to serve as co-guest editor of a special cluster of *Exemplaria* (19.2) on movie medievalism (edited by R.A. Shoaf). Richard's comments on chapters 4 and 5 of this book have been invaluable. Edward Risden chimed in at a crucial moment with practical advice and personal conviction. The indefatigably supportive members of the Medieval Association of the Midwest have listened to some of these ideas far too many times and have helped me stay connected to the wider world of medieval studies up north. And members of the College English Association of the Caribbean have given me a friendly forum in Puerto Rico. My students in a series of courses on the topic at the University of Puerto Rico, Mayagüez, have kept the home fires stoked with their challenging responses to these films, and my colleagues in the Department of English have all been, in various ways, a constant source of inspiration. The Faculty of Arts and Sciences, under the leadership of deans Waded Cruzado and Moises Orengo, provided release time from teaching and two sabbatical leaves, which allowed me to complete this and other projects. I also want to extend my thanks for permission to use revised versions of essays, originally published by *Studies in Medievalism*, *Exemplaria*, and Blackwell, which comprise respectively chapters 3, 4, and 6 of this book. Nandita Batra first taught me that the possibilities on this island to be a part of a remarkable community are as boundless as the view from her terrace. José Irizarry became the older brother I never had and continues to believe in me more than I will ever dare to believe in myself. Some debts of gratitude, of course, defy simple acknowledgment. I can only wish my father could have seen this book and give thanks that my mother will find a prominent place for it on her shelf. My wife, Socorro Rodriguez Santaliz, knows that this is her book as well as mine, for she was there for its conception and suffered along with me through the labors of bringing it to light.

Table of Contents

Preface

Though lines snake from my office door well down the hallway once a year with students asking and sometimes demanding to be added to the roll for my film class, they often have difficulty saying exactly what it is they want to study. The class lists are no help: they simply say "Special Topics in Film." As Umberto Eco archly quipped: "It seems that people like the Middle Ages." My students *love* film and are often deeply invested in their own ideas of the Middle Ages, so they find this combination very exciting. I can sympathize with their uncertainty about what to call this combination, because I'm far from sure what to call it myself. Though the study of these films has grown from a cottage industry to an influential and growing concern both inside and outside academia, the issue of terminology is far from settled. Kevin Harty offered the catchy "Reel Middle Ages," which has a number of advantages, as long as one is writing and not speaking. Lynn T. Ramey and Tison Pugh recently settled on "'Medieval' Cinema," the very preposterousness of which is wonderfully provocative. When Richard Burt and I were invited by R.A. Shoaf to serve as guest editors of a special cluster for *Exemplaria*, we chose "Movie Medievalism" to describe just what it was we and our contributors thought we were doing. We were also partial to "cinémedievalism." For me either one does just as well, but I prefer the former because it sounds a bit less exclusive. What is essential, it seems to me, is to recognize that these films are doing an especially potent form of "medievalism," which deserves to be studied for its own sake but also challenges and opens up traditional medieval studies in a number of fascinating ways.

The long and winding road that led to this book began when Tom Shippey invited me to give a paper at Leeds and then to turn that paper into an essay for *Studies in Medievalism*. By the time this published essay prompted Richard Burt to invite me to give a talk at the University of Florida conference "Getting Medieval on the Movies" (2005), I was well and truly hooked.

1

The eclectic nature of my approach relies upon the fact that there are fewer and fewer barriers between the study of the Middle Ages and the study of medievalism. Indeed, all of us will one day be accused of having done medievalism rather than medieval studies, because the word "medievalism" has grown from denoting a period style (nineteenth-century Gothic) to something like a *mode* into which collapse the scholarly, the popular, and the artistic with the passage of time. I hope that there will be much here to interest medievalists and their students, but I have also tried to engage those interested primarily in film and media studies, as well as theorists and commentators on the contemporary scene. Two fairly long chapters intended to introduce this rapidly burgeoning field through the lenses of Lacanian psychoanalysis and the Deleuzian philosophy of the time-image precede my readings of particular recent films. The first of these introductory chapters explores how a vast array of films (including both auteur cinema and popular movies) contributes to what I call our "medieval imaginary." The second chapter is concerned with how time itself functions in cinematic representations of the medieval. The final five chapters offer detailed considerations of specific examples of movie medievalism, for the most part released after the year 2000 in more or less chronological order: *First Knight, A Knight's Tale, The Messenger: The Story of Joan of Arc, Kingdom of Heaven, King Arthur, Night Watch*, and *The Da Vinci Code*.

PART ONE

*An Introduction to
Movie Medievalism*

1

The Medieval Imaginary

To recoin a phrase, movie medievalism is history in a hurry, driven by the nostalgia of popular culture, as well as the commercialization of paranoia in global capitalism. Such haste makes for an intriguing mélange, which by turns fetishizes the alterity of the Middle Ages as a temporal Other while compulsively retooling imagined continuities to fit the rapidly changing priorities of the contemporary world. Like Sigmund Freud's little grandson, what Kevin Harty has dubbed "the reel Middle Ages" plays compulsively with its reel and celluloid tether, making the medieval "gone" (*fort!*) and then staging its returns (*da!*) in attempts to master an abiding sense of loss.[1] As Freud noted, pleasure and aggression are both integral to this game. The same holds true of the *pastime* I am calling movie medievalism, which is as much about making the past gone as it is about the endlessly renewable surprises inherent in finding it again. In fact, movie medievalism is perhaps best understood as an egregious example of how Jacques Lacan suggests memory itself functions, as a series of assertions about the past in the future perfect tense: it screens what will have been, and therein lies its (*un*)*heimlich* quality. Yet this uncanny future perfect deserves to be read not solely as a contemporary pastime, but also as a production of the cinema apparatus, profoundly influenced by cinema's own history.

The study of these films was initially and perhaps inevitably centered on the reel/real distinction. The high watermark of this approach is Harty's admirable work *The Reel Middle Ages* (McFarland, 1999), which has helped to establish movie medievalism as an academic concern. Harty's book is an indispensable guide to more than 900 films and the corpus he establishes therein represents the core of this rapidly growing discipline. Here the reel/ real distinction has obvious advantages, not least of which is the brief contextualization and evaluation of films, based chiefly upon their fidelity to medieval sources. Yet if Harty demonstrates the value of such an approach,

John Aberth's *A Knight at the Movies: Medieval History on Film* (2003) reveals its limitations. Aberth treats films not according to genres, directors, or any other cinematic classification, but rather simply groups them under rubrics such as: "Viking Films," "Crusade Films," Robin Hood Films," and "Joan of Arc Films." The organization of each chapter is the real/reel distinction writ large, beginning with a survey of received opinion on the relevant topic entitled "The Background" (note the definite article and the singular noun), followed by some engaging discussions of particular films. Still, one cannot help but conclude from the structure of his argument that these films are interesting chiefly as curios in their benighted approximations of historical reality.

Certainly we can widen our notions of what counts as background to include the film apparatus itself, film genres, the history and theory of film, its relationship to movements inside and outside academia, as well as the social and economic forces that subtend the production, distribution, and reception of these films, yet the question persists: Are the reel Middle Ages to be defined and studied chiefly in terms of error? And where exactly are to be found the real Middle Ages that this terminology presupposes? Not surprisingly the reel/real distinction ends by reifying the traditional medieval studies it seems designed to partition. In classic Derridean fashion the pun marks a difference deferred, not least in rear-guard attempts to define philology or history as above and beyond such trivial pursuits. I do not advocate abandoning the real/reel distinction altogether, yet I will argue that it is considerably more useful as an analytical tool when reinscribed within the Lacanian orders of the Real and the Imaginary.

It was Freud, among his many analogies between technologies of communication and the mind, who first fleshed out the parallels between creative writing and daydreams (1989). But it was left to Christian Metz to explore the more thoroughgoing analogy between film and waking fantasy, to place the accent upon the audience rather than the author/auteur, and to locate this analogy in the realm of Lacan's Imaginary order.

> In the filmic state as in the daydream, perceptual transference stops before its conclusion, true illusion is wanting, the imaginary remains felt as such; just as the spectator knows he is watching a film, the daydream knows that it is a daydream. Regression is exhausted in both cases before reaching the perceptual agency; the subject does not confuse the images with perceptions, but clearly maintains their status as images ... (not to speak of the true daydreams, mental images, mental images recognized as such, accompanying the viewing of the film and embroidered around it; they are never taken for real; on the other hand, the subject sometimes has trouble distinguishing them from the diegesis, but this is because both belong to a rather closely related mode of the imaginary). In all of this, the filmic state and the conscious fantasy clearly belong to waking [p. 133].

Metz's *praeteritio* ("not to speak of the true daydreams...") passes over the imbrication of screened fantasies with the daydreams they provoke in audiences — a nexus of the Imaginary that perhaps accounts at least in part for the power the Hollywood dream factory is thought to have over the film-going public. If classical editing techniques suture the viewing subject into the world projected on the screen, these sutures also encourage sur-fantasies of identification with actors and the worlds they inhabit. While Metz is surely correct that screen dreams "are never taken for real" (after all, no one jumps up to defend Arthur from Mordred or Joan from her judges), the mutual implication of screen dreams and daydreams — which we might understand as an overdetermined form of reverie — helps to frame our perception of the real world we encounter when we leave the theater.

With historical films this production of reverie is considerably more powerful because the "reality-effects" of film are not immediately contravened by the reality principle. That is to say, ideas formed during a film set in contemporary times may linger beyond the cinema experience, but soon give way to more mundane experiences that are not packed with heroic action, beautiful people, or poetically just consequences. Our ideas about the distant past are perhaps more vulnerable to the lure of cinema because there is no immediate access to falsification. The very alterity of the Middle Ages works to make it an especially potent preserve of fantasy, the realm par excellence of the Imaginary. Certainly, one can go to the cinema or rent a DVD already armed with sufficient information to reject film (re)visions of the Middle Ages, or one can be provoked to seek out scholarly background or expert judgments, but there are very few people indeed who do not imagine Arthur fighting on horseback in plate armor, Joan of Arc as a battle-hardened proto-feminist, or William Wallace as a short, tartan-clad peasant.

A great deal of writing about historical films in general and about movie medievalism in particular is concerned with the problem of historical accuracy.[2] In criticism of films about the Middle Ages such work is often provoked by pre-release claims of rigorous fidelity, new discoveries, or fresh interpretations of all the available evidence. These claims almost never withstand even superficial scrutiny because the purpose for making them in the first place is not to engage sober academic reflection but rather to lay the framework for the film's reality effects and to authorize it as a site of what Lacan calls "imaginary identifications" for a mass audience. In Malcolm Bowie's succinct explanation:

> The Imaginary is the order of mirror-images, identifications and reciprocities. It is the dimension of experience in which the individual seeks not simply to placate the Other but to dissolve his otherness by becoming his counterpart.... The

> Imaginary is the scene of a desperate delusional attempt to be and to remain "what one is" by gathering to oneself ever more instances of sameness, resemblance and self-replication, it is the birthplace of the narcissistic "ideal ego" (*Idealich, moi idéal*). Lacan's "Imaginary" thus creates a bridge between inner-directed and outer-directed mental acts, and belongs as much to the objects of perception as to those internal objects for which the word is usually reserved in ordinary speech [p. 92].

For the penchant of the Imaginary to blur the distinction between fantasy and perception Lacan retained an abiding scorn. Critics of ideology as false consciousness have also been quick to see in the cinema apparatus an especially potent technology of the Imaginary, which, as Jean-Louis Baudry put it, "lives on the denial of difference: difference is necessary for it to live, but it lives on its negation" (p. 290). Baudry here references film's reliance on the persistence of vision, but calls this particular phenomenon "exemplary" and notes the disturbing effect of mechanical breakdowns in which the technology accidentally screens for audiences its own artificial process of creating movement and continuity from distinct frames of film. This denial of difference is also a crucial feature of Walter Benjamin's famous diagnosis of a "decay of the aura" in modern societies in which "the desire of contemporary masses to bring things 'closer' spatially and humanly ... is just as ardent as their bent toward overcoming the uniqueness of every reality by accepting its reproduction" (p. 223). Certainly no experience before the advent of virtual technologies has so thoroughly exemplified the loss of the aura in modern mass society than the screening of moving pictures about distant times and places in a dark theater. Theorists like François Lyotard (1984) or Frederick Jameson (1991) have also lamented the decay of historical consciousness accelerated by postmodern simulation and pastiche in analogous terms, as a collapse of what Benjamin called "the unique phenomenon of a distance."

The elision of differences is perhaps especially problematic in movie medievalism because the period, since its delineation by early modern thinkers, has been most often conceived as a radical alterity. The term "medieval" in popular culture often refers to that which is abjectly or shockingly outside the legal and customary constraints of post–Enlightenment civilization. As an expression of contempt or condemnation the term exiles the abject to the distant, other country of the past. Yet these chronological others somehow remain always and immediately the sum of all fears. In the celebrated phrase of Quentin Tarantino's *Pulp Fiction*, one "gets medieval" on someone else's hind quarters. The threat neatly combines racial and homophobic slurs (the perpetrators are to be "a coupla pipe-hittin' niggers" [sic] and the victim a good old boy same-sex rapist), while locating the medieval as an extreme beyond modern limits and perhaps even beyond the limits of language itself.[3] This "medieval" represents a species of violence that even in a hyper-violent film cannot be shown or even clearly described. To "get medieval" then is to step outside the Symbolic order into an Imaginary that collapses directly into an unspeakable, even unimaginable Real.

Certainly the most programmatic setting forth of the Imaginary/Real distinction in recent cinema is that by the theorist/director Jean-Luc Godard in his *Notre Musique* (2004). Near the middle of the film Godard himself offers a neat synopsis:

> In 1938 Heisenberg and Bohr were walking in the Danish countryside, talking about physics. They came to Elsinore castle. The German scientist said: "Oh there's nothing special about this castle!" The Danish scientist said: "Yes, but if you say 'Hamlet's castle' then it becomes special." Elsinore the Real, Hamlet the Imaginary. Shot-reverse shot. Imaginaire: certainty; Reality: uncertainty. The principle of cinema, go towards the light and shine it on our night. Our music.

The distinction holds true for the film itself in which "our music" is divided not simply into three movements but roughly into past, present, and future — structured by the tripartite realms of Dante's *Divine Comedy*. In the past, which runs right up through 9/11 and the invasion of Afghanistan, war is quite literally hell ("Royaume 1: Enfer"), a wrenching collage of horrors that freely mixes newsreel and cinema footage. Two comparatively extended sequences from Sergei Eisenstein's *Alexander Nevsky* (1938) and Akira Kurosawa's *Kagemusha* (1981) — both discussed in some detail in later chapters of this book — represent the medieval past in Godard's film. There are two ways in which one can read Godard's juxtaposition of reel and real history in this hell of images, namely, as a distinction between the cinematic spectacle and the terrible reality of human suffering or as a collapsing of the newsreel and the cinematic reel. Godard's version of the anecdote doesn't help matters much because it appears to reverse the positions we might expect Heisenberg and Bohr to take. More ambiguous still is the fact that Godard doesn't leave well enough alone; instead, he works on the newsreel footage, fashioning images that become more symbolic than documentary. I suspect Godard's point is actually a very complex and ambivalent answer to the problem of the reel versus real. Certainly we can lament the failure to separate the real from the imaginary (as we might expect Bohr to do), whereby cinematic images of the past before photography assume a status in cultural memory indistinguishable from the products of photojournalism. Yet we can also, with Heisenberg, insist that even the most precise attempts to capture reality must themselves be measured as part of the equation. For Godard, there is a difference between the imaginary and the real (the reel and the real) but it lies precisely in this uncertainty about the extent to which the latter is a product of the former. Umberto Eco's nominalist detective William of Baskerville puts all this much more succinctly. When asked what he most fears, he quickly replies, "certainty."

I will have more to say about the Real Middle Ages below, but here I want to return to the Reel Middle Ages, that is, the medieval imaginary and its expression in cinémedievalism. This imaginary is perhaps most glaringly obvious in its breach rather than its observance, most pointedly in the parodic anatomy of these films offered up in *Monty Python and the Holy Grail* (d. Terry Gilliam and Terry Jones 1975).[4] If we recall Christian Metz's point above about the exemplary nature of cinema's "denial of difference" both at the level of distinct pictures projected at 24 frames per second and in the extended sense of the elision of historical and cultural alterity, we are poised to see in the film's carnivalization of Arthurian cinema a denial of these conventional denials. Three brief examples should suffice to demonstrate this. The opening credit sequence (or rather sequence of credit sequences) is ontologically erratic: The film begins with what poses as a confusion of reels (reals?) where the opening sequence from what appears to be a black-and-white situation comedy set in postwar suburbia leads off a desultory pastiche of jarringly disjunctive introductions. The initial sequence follows the packaging, loading, and distribution of a detergent called "Dreem." This misspelled command reads like a clumsily inserted subliminal message, but of course it also travesties the idea of a mass-market dream factory. Inapposite montage always poses an implicit question for an audience: exactly what do sponsored sitcoms and their egregious product placements have in common with yet another film about King Arthur? Perhaps the profit motive is at the bottom of all cultural production, as the Marxist peasant will later maintain. But the palpable nostalgia in this "Pleasantville" depiction of peaceful suburban life in simpler times does in fact set the stage for the more deep-seated nostalgia of Arthurian cinema. Yet before we can ponder these matters in any depth, the film splice "breaks" and we watch as the reel slows down and the picture is cancelled by a naked white light. In simulating failures of continuity — both historical and technical — the film begins by literally exposing the seams (seems?) of its own simulation.[5]

The effect of the first of the opening sequences is not so much a frame-break as a frame exposure that lays bare both the apparatus as well as its attendant anachronisms. When what might loosely be termed the diegesis finally commences, we watch as Arthur and his squire ascend a hill that gradually obscures less and less of our view of them. As they reach the hilltop, another apparatus gag is revealed, this time defamiliarizing the synchronous presentation of image and sound tracks. The knights are not on horseback, as we

Arthur (Graham Chapman) and his squire Patsy (Terry Gilliam) emerge from the mists of time without horses in Terry Gilliam and Terry Jones's *Monty Python and the Holy Grail* (1975).

were led to assume, but rather hopping up and down and hitting cocoanut shells together to simulate the sights and sounds of warriors on horseback. Of course by slowly exposing the ruse of cinema realism the gag also denaturalizes the framing of shots, making us aware that the camera conceals as well as reveals. As Siegfried Kracauer remarks:

> Unlike the immediate past, the historical past must be staged in terms of costumes and settings completely estranged from present-day life. Consequently, it is inevitable that any moviegoer susceptible to the medium should feel uneasy about their irrevocable staginess. [...] Identifying himself with the camera, that is, he does not naïvely succumb to the magic of the allegedly recaptured past but remains conscious of the efforts going into its construction [1960, p. 77].

Yet Monty Python's rather erudite joke about scarcity of warhorses in Dark Age Britain is in turn undercut by the film's recurrent elision of historical difference *within* its own diegetic Middle Ages. Arthur wears a crusader's tunic and witnesses first a nascent Peasant's Revolt and later the Black Death. He lives, as it were, simultaneously in the sixth, twelfth, and fourteenth centuries — an embodiment of the contradictions inherent in the popular understanding of a thousand years as a single historical period. "Spam!" is not only the Monty Python mantra, but it also nicely symbolizes what the sausage press of popular culture makes of the Arthurian legend. Again, the parody of the film apparatus itself is perhaps the most belabored joke of all. One of Monty Python's favorite butts is Robert Bresson's *Lancelot du lac* (1974), an experimental film that often frames shots of bodies from the torso down, and includes a great deal of un-synced, extradiegetic sound. In mocking Bresson's idiosyncratic film (and avant-garde cinema as a whole) the Monty Python troop settle some very old scores about the French appropriation of Britain's nationalist myth, albeit within the diegesis the Arthurian knights are unable to breach the walls of the stubbornly French grail castle. The cocoanut joke also constructs its own representational genealogy, alluding to the long theatrical history of sound effects, stretching back even to medieval drama itself; but this nice detail (in both medieval and modern senses) is egregiously out of place. Like certain species of swallow, the cocoanut was not indigenous to the British Isles. In sum, the opening scene rides Python's favorite hobby-horse: the idiocy of the imaginary Middle Ages.

If the medieval imaginary consists in the denial of historical difference or in too firm a belief in the coherence and continuity of historical development, then the final scene of *Monty Python and the Holy Grail* travesties not only anachronism but also facile assertions of causation and consequence. Near the end of the film "A Famous Historian" (in a nod toward BBC–style documentaries) attempts to provide a context for the historical siege of the castle seen in the background. A knight in armor (probably Lancelot) rides into the frame to cut him down. The parody cuts in a number of directions at once. The Famous Historian is both pretentious and pompous: as in many documentaries, he assumes the status of a news reporter. His position in front of the castle lends authority to his narration about what we are told to imagine is actually going on behind his back. He pays with his life for being all too successful in making the past "come alive" for his audience.[6] There are probably few directors who fail to relish the scene for its humorous punishment of this academic intrusion of the symbolic into the imaginary. Yet in the final scene of the film, the symbolic reasserts itself as the police arrive to arrest Lancelot and disperse the army besieging the castle, just as they would a rowdy group of neo-medievals on the grounds of a National Trust site. The final shot of a policeman putting his hand over the lens of the camera makes the film end as it began, by defamiliarizing the apparatus. We have bumped smack into a modern world that easily polices and contains the actualization of medieval fantasies.

Repeatedly in the medieval imaginary, though, the distant past looms threateningly at the frontiers of contemporary society. Two recent commercials — for wood stain and credit cards — position modernity as being separated from a barbaric Middle Ages by the thinnest of veneers. In a spot for Cabot varnish a homeowner daydreams that his backyard deck is being assaulted by a veritable storm of medieval weapons, including swords, spears, axes, and fireballs, though a double-take reveals an immaculate deck still beading water. In a series of commercials for Capital One, using a credit card unleashes a swarm of Viking raiders who represent the exorbitant interest fees charged by other companies. Paying with the Capital One Card stops the charging berserkers in their tracks, whereupon one turns threateningly to the camera to ask: "What's in your wallet?" Pure examples of commodity fetishism, these ads imagine medieval barbarians at the gate, held at bay by the discerning consumer. Such spots are also positioned within the siege mentality of a post–9/11 America, when George Bush quickly proclaimed that Americans could help fight the war on terror by refusing to allow the attacks to disrupt commerce.

Another prevalent trope of liminality makes wardrobes a direct portal between past and present. As the deeply cathected locus of childhood bedtime fears and fantasies, the wardrobe serves as the gate to the past in the recent *The Lion, the Witch and Wardrobe* (d. Andrew Adamson 2005) and Terry Gilliam himself, no doubt inspired by C.S. Lewis's *Narnia* series, has a medieval knight on horseback crash through a wardrobe and into the twentieth-century bedroom of a young boy in *Time Bandits* (1981). Gilliam would go on to explore the intrusion of the medieval into modern life in two later films, *Brazil* (1985) and *The Fisher King* (1991). Here the phantasmagoric medieval is partly nostalgic preserve and partly a ghost in the machine of modernization. *Brazil*'s hero is trapped in a bureaucratic information-age that coils its way into every corner of human life. His only escape is through dreams in which he soars above the constraints of a nightmarish city like an armor-clad Icarus. There he meets a damsel in distress (who bears every resemblance to the real-world leader of a terrorist conspiracy) and does battle with supernatural foes — monsters that represent the spiritual hazards of postindustrial society, such as the transistorized Samurai who bleeds fire. Sam's quest (at least in the director's cut) is unsuccessful: The romanticizing of the mind as its own place that can make a heaven of hell is finally accessible only in a lobotomy-induced, psychotic break with reality.[7] The final words of the film are "he's gone."

This conclusion prompted Slavoj Žižek's Lacanian reading of the film that, while certainly tenable, is perhaps still too optimistic:

> Although functioning as a support for the totalitarian order, fantasy is then at the same time the leftover of the real that enables us to "pull ourselves out," to preserve a kind of distance from the socio-symbolic network. When we become

> crazed in our obsession with idiotic enjoyment, even totalitarian manipulation cannot reach us [Žižek 1991, p. 128].

While I endorse and will pursue in more detail in the next section Žižek's point about fantasy becoming a "leftover of the real," his interpretation of the film takes hold of the wrong end of the cranial probe. The hero's attempts to intervene in the totalitarian state, to pull himself and his ladylove out of it are repeatedly thwarted. His distance at the end of the film from the "socio-symbolic network" does not represent the preservation of personal liberty (even of the "idiotic" variety) but rather a forced internal exile within his own mind (the result of an overzealous probing of his brain for "information") to exactly the phantasmagoric happiness the state insists all its citizens must inhabit. The view from the clouds that opens and closes the director's cut is in fact a quotation from Leni Riefenstahl's *Triumph of the Will* (1935). Psychosis is no basis for social change or individual enlightenment.

Or is it? Gilliam's later film *The Fisher King* (1991) offers a truer instance of Žižek's thesis, in which hallucinations and even catatonia provide a path through the wasteland of modern society to redemption. Of course T. S. Eliot's *The Wasteland* first transposed Jessie Weston's anthropological readings of the myth of the grail onto the late-capitalist city, but Gilliam found in the myth's original theme of renewal an imaginary space in which even the cold, violent city of New York could serve as a meeting ground for a self-destructive shock-jock and a homeless schizophrenic. The wasteland is symbolized by (but not confined to) the city dump where the human refuse of society is discarded before New York made even homelessness a crime. The grail remains ensconced in a neo-medieval castle rising incongruously from the streets of twentieth-century Manhattan. In front of that castle, as Jack (Jeff Bridges) tries to reason Perry (Robin Williams) out of his delusions of chivalric grandeur and back into the real world from which his tragedy has exiled him, the Red Knight makes his first appearance. He breathes fire and embodies the traumatic memory of a quite literally unthinkable tragedy that keeps Perry locked in his imaginary world. That the blocked memory itself takes the form of a forbidding dragon-knight, who both guards the grail castle and prohibits Perry's access to his own past, is then a richly overdetermined example of medievalism as paranoia. Like *Brazil*, *The Fisher King* explores the dark side of the medieval imaginary, wherein the traumatic kernel of the real — in exceeding the possibility of the symbolic to express or bind it to memory — takes on the hard shell of psychotic fantasy. Encased in tempered steel and flames, the Red Knight embodies the sum of all modern fears, of senseless, faceless, motiveless violence — a repressed image that continues to return in the form of an *unheimliche* figure of medieval savagery. Yet Perry's

The transistorized Samurai atop a heap of broken images in Terry Gilliam's *Brazil* (1985).

The Dragon-Knight who guards access to both the Grail Castle and the traumatic past in Terry Gilliam's *The Fisher King* (1991).

psychosis is also bountifully contagious; it possesses the magical capacity to transform drab and empty life into graceful splendor.[8] Near the end of the film Perry, like Sam in *Brazil*, has lapsed into a deep coma. Jack tries to pull him out of it by choosing to identify with Perry's fantasy. When he steals the "grail" from the rich man's castle, three men's lives are redeemed — if not by the worthless plastic trophy itself then by the sympathetic quest involved in taking it and the leap of faith this entails. The film ends with Jack and Perry lying naked in the dark of Central Park — itself a kind of preserve from the modern city — where they practice moving clouds with their minds.

There is little room in Lacan's notion of the imaginary for this kind of quixotic fantasy that creates a place for hope by denying both history and reason. The hallucinatory co-presence of the Middle Ages and the modern world is seldom as benign ideologically as it is in *The Fisher King*. The denial of difference in both the film apparatus and the living history it simulates is perhaps most evident in double-exposure or back-projection photography, which screens the spiritual presence of the past within the present. Parallel montage can also suggest not only a concurrence but also a synchronicity between widely disparate events. An early example of the first kind of denial of difference is Cecil B. DeMille's *Joan the Woman* while D. W. Griffith's *Intolerance: A Sun Play of the Ages* is a thoroughgoing example of the second kind. Both films were released in 1916 as America readied itself to enter World War I, the former opening in American theaters just as the latter was closing its unsuccessful run; both films evidence well an abiding concern with historical continuity and analogy.

Joan the Woman was the first of DeMille's grandiose historical spectacles, exploring what would be contemptuously called the "sex motive in history." Two very different versions of the film were released: an American cut, which featured a contemporary frame set in the trench warfare of twentieth-century France, and a French version, which deletes most of this frame as well as severely curtailing the role of Joan's romantic interest, Eric Trent. The term "frame" then is misleading since the bracketing scenes in the American version set in the contemporary world serve not to contain or set apart Joan's brief life in the early fifteenth century but rather to open supernatural lines of communication between the past and the present. As Robin Blaetz's engaging discussion points out: "With these abrupt temporal leaps between centuries, the film simultaneously transports the viewer into the past and brings the medieval into the present with a startling immediacy" (p. 58). This immediacy of past and present is carried out at the level both of the shot and of the diegesis. Trick photography using mirrors in the opening and closing scenes superimposes Joan as a spiritual presence within the front-line barracks of a British soldier who has discovered her sword hidden behind the wall of his hut. His vision inspires him to take on a suicidal mission in expiation for a crime against her that is initially left unspecified. The uncanny nature of this need for expiation is clarified as the historical drama unfolds: The British soldier is the reincarnation of Joan's putative lover, Eric Trent, who betrayed her to her enemies. The vision of Joan returns at the end of the film after Trent-redux has been shot in the act of planting the bomb that destroys a German trench, as Joan floats over a graveyard of the English dead sanctifying their sacrifice. Hence, while the frame, in casting Joan as a kind of tutelary deity, opens up imaginary pathways between the past and the present, the French and the English, it also forecloses any further advance of the Germans into France.

The film's imaginary projection of national alliances through romantic love relies upon a thorough sifting of national identities and affinities. The central problem becomes how to read the double identity of Eric Trent, the film's foremost invention, ideologically. The imaginary construction of Trent's dual existence (fifteenth- and twentieth-century soldier, betrayer, and redeemer) reflects a vision of English identity as constituted by a fundamental duality. In the trench warfare of the early twentieth century the constituent parts of an English character formed in the Middle Ages are violently opposed: (Saxon) German versus (Norman) French. This dual identity is the inheritance of a nineteenth-century nationalist medievalism so evident in the novels of Sir Walter Scott such as *Ivanhoe*, though here the moral valances are reversed. The medieval Trent's duplicity and the altruism displayed by his modern reincarnation are thus cast as a spiritual conflict within English national identity itself, a Manichean conflict between good and evil, between French and Saxon, which plays itself out across the centuries in a narrative of guilt and expiation. However, the more problematic issue remains of how this imaginary construction of English identity was supposed to arouse — as it undoubtedly was designed to do — American patriotism and to champion America's entrance into World War I. The French-American DeMille made a film that imaginatively collapses not only historical distinctions but geographical ones as well. His heroine, Geraldine Farrar, made the point distinctly when she appeared at the Boston premiere of the film wrapped in an American flag. Though a nation composed of immigrants from many nations, America's national character was symbolized, apparently once and for all, by the French gift of the Statue of Liberty — a personification that transcends temporal and spatial differences. In rising to defend England and France, America was defending a vital spirit of *libertas* that, while transcendent as embodied in Joan of Arc, represents what is best in the English themselves, and finds its supreme realization in the United States. As the opening title sequence of the film itself has it, Joan is "the soul of France" and "her spirit fights today."

Manufacturing continuity, analogy, even the fundamental identity of different epochs and nations by denying the aura of specific historical events depends upon abstraction just as surely as the technology of moving pictures depends upon the persistence of vision. While spectacles such as those of DeMille and Griffith offered an unprecedented abundance of visual detail in representations of history, these details were often in the service of transcendent abstractions that determined the moral relevance of these spectacles for modern audiences. One such abstraction is "love through the ages," which transcends both war and time in DeMille's *Joan the Woman* and in Griffith's two most controversial films, *Birth of a Nation* (1915) and *Intolerance* (1916). The almost limitless influence of *Birth of a Nation* not only did much to revive the Ku Klux Klan, it also established a formula for the imaginary reconstruction of the past that continues to dominate Hollywood historical spectacles up to the present day. As David A. Cook explains, its financial success "seemed to valorize Hollywood's taste for the emotional, sensational, and the melodramatic as opposed to the rational, philosophical, and discursive at the very moment of its birth" (p. 73). From Griffith's perspective though, it was the bias of his critics that prevented them from sympathizing with his nostalgic vision of "the Old South," the last bastion of a feudal order that connected the aristocracy of the agrarian South with the chivalric idealism of the Middle Ages.[9] The victory of the North in the Civil War represented the final defeat of a way of life championed in nineteenth-century medievalism by the wave of modern industrialization. Griffith's response to the charges of prejudice and the view of history as a process of progressive emancipation was *Intolerance*. The film employs at times frenetic cross-cutting, parallelism, and analogy in its recursive montage of four separate stories (set in ancient Babylon, Jerusalem in the time of Christ, sixteenth-century Paris, and contemporary America) in order to envision history as an ongoing though repetitive Manichean struggle between the forces of love and prejudice. While none of Griffith's epochs are precisely "medieval" (the nearest in time is the massacre of the Huguenauts in 1572 Paris), his insistence that "lives run parallel in their hopes and perplexities" and that the modern age compulsively repeats the past is an ideology that continues to underwrite the production of Hollywood's historical spectacles unto the present day. A recent example of a film that less explicitly casts present conflicts as a compulsive repetition of the medieval past is Ridley Scott's *Kingdom of Heaven* (2006) discussed in chapter 5 below.

Indeed, the notion of the Middle Ages as an essence abiding in the modern world beneath differences rendered superficial by the recursive or synchronistic nature of history is a continuous theme in many films throughout the last hundred years. Two brief but very disparate examples should suffice to demonstrate this. In both *A Canterbury Tale* (d. "The Archers," i.e., Michael Powell and Emeric Pressburger 1944) and *Hannibal* (d. Ridley Scott 2001), the endurance of the Middle Ages is expressed through the essential nature of character and its recursive journeys through the ages. *A Canterbury Tale* takes its clue perhaps from the unfinished state of Chaucer's work and the long tradition of supplementary tales that began in the first decade after the poet's death and continues into the present day.[10] Figuring the progress of English society as an ongoing journey to which each age contributes its own installment has imaginatively bound generations to Chaucer's *compaignye* and encouraged many to add their own stories. From Dryden in the seventeenth century through Blake in the nineteenth, Chaucer's cross-section of English society was repeatedly cast as an enduring anatomy of "God's plenty."

> 'Tis sufficient to say according to the Proverb, that here is God's Plenty. We have our Fore-fathers and Great Grand-dames all before us, as they were in Chaucer's Days; their general Characters are still remaining in Mankind, and even in England, though they are call'd by other Names.... For Mankind is ever the same, and nothing is lost out of Nature, though every thing is alter'd [qtd. in Brewer 1978, p. 167].

> Accident ever varies, Substance can never suffer change nor decay. Of Chaucer's characters, as described in his Canterbury Tales, some of the names or titles are altered by time, but the characters themselves for ever remain unaltered, and consequently they are the physiognomies or lineaments of universal human life, beyond which Nature never steps. Names alter, things never alter.... As Newton numbered the stars, and as Linneus numbered the planets, so Chaucer numbered the classes of men [qtd. in Brewer 1978, p. 251].

Blake's comparison of Newton, Linnaeus, and Chaucer is especially apropos because the latter not only "numbered the classes of men" but also repeatedly linked their *complexiouns* and their destinies to astral or planetary influence. Understanding the composition of modern society and of modern subjectivities as the expression of an abiding reality "beyond which Nature never steps," allows cinémedievalism to plot the contemporary trajectories of people and nations as the fulfillment their destinies.

The justly famous framing sequence of *A Canterbury Tale* welcomes the challenge of tracing essential continuities beneath the shock of the new. A printed page of the first sentence of the "General Prologue" in Middle English is deliberately misread in voice-over using post–Great Vowel Shift sounds and replacing archaic words with their modern equivalents so that "ferne halwes" becomes "distant shrines" and the pun in Chaucer's final couplet "seke/

seeke" becomes "seek/weak." The sickly sweet, weak metaphrase is not really modern either, but rather a kind of audio lap-dissolve that preserves some characteristics of Middle English ("perced" and "fowles" are disyllabic) to lend an archaic cadence to the deliberate, Received Pronunciation that predominates. The lesson in modernized Middle English is clear: what first appears old-fashioned or strange possesses a vital continuity with the present. Having "translated" Chaucer's sentence about natural and spiritual regeneration into a modern idiom, the montage then cuts to the pilgrim road itself along which the medieval pilgrims, to quote e.e. cummings, "come up from the never of when/come into the now of forever come riding alive."[11] The appearance of the pilgrims suggests less a flashback than a resurgence, a sense later confirmed when the contemporary "land girl" Alison (!) hears their laughter and music while caught in a reverie on that same road. Next, a legendary form cut matches the flight of the medieval Squire's hawk to a present-day German Spitfire soaring above the same landscape. The shot is widely thought to have inspired Stanley Kubrick's even more radical montage of times in *2001: A Space Odyssey* (1968), in which a bone hurled into the air in prehistoric times morphs into an orbiting space station. But the *Canterbury* sequence actually includes a double montage, that of the hawk/Spitfire, as well as a pairing of shots that perhaps takes its clue from the reincarnation of Eric Trent in DeMille's *Joan the Woman*. In the Archers' version of the time trope, the medieval squire stares up into the sky following the flight of the hawk, only to be replaced by a shot of the same face in the contemporary world — now wearing a combat helmet and British uniform. This doubling of heavenly gazes establishes what will become the signature shot of the whole film. Each of the major characters repeatedly appears to be searching for something in the heavens, but their gazes have no object, no point of reference, until the end of the film when this pose of rapt contemplation at last finds its object in the fan-vaulted ceiling of Canterbury Cathedral. The opening sequence, though, presents the modern world as a horrifying rupture. As the voice-over narrates, the newest pilgrim on the idyllic roads of Kent is an armored tank. It is just this sense of a ruptured continuity, out of touch with the spiritual resources inherent in England's landscape and architecture, that the film seeks to repair.

Certainly a candidate for the quirkiest, most idiosyncratic piece of wartime propaganda ever made, *A Canterbury Tale* takes some very odd detours indeed on its journey toward the blessings the major characters receive once they finally complete the ten-minute train ride to Canterbury. The film's hero (played by a real American soldier, not a film actor) mistakenly gets off the train one stop too early in the fictitious "Chillingbourne." For most of the film Canterbury Cathedral is seen only in prospect, just as it is in the prologue to the last of Chaucer's *Canterbury Tales*. Significantly, Chaucer's own pilgrims never reach the cathedral. This final distance between prospect and fulfillment is reached in the film, but only after the characters and audience have been instructed in the natural beauties and spiritual resources inherent in the journey itself. The didactic nature of this comedy in some sense reproduces the uneasy alliance of "sentence and solas" or jest and earnest in Chaucer's own work. For many, the Archers' tale is a restrained and loving anthem to the beauty of the English countryside, where Powell himself was raised. However, its wartime melodrama of sweethearts lost and found, of an easy cooperation between English and American soldiers, teamed with an irrepressible English "widow" to solve a mystery, is belied by the reality of a quarter million American soldiers billeted throughout England in 1943, who notoriously had little sympathy for the backwardness of the English countryside and rather too much for lonely English women themselves.

The joker in the deck of modern pilgrims is played by Thomas Colpeper (Eric Portman) a local, organic intellectual, and regional magistrate. Colpeper plays Man of Law to the film's "new woman," a (supposed) widow and city girl quaintly dubbed Alison. The Man of Law's double business is to teach soldiers an appreciation for the rural history of Kent and English women the patience of Constance. The latter duty he accomplishes by pouring glue into the hair of any woman caught out after dark. Our first sight of Alison is internally framed in the backlit doorway of the stationhouse, clad seductively in a short skirt and smoking — the epitome of the film-noir femme fatale. She offers to lead the two soldiers through the wartime blackout to their destinations in town, lighting the way with her "torch." She pays for "carrying the torch" and attempting to lead the soldiers (astray) when "the glue man," who as it turns out has punished seven other fraternizing women with this gooey fetish of his, assaults her. (An earlier draft of the screenplay had the assailant slashing women's dresses with a knife, though this was abandoned as being too overtly sexual.) The splash of sticky goo in the dark ultimately reveals a disgusting remainder, misogyny's adhesion within nostalgic attempts to preserve national identity.

Though it is perhaps difficult to imagine anything more foreign to the pastoral melodrama of *A Canterbury Tale* than the recent installment in the career of Dr. Hannibal the Cannibal Lecter (*Hannibal*, d. Ridley Scott 2001), the two films do share a vision of historical recurrence channeled through the literary and architectural monuments of the past. They also share a scene featuring a public history lecture, complete with slides, given by a morally compromised protagonist about the immediate relevance of the medieval past to the contemporary world. Albeit in much more horrific ways, Dr. Lecter, like Colpeper, orchestrates the very recursiveness of "character" that his lecture attempts to demonstrate. Lecter's academic specialty — apart from his infamous culinary expertise — is the iconographical tradition in Dante's *Commedia*, specifically the oddly overdetermined detail in medieval art of Judas's suicide by hanging *and* disembowelment. For Lecter, Judas represents a betrayal committed because of avarice, which thus explains the representation of the apostle's death as a combination of suicide and execution for treason. The last slide, which he waits to show to the Italian *commendatore* Rinaldo Pazzi until the hall has cleared, depicts the execution of Francesco de Pazzi, the detective's medieval ancestor who committed the same mortal sins of greed and suicide. The sequence begins with an outdoor performance of the opera *La Vita Nuova* in which Pazzi imagines a new life of leisure with his beautiful young wife, aptly named Allegra. At the intermission Lecter gives Allegra an italic copy of Dante's first sonnet in *La Vita Nuova*, though his overtures to her husband threaten to literalize the allegorical dream of eating human hearts. The polite flirtation between Allegra and Lecter over the sonnet includes the *questiones amoris* of courtly love, menaced by the more chilling, literal sense of love as hunger to which Pazzi now knows Lecter is devoted. Pazzi's virtual futures appear represented in the two works of Dante, yet in choosing cupidity he finds himself bound to the "divine" justice of the seventh circle of Dante's Hell with those violent against themselves — the godlike verdict of Lecter (posing as "Dr. Fell"), which deems all opposition to him as a form of suicide. A close-up of the final slide shows the medieval Pazzi (which Lecter affectedly pronounces "patsy") hanging disemboweled from the walls of the very building in which Lecter had given his lecture. The medieval Pazzi's modern descendent, who was conspiring to sell Lecter to his enemies, swings by his neck like his ancestor from the walls as his entrails also dangle from a gash in his abdomen. In painterly style Lecter deliberately crafts what is in effect a match cut to reproduce the mise-en-scènes of the slides illustrating the suicides of Judas, Pietro della Vigne and Francesco de Pazzi. If as Marx claimed, history twice repeats itself, first as tragedy and then as farce, this scene partakes of both. Pazzi of course is made to confirm the proverb that those who ignore history are destined to repeat it. Although both *A Canterbury Tale's* Colpeper as well as Hannibal Lecter prove true its converse: Those who teach history are compelled to repeat it by enforcing a kind of genealogical imperative.

The self-consciousness of *mise-en-abyme* structures in which films screen images of the medieval past within their own diegesis — such as the slide shows given by Colpeper and Lecter — should give us pause.[12] In both films the question of the use of the past is posed within the tangle of motives implicit in its representation, be they patriotic and misogynistic or the sadistic pursuit of poetic justice. The association of the monstrous and the intellectual, science and the diabolic, reanimation and reincarnation stretches back to cinema's infancy, into its dual inheritance in the realms of technology and sideshow illusion. In the early film, *The Golem* (d. Paul Wegener 1920), the Jewish magician not only creates the monster, he also screens a back-projected "movie" of the Jewish exile for his king. In the film within the film, Moses turns aside from his long journey to speak directly to his astonished medieval audience, though his message "let my people go" is clearly addressed to the early twentieth-century audience of the film as well. The magic of historical cinema, such *mise-en-abyme* structures seem to insist, resides in its séance-like summons of ghosts from the past, which have distinct messages for the present.

In surveying the Imaginary's "denial of difference" through cinematic devices like double-exposure photography, associative montage, and back-projection, I have neglected perhaps the simplest and most prevalent device for the production of "imaginary identifications," the close-up. Let me close this section, then, with a final example from an almost universally acknowledged masterpiece of movie medievalism, Carl Theodore Dreyer's *The Passion of Joan of Arc* (1921). The stark, empty mise-en-scène of Dryer's film emphasizes Joan's isolation, while the unbalanced, off-kilter nature of the few physical elements that do furnish the scenes take on nightmarish, Daliesque proportions. The film is dominated by the dream-like play of floating faces, disengaged from their bodies and unattached to any physical point of reference. Essentially the film is reduced for long sequences to Marie Falconnetti's seemingly limitless expressions as they pass across her face, only tangentially connected to the physical world around her. The film begins, like *A Canterbury Tale*, with a book — here a manuscript record of the heresy trial — from which we cut immediately to the scene of Joan's interrogation. This cross-media translation from manuscript to moving image brings the past into a longing, aching proximity with the present. If the imaginary draws the past closer, Dreyer's close-ups are the degree zero of identification where historical difference disappears completely. As a number of critics have remarked, the close-up blurs rather than defines individual identity — recall the famous anecdote about Bibi Andersson and Liv Ullmann in Berman's *Persona* (1966), who, when the film was screened for them, couldn't tell in places who was who. For Gilles Deleuze these close-ups "have pushed the face to those regions where the principle of individuation no longer holds sway" (1986, p. 108).

Joan of Arc's (Marie Falconetti) transcendent gaze sees beyond the looming menace of her judge (Maurice Schultz) in Carl Theodore Dreyer's *The Passion of Joan of Arc* (1928).

Joan's face comes loose from the past and even from the period in which the film was made, and becomes a specter haunting all futures: her shaved head, hollow cheeks, and blackened eye sockets cannot but remind us of the Nazis' final solution; the implements of her torture, filmed as shadows and crazy-wheel mechanisms, hint at the surreal ubiquity of torture; and her guards wear World War I helmets and horn-rimmed glasses. This deterritorialization is furthered even in the close-ups of Joan's gazes and expressions, unbalanced by reverse shots that would have served to orient them. What Joan sees and responds to exceed her physical environment, that is, we see her reacting not only to the inquisition but also to her own thoughts, memories, and visions of the divine — all of which remain hidden from us. The isolation and reticence of Dreyer's close-ups bring us painfully close to Joan without ever allowing us any real insight into her soul. Her very opacity to her medieval judges and to the cinema audience as well is the sign of her sublimity. What we see of Joan, we see through a lens that brings her anguish and uncertainty, her courage and resolution so painfully close that watching the film becomes its own exquisite form of torture.[13]

The Real Middle Ages

Lacan saw in modern society a waning of Symbolic efficiency, a Western world whose systemic malady is paranoid narcissism. For his celebrated contemporary avatar Slavoj Žižek, "when Symbolic efficiency is suspended, the Imaginary falls into the Real" (1999, p. 374). As belief in the big Other disappears from the horizon — that is, as faith in God, democracy, or even knowledge itself is increasingly undermined by suspicion and cynicism — postmodern subjects fantasize unfettered access to the Real. Incursions of the Imaginary into the Real are especially evident in cinema and popular culture. Three expressions of this postmodern cultural collapse for Žižek are: (1) the imaginary bridging or filling of gaps within the symbolic, (2) the reduction of the other to an imaginary counterpart of the subject, and (3) the widespread belief in conspiracy theories.[14] I mentioned above the extent to which Benjamin's "unique phenomenon of a distance" is compromised by the cinema apparatus as well as the common impression (canonized in Jameson's *The Postmodern Condition*) that the postmodern world is suffering from the lack of "historical consciousness." This loss of distance and distinction is especially striking in postmodern movie medievalism because the gap these films bridge is so profound. Our knowledge about the Middle Ages contains many lacunae and our sense of their alterity is perhaps the founding distinction of the historical consciousness Jameson laments.

But these gaps are quickly filled and distinctions quickly erased in contemporary "medieval cinema," though it is perhaps the penetration of psychology itself into popular culture that is at least partly to blame. For instance, our evidence about the lives of comparatively well-documented individuals such as Joan of Arc or William Wallace tells us relatively little about their childhood — an age that for contemporary society is the master key to the secrets of personality. Films like *The Messenger: The Story of Joan of Arc* (d. Luc Besson 1999), *Braveheart* (d. Mel Gibson 1995), *Tristan and Isolde* (Kevin Reynolds 2006), *First Knight* (d. Jerry Zucker 1995), and even *Ivan the Terrible II* (d. Sergei Eisenstein 1958) offer imaginary back stories that supplement the historical record by uncovering psychological traumas in a troubling mimicry of clinical psychoanalysis itself. In what might be called a cultural projection of counter-transference, historical lacunae, particularly those concerning the motivations of character so essential to popular cinema, become repressed content whose revelation permits "insight" into historical psyches. Indeed, in a culture where "false memory syndrome" has now become a recognized clinical disorder, we should perhaps not be surprised to see Joan of Arc and William Wallace or Tristan and Lancelot as traumatized children. But this movement "from the void of subjectivity to the inner wealth of personality" (Žižek 2001, p. 148) in fact empties the past of its enigmas and contributes considerably to the paranoia of a culture that, not content with its sum of victims, multiplies them in its imaginary diagnoses of the past. Indeed, perhaps cinema's determination to invest medieval childhoods with psychic trauma is the microcosmic expression of the grand metapsychological narrative whereby the modern world finds the source of its problems in the traumatic childhood of the Middle Ages.

The most revealing projections of movie medievalism are in the phantasmagoric filling of gaps opened in the past by modern rationalism. Here evolutionary biology and even genetics are made to offer what are in essence euhemeristic interpretations of the supernatural, analogous to the medieval tradition of interpreting pagan gods as exceptional, though human, beings. The Anglo-Saxons apparently found the existence of trolls and dragons considerably less problematic than some moderns do. The Anglo-Saxon Chronicle for the year 793 dutifully records the appearance of dragons in the sky; and Tolkien was still insisting in 1936 upon a literal reading of the dragon in *Beowulf* in his famous lecture "*Beowulf:* The Monsters and the Critics" (Tolkien 1991, p. 14–44). However, more recently in the battle between the monsters and the screenwriters, euhemerism has once again come home to roost. The film made from Michael Crichton's novel *The Eaters of the Dead* (*The Thirteenth Warrior,* d. John McTiernan 1999) is based on the pseudoscientific proposition that the reality behind the "*Caines cynn*" in *Beowulf* was the miraculous survival of pockets of Neanderthals into Dark Age Denmark. The *fyr-draca* is also explained by rational euhemerism: It is not a fire-breathing dragon but rather a slithering line of cavalry who attack at night and hurl incendiary spears. The evolutionary contradiction of Neanderthal cannibals who also domesticate horses doesn't trouble Crichton or McTiernan.

John Gardiner's sympathetic portrayal of the monster as an existential antihero in his superb novel *Grendel* (1971) has recently inspired yet another gap-filling euhemerism, which combines genetics and the psychology of victimization. According to *Beowulf and Grendel* (d. Sturla Gunnarsson 2006), trolls were actually those ostracized by society because of congenital birth defects. Grendel's unending feud against Hrothgar is not simply motiveless malignity but rather the creature's revenge for the king's senseless murder of Grendel's similarly handicapped father. In this ruthlessly euhemeristic world, the Irish missionary Brendan is a self-deluding charlatan who represents for Hrothgar a desperate last resort. Both Christianity and Germanic paganism become "coloring" in an imagined "real" story of the Other, transformed into a lower-case "other." False memory syndrome is extended not just to the imaginary childhood traumas of nationalist freedom fighters like Joan of Arc or William Wallace, but even to mythical monsters like Grendel, who witnesses as a boy the murder of his father. As we might expect, Beowulf finally kills Grendel, though the monster lives long enough to get a child upon a human witch, thereby ensuring that the bloodline stretching back (we imagine) to the similarly challenged Cain himself will continue to haunt civilization into the future. The film actually has provocative (if predictable) things to say about the irrepressible nature of resistance movements and their "monstrous" tactics, as the traumatic offspring of dead fathers. However, politically correct back stories about how we create monstrous others are not an isolated phenomenon. Take for instance the futurist-medieval *Beowulf* (d. Graham Baker 1999), where Hrothgar himself fathers Grendel upon the demonic ghost of a woman whose whole city he has annihilated. But such cross-species or cross-ontological miscegenation is perhaps not as benign as it first appears. That imperialism and manifest destiny create others not only by dint of arms but also through the deployment of evolutionary and genetic discourses is beyond debate.[15] So too is the notion, potent already in the Old English *Beowulf* and prevalent in today's world as well, that conflicts (be they tribal, racial, or religious) have a kind of immortality because they breed alienated, vengeful children.[16] The Grendel of the Old English poem descends from a line of monsters who mated with human women, just as in the films *Beowulf* and *Beowulf and Grendel* monstrous offspring are sired upon a woman-turned-demon and a witch, respectively. In *The Thirteenth Warrior*, as Lynn Shutters reminds us, the *Wendol* are a matriarchal society but one perversely fecund with death — the lair of the mother is a cave teeming with human skulls (pp. 83–87). In these politically correct fantasies, vengeance and hatred, in a rare paroxysm of fidelity to the medieval poem, are a function of the horrible fertility of the monstrous feminine.

The second manifestation of the collapse of the Imaginary into the Real is, as Tony Meyers explains, "the Other reduced to the other, an imaginary counterpart who is not a subject in his/her own right but, in effect, an aspect of a self-sufficient ego (the other) with a message for him/her" (p. 59). Certainly the secret that Hrothgar is really Grendel's father in Graham Baker's *Beowulf* is such a message. So is the brooding offspring Grendel leaves behind in Gunnarsson's *Beowulf and Grendel*. A naked Lancelot in *Excalibur* (d. John Boorman 1981) does battle with an armored double of himself as his internal struggle between desire for Guinevere and loyalty to Arthur reaches a fevered pitch in his dreams. The message this double conveys is Lancelot's self-betrayal: the one opponent he cannot defeat is his ideal self with whom his desires have placed him in deadly conflict. In *Brazil*, when the hero unmasks the transistorized Samurai, he also finds his own face beneath the helmet. That Sam sees himself beneath the mask of a Japanese boogeyman *is* an insight: It travesties Western fears about the menace of the "impersonal" Japanese and their technological power. But that Sam's victory is ultimately revealed as self-destructive underscores as well the futility of his resistance. Doubling and "imaginary counterparts" is also recurrent theme in my discussion of Luc Besson's *The Messenger* in chapter 4; here I would only note how the multiple identities of the figure "Conscience" (Dustin Hoffman et al.) first appear to be versions of the Big Other, that is, God himself, who instructs and later rebukes Joan, only to be revealed finally as the mere phantoms of a suggestible psyche. Her message then is not from God but rather the manifestation of her own tortured Conscience, whose appearance also makes abundantly evident postmodern cinema's colonization of visionary, spiritual experience by an agnostic, psychoanalytic rationalism. And it is this personified part of herself, this little other that provides Joan with the answers she seeks and that leads her to insight about her self, a self that the imaginary psychobiography poises between the pathos of victimization and the psychopathology of religious zealotry. In its relentless production of pseudo-scientific euhemerisms, movie medievalism is in the business of projecting messengers with messages that contemporary audiences will receive as "relevant."

Finally, perhaps the most symptomatic characteristic of a modern age grown skeptical of the master narratives that lent meaning to historical change is the current fascination with conspiracy. The conspiracy mentality is in many ways the converse of the process outlined above in which supernatural Others are naturalized into little others, medieval counterparts with messages for modernity. Here the Big Other reappears as a secret the past has withheld from the present. Žižek is quick to remind us that the "paranoid construction" of conspiracy theory is a *symptom* and not the pathology itself. It is "on the contrary, an attempt to heal ourselves, to pull ourselves out of the real 'illness,' the 'end of the world,' the breakdown of the symbolic universe, by means of this substitute formation" (1991, p. 19). Here Žižek seems to ignore the role of apocalyptical thinking in much conspiracy theory and, perhaps like many adherents of the "hermeneutics of suspicion," falls prey to it himself. In a number of recent films a figure of modern rationality, set incongruously within a medieval world of pagan and/or Christian superstition, manages to debunk medieval conspiracy theories only to uncover a more deep-seated continuity between medieval and modern.

In Jean-Jacques Annaud's *The Name of the Rose* (1986), William of Baskerville incarnates a tradition of investigation that stretches from a fourteenth-century inquisitor/nominalist through the nineteenth-century empirical detective Sherlock Homes and down to Umberto Eco's own potent combination of semiotics and medieval scholarship. William's nemesis, Jorge de Burgos, attempts to repress at all costs a secret book — the authority of which could profoundly alter the course of Western society, perhaps even stemming the tide of religious intolerance and totalitarianism that washed over later ages. But William and Jorge are angels of history battling over a future always already determined by the world to which the audience returns when they walk out of Annaud's movie or close Eco's book. This elegiac fatalism is its own form of apocalypse, one which reveals the past's complicity in the present.

Eco himself would later send up conspiracy theories in *Foucault's Pendulum* (1989), but already in *The Name of the Rose* (1983) he can be seen forging his own conspiracies, as well as the book whose loss supposedly changed the world. Of course it is not really the putative second book of Aristotle's *Poetics*, on comedy, that Jorge partially ingests and which ultimately burns along with him in the labyrinth, but rather M. M. Bakhtin's *Rabelais and His World* (1984). Like the Derridean postcard, Bakhtin dictates to Aristotle a text whose authority and coherence would have produced the truly dialectical polyphony so effectively marginalized in the medieval synthesis.[17] Jorge's suicidal rumination on this post-book uncannily echoes the painful, perhaps apocryphal story of a censored and exiled Bakhtin, who died of emphysema, smoking his own manuscripts, page by agonizing page, in a Soviet gulag. Bakhtin's valorization of the marginal in medieval culture as a potentially revolutionary comedy erases its own traces in the film — all who read it are swept up into an apocalyptic pattern, their corpses becoming signs in Jorge's forgery of God's book of nature, which threatens to foreclose the future. Jorge is at war with the future itself; he attempts to incarnate a world of the future-as-same, "a divine recapitulation," where repetition is without significant difference. In this we might argue that from Eco's point of view he is at least partially successful. Certainly Eco himself is far from sanguine about the dialectical possibilities of Bakhtin's "carnivalesque" lower stratum; he sees the festive spirit as a safety value for popular discontent rather than as a revolutionary heterodoxy.[18] Yet the contest for the future between William and Jorge de Burgos echoes the playful conflict between Eco and Jorge Luis Borges. One abiding characteristic of medievalism, as we have seen, is its future perfect, teleological constructions: The present constructs the past by which it will have been determined.

Annaud's discussion of filming *The Name of the Rose* in the audio-commentary to the DVD reveals a great deal about his "pastiche" of Eco's novel. One thing it reveals is the pastiched nature of historical filmmaking. Annaud

Sean Connery (as William of Baskerville) and F. Murray Abraham (as Bernardo Gui) battle over which book will determine the future in Jean-Jacques Annaud's *The Name of the Rose* (1986).

delights in demonstrating the seams of his illusion, from the detailed richness of the mise-en-scène to the continuity editing between built sets, authentic dressed interiors, and establishing shots of historical locations. The director adds the mandatory fog to exterior shots of his medieval monastery, though the climate itself cooperates in the end and gives him snow on the last day of principal photography, when he shoots the film's final sequence. The fire he has set within the labyrinth rages out of control, endangering the actors and consuming most of the set. He takes his clue for the herbalist's cell from a painting by Holbein and has dozens of reproductions cast from objects in museums. In this most bookish of films, a team of monks is employed to reproduce the pages of illuminated manuscripts seen in the film, each of which reportedly took a single monk six months to accomplish, yet these precious simulacra also have a way of disappearing from the set! The value of these copies seems for Annaud evidence of the film's authenticity, its attention to detail.[19] Yet, wittingly or not, the director's audio commentary on the film's production yields a real world of filmmaking haunted by its own imaginary.

It is at the level of the film's thematics that the medieval as the Lacanian Real of modernity is most apparent. The quietly momentous debate over

Christ's ownership of the clothes he wore is for Annaud a distant echo of the battle between capitalism and socialism. The Franciscans lose the debate (which is a loss for socialism as well) not because of the poverty of their arguments but because of the threatening appearance of Bernardo Gui and the Inquisition. The formation of a persecuting society, said to have begun in the late Middle Ages, can then be seen behind the rise of capitalism but it is responsible for the failure of socialism as well. Annaud's apocalyptic film then is not only about a book lost in the conflagration, but just as crucially about the book that survived, Bernardo's treatise on torture, which Annaud tells us "became a source text for the Nazis."

The popularity of *The Name of the Rose* and *The Return of Martin Guerre* (d. Daniel Vigne 1982) has spawned a number of films centering on the precocious modernity of detective clerics. These figures embody the contradictions inherent in the modern wish to know the medieval past directly from a perspective that is at once within and yet impervious to its radical alterity. They are also, I submit, filmic attempts to implicate modern scholars in the medieval worlds they reconstruct. In films such as *The Reckoning* (d. Paul McGuigan 2003) and *The Advocate* (alt. title *The Hour of the Pig*, d. Leslie Magahey 1993), these figures are poised at the cusp of the transition between medieval and modern. Their personal itineraries spatialize chronology in journeys from metropolitan centers to an interior that is also temporally anterior in its cultural development. In these films the sexual abuse and murder of children provide the central mystery and, in both, blame must be shifted from an innocent witch onto a guilty aristocratic male. *The Reckoning* stages the transition to modernity in a *mise-en-abyme* of dramatic evolution: The traveling troop of actors progresses from mystery to morality play and finally to a proto–Brechtian epic theater in its quest to make drama relevant to the lives of its audience. Traditional theatrical genres fail to reveal and even serve to uphold an aristocratic privilege that extends to the bodies and lives of young boys. The peasantry, well-fed and prosperous thanks to their generous lord, maintain a conspiracy of silence until a representation of the boy's rape and murder stirs them to beat the appropriately named Robert de Guise to death with their bare hands. Hence, there are two mysteries solved by the anachronistic intrusion of political street theater into the past. First, a murderer is unmasked, and, second, the scapegoating of witches and Jews for the mutilated corpses of children is debunked. We "know" that serial rapists and murderers of children are almost invariably males who kill within their own ethnic group, and so the theater troupe is licensed to perform a reenactment that establishes in the style of a contemporary docudrama, complete with the voice-over narration and flashback, the truth behind medieval paranoias about witches and Jews. But of course to transfer the crimes to which Gilles de Rais confessed under the threat of torture from fifteenth-century France to four-teenth-century England — the film's fictional Lord Robert de Guise is played by the same actor (Vincent Cassell) who took the role of de Rais in the earlier film *The Messenger* — is less a debunking of medieval paranoias than a blatant projection, designed to source modern configurations of deviancy. In his revelation of the real culprit, the frockless monk Nicholas rouses the crowd to vengeance with the claim that now they finally know the truth and "truth has power." The collocation knowledge-power should provoke us to look beyond the film's attempt to associate its rebellion with that which would occur in England a year later in the Peasants' Revolt (1381) and to read from a Foucauldian perspective the ways in which such truths are manufactured by an industry asserting its own form of control over the past. To misuse T. S. Eliot, we know more than people living in the past, they are what we know.

In its frothy brew of fabliau humor and dark conspiracy *The Advocate* likewise foregrounds the alterity of the Middle Ages behind which lurk unexpected links to modern capitalism and sadism. The film's hero is a lawyer who retires from Paris in the hopes of finding the peace and quiet to be had in the simple life of a peasant village. His wish to leave the chaos and corruption of the city behind thus calques modern nostalgia for the medieval. What he finds is a world he repeatedly misinterprets is a legal system dominated by "custom and practice" that obviates his advanced training in forensic rhetoric and Abelardian logic. As the representative of the dawn of a modern world exiled to a medieval village, his struggle is cast in frankly Manichean terms. The opening title sequence remarkably calls fifteenth century France "the Dark Ages" and Matrie's mission to reform the village is cast in progressive terms. However, his attempts to reveal the truth and do justice meet with only ambivalent success. As he leaves the village, "the shining knight" enters in fulfillment of the prophecy that his coming would end their suffering — he comes bearing the plague. This Poesque coda undermines the narrative of enlightenment that the film had seemed poised to deliver.

Modernity does not shed light on the past; rather, feudalism's easy transition into market capitalism casts its long shadow into the modern world. Early on, the witch tells Matrie: "There is darkness all about you. You can bring the light." He discovers a secret order, connected to the Cathars, that has transitioned seamlessly into a monopolistic, price-fixing guild established to control wages and protect domestic markets from foreign competition. The "vanishing mediator" between feudalism and capitalism is not Puritanism, *pace* Weber, but rather the heretical worship of excess as an end in itself — a conclusion, as Bruce Holsinger has amply demonstrated, about the transition between medieval and modern with which Georges Bataille would have heartily agreed (pp. 26–56 and 204–20). Like Tom Cruise's character in Stanley Kubrick's provocative *Eyes Wide Shut* (1999), Matrie's sexual misadventures lead him to stumble upon a secret brotherhood of Catharists turned capitalists. His intrusion on the Lacanian Real allows a glimpse of an essential, timeless base that orders and constructs the apparent realities of superstructural dynamics.

In essence the failure of all three detective monks to defeat the conspiracies they uncover calques the incapacity of post–Enlightenment rationalism to contain or repress the medieval, as well as confirming as a definitive part of the Real capitalism's genealogical descent from the feudal and ecclesiastical estates of the Middle Ages. Gilles Deleuze notes that cinema's fascination with surveillance, investigation, and conspiracy marks its status as the most commercial of art forms:

> The cinema as art itself lives in a direct relation with a permanent plot (*complot*), an international conspiracy which conditions it from within, as the most indispensable enemy. This conspiracy is that of money; what defines industrial art is not mechanical reproduction but the internalized relation with money [pp. 77].

In all three films we have been discussing (*The Name of the Rose*, *The Reckoning*, and *The Advocate*), the detective finds himself situated at the nexus between feudalism and capitalism, at a point where historical determinism seems momentarily suspended. The elegiac tone common to all three films comes not from simple nostalgia but from a fissure in historical continuity that has the potential to render the future present of the audience virtual. But as we know and the detectives soon learn, the spark must jump that gap because the Real of history demands that development from feudalism to capitalism leave largely undisturbed the realities of sexism, racism, gross economic inequality, and commercial religion.

The unprecedented success of Dan Brown's novel as well as the initial box-office earnings of *The Da Vinci Code* (d. Ron Howard 2006) perhaps lie in the positioning of this gap of virtual history not at the always already determined cusp of transition from medieval to modern but in the contemporary world of the audience. Brown teams a detective and a scholar, who together uncover fantastically protean conspiracies of history locked in a Manichean struggle, whose contemporary incarnations (Opus Dei and the Priory of Sion) continue the battle into the present day over how the "Middle Ages" will end. The success of Brown's warring conspiracies deserves and will receive a fuller treatment in my final chapter, but here let us simply conclude this chapter by relishing the ironies of a fiction about conspiracy that has become one of the best-selling books of all time. There could be no more compelling example of how the conspiracies of commercial art are "conditioned from within" by money, its "most intimate and indispensable enemy." Nor could there be any more complete demonstration of the paranoid narcissism that drives postmodernity's imaginary colonization of the Real. Understood in broad terms, conspiracy is cinémedievalism's defining cliché.

2

Time Machines

Time has always put the notion of truth into crisis. — Gilles Deleuze

In the foregoing chapter I attempted to reframe the problem of historical accuracy in cinémedievalism within what seem to me the more heuristic terms of psychoanalysis and the cinema apparatus. By reformulating the debate in terms of Lacan's orders, I hoped to shift the focus from anachronism to a locus of cultural fantasy wherein the reel/real divide is reinterpreted as the Imaginary/Real. As we have seen, Lacan's orders do not remain distinct, particularly in popular cinema; rather, the point is to parse the varieties of cultural signification and obfuscation the medieval is doing in cinema. Hence, I have discussed not only films set exclusively in the Middle Ages but also those in which the medieval plays only a supporting role because these films also contribute to and rely upon an imaginary Middle Ages, an imaginary that at times threatens to overwhelm the Symbolic completely, spilling over into and saturating our sense of the Real. In this chapter, taking my terms from Gilles Deleuze's two *Cinema* books, I want to reframe the question yet again by moving from the Imaginary/Real to the virtual and the actual.

Deleuze's cinematic philosophy as outlined primarily in *Cinema I: The Movement Image* and *Cinema II: The Time-Image* relies upon what can only be called a grand metanarrative. I say "cinematic philosophy" because the books are neither a theory nor a history of cinema, but rather a challenging attempt to confront philosophy with the revolutions in thinking that film makes possible. I say "metanarrative" without meaning to condemn, but rather to point to this work's tactic of drawing large conclusions about the development of cinema from particular films or from specific characteristics in films. Deleuze attends rather exclusively to what in the United States is often called "art-house" or "auteur" cinema and within this canon to indirect or direct representations of time. The central distinction in this cinematic philosophy is drawn between classical and modern films, the rupture having been precipitated by a crisis in the perception of time that followed World War II. Deleuze attributes this rupture to:

> the war and its consequences, the unsteadiness of the American Dream in all its aspects, the new consciousness of minorities, the rise and inflation of images both in the external world and in people's minds, the influence on the cinema of the new modes of narrative with which literature had experimented, the crisis of Hollywood and its old genres [1986, p. 206].

Before the war and more ambivalently in its aftermath cinema's innovations were embodied in the "movement image," a realistic, organic system of relations within a milieu, the qualities of which create a world of situations and actions strung together in casual chains. Such a cinema does not preclude discontinuities, flashbacks, or dreams but rather these disruptions are contained within what Deleuze calls the "sensory-motor schema." Gregory Flaxman succinctly outlines the typology of this schema and the interrelation of different kinds of images: "Situations present essences (*perception-images*), which then give rise to actions (*action-images*), while the interval (*affection-images*) marks the moment between the perception and the action" (p. 101). Traditional cinema narration in the classic Hollywood style produces continuity by rational combinations of these three image types. The sensory-motor schema also "regulates the images by deflecting them into certain habitual paths" (Flaxman, p. 21), whereby are formed for Deleuze the clichéd "old genres" of Hollywood such as *film noir*, the melodrama or the western.

The crisis in the sensory-motor schema occurred when the rational connections between situation, action, and affect began to break down in the aftermath of World War II. For Deleuze, "the soul of cinema" is profoundly transformed during this crisis in a reflexive involution from the world of action-reaction toward an exploration of inner, psychic temporalities. In postwar films action is typically paralyzed or reduced to directionless wandering through the "any-space-whatever" of a Europe laid physically and spiritually waste. Perceptual situations have grown too overwhelming for the sensory-motor link and the affective interval expands to the point of impotence or spasms of random action. This expansion and dominance of the interval, which we might with Eliot call the shadow that falls between excitation and response, was always inherent in Deleuze's developmental typology.[1] He also uses it to establish the distinction in the early history of cinema between European films like Dreyer's *The Passion of Joan of Arc*, which are dominated by the affective interval, and American films like Griffith's *Intolerance*, which are driven forward at breakneck speed by the parallel montage of action-images. Deleuze pays grudging respect to the triumphs of American cinema, which are all the more impressive since it has recklessly turned down the blind alley of the action-image and taken much of the rest of the world with it: "the greatest commercial successes always take that route but the soul of the cinema no longer does" (1986, p. 206). The progress of this "soul of the cinema" argument is troublesome not only for its essentialism but also because there can be no "beyond movement" in cinema, the result would be a still photograph. Also, as David Bordwell abundantly demonstrates, art-cinema's "inquiry into character" at the expense of causation and action is no less conventional than classical cinema, it simply relies upon a different set of conventions (1985, pp. 205–33). Instead of a Foucault-inspired historicism based on a single transition from the "classical" to the "modern," we would do better to trace the interplay of intervals and actions throughout the history of cinema, as Deleuze himself traces the dominance of situation and action through classical cinema. Intervals surely prompt and influence responses no less significant for being delayed, just as surely as actions create intervals. Certainly in Italian Neo-Realism and the French New Wave the interval oppresses and delays action, time seems to curve back on itself as objects lose their utility, human beings their sense of purpose. Though there is sometimes a great deal of movement in these films, in Eliot's terms the shadow falls between mere action and the act. But even in Godard's paradigmatic *Breathless* (1960) the wanderer is pinned down because he commits a series of murders and the couple does eventually get up out of bed and go into the street — with disastrous consequences.

Another problem with Deleuze's developmental typology of course is what exactly happens *after* cinematic modernism? Many readers of Deleuze have seen the soul of cinema as having moved in recent decades to the Third World. This is an intriguing hypothesis and perhaps marks yet a second fundamental break in thinking through images. Yet the application of Deleuze to non–Western contexts is problematical. Also, within the Western context, postmodernism has seen the breakdown of the very distinctions upon which the theory rests, for example, the growing "incredulity toward metanarratives," the willful pastiche of high and low culture, and particularly the wholesale pillaging of modernist avant-gardes by popular culture. What has in fact happened to the revolutionary time-images Deleuze so brilliantly anatomized is their gradual cooptation by popular culture, and their transformation into the clichés he so abhorred. The interval, the time-image (I am collapsing the two in a way Deleuze did not) has been reintegrated into the dominant sensory-motor schema, though I might argue in a Deleuzian manner though against Deleuze himself, that the action-image was always there potentially within the oppressive intervals of art-house cinema, waiting to stage its return.

This is most certainly *not* to say that these more recent time-images are not misprisions — citations out of context and with an attendant loss in depth and resonance — but rather that the image schemas Deleuze traced have their own trajectory, one that lands them squarely in the postmodern "matrix." In what follows I outline the characteristics of Deleuze's time-image and trace its manifestations across the last fifty years in some justly revered films about the Middle Ages. My argument attempts to be historical in two ways: first, it tracks developments from what Deleuze would call modernist films through to popular film's reincorporation of the time-image within a classical sensory-motor schema, and, second, it treats the time-image itself as an historical phenomenon (not as the "soul of the cinema") whose horizons are now more apparent.

For Deleuze the organic realism of the movement-image regime is replaced by inorganic, crystalline images wherein the fundamental binary of real versus imaginary is pushed to a point of uncertainty. The crystal image is structured by three sets of poles or oppositions that are themselves unstable: actual/virtual, limpid/opaque, and seed/environment. Following Henri Bergson, Deleuze sees time gushing forth in a double arc, a present that passes and a past that is preserved. The two-sided "mutual" nature of the crystalline image tracks these flows but also sets up circuits of exchange wherein the distinction is maintained but the identity of any facet of the image as actual or virtual is indeterminate. Put more simply, the past that the present is always becoming and the present nature of recollections mirror one another. The relevance of this to medievalism should be apparent. As Gregory Flaxman explains, "the present in the modern cinema seems almost to lapse into the past, or the past to overtake the present [...] What this means is that at the most contracted point of these circuits, present and past, actual and virtual converge" (p. 32). Clear distinctions such as real/imaginary or present/past become actual/virtual, characterized by unstable exchanges because "the virtual is *not* imaginary, it is the reservoir that thought draws on to bring about the actual." The same is true for the limpid and the opaque: as in the crystal itself, changes in temperature, light, or angle of vision can cause clear or reflective surfaces to dull or darken. In the relation between the seed and environment we have a way of tracing these exchanges and reciprocities through entire films, as well as the relationship between films and the wider world. The environment produces the seed and influences its growth into a milieu, which is in turn transformed by that growth: in every seed is a potential environment, but there are environments in which seeds cannot actualize themselves. The carnival house of mirrors in *The Lady from Shanghai* (d. Orson Welles 1948) is perhaps the clearest and most famous example of these interchanges. The presence of the *femme fatale* and her jealous husband is reflected in multiple virtual images. Shooting at these reflections opens black holes as the mirrors shatter, until the actual killers finally emerge from their virtual representations and shoot each other to death. The recent *Timeline* (d. Richard Donner 2003) begins rather than ends with a citation of this famous time-image, though here the house of mirrors is a real time machine blasted into fragments by a concussion grenade dropped into fourteenth-century France, which is transported back to the future twenty-first century and explodes in a lab in New Mexico. The remainder of the film is spent repairing the time machine in order to retrieve a crew of modern time tourists who, despite all prohibitions to the contrary, operate in the virtual archive of the past — like the oblivious "historical consciousness" they seem to represent — by actualizing incompossible romantic fantasies. In the trajectory from Welles's film to Donner's we trace that of the time-image itself from the avant-garde to action cinema.

A number of conclusions can be drawn from unstable divisions within the crystalline regime, which Deleuze dubs "mirrors or seeds of time." These signs produce pure optical and sound situations, distinct from the sensory-motor link and characterized by immobility, indecision, and confinement. They also facilitate rhymes or exchanges between internal and external worlds. This regime favors self-referential, mirror, or *mise-en-abyme* structures (representations of theater, art, illusion, doubling, etc.), such that the film becomes a pseudo-story or the simulation of a story. Finally, the crystalline regime collapses time into contemporaneity "of the present with the past it will be, of the past with the present it has been" (Deleuze 1989, p. 274). Even though Deleuze has surprisingly little to say about historical films, his philosophy of the crystalline time-image offers an intriguing perspective from which to survey postwar cinémedievalism. Perhaps the ideal place to begin an admittedly partial survey is with Ingmar Bergman's *The Seventh Seal* (1957), the film that has had perhaps the greatest influence on subsequent movie medievalism over the last fifty years.

The Seventh Seal

The omission of *The Seventh Seal* from Deleuze's *Cinema* books is glaring because it represents quite a thorough example of the time-image. The film opens on the boundary between the sea and a black-shale shore where both the knight and his squire lie asleep. This freezing of the sensory-motor link rhymes with the internal, spiritual life of the knight Antonius Block as well: he kneels to pray but finds he cannot. Block's situation at the border of sea and shore marks a kind of midpoint in his transition between a genocidal holocaust (the Crusades) and the threat of an apocalypse (the Black Death), analogous perhaps to Bergman's own situation in 1957 between World War II and the prospect of all-out nuclear war. A chessboard is laid out upon the rocks with a match apparently in progress, though it is difficult to imagine where the knight has found an opponent — his squire Jöns is certainly given to less cerebral pursuits. I like to imagine he has been playing against himself. The overlap of white and black in the squares and pieces of the chessboard is doubled by the sea and shore, the surf rushes in and black rocks jut from the surface of the water — an effect intensified later when a double-exposure projects the chessboard onto the raging sea. This falling together of limpid and opaque, actual and virtual heralds the first appearance of Death at the seashore — looking every bit like a chess piece himself — and launches the film's many-faceted crystallization of time. The foregrounding of Death's appearance as what Deleuze would call a "pure optical situation" is emphasized in the sound track by the sudden silencing of the crashing waves. The chessboard then is the seed of a crystal image that continues to expand throughout the plot: The virtual match the knight plays against death threatens to embrace all the actual characters and places in the film. The final shot in the scene raises the image to the level of a transcendent reality when the chessboard is superimposed upon the heavens' already gaseous interplay of dark and light, cloud and sky. In the course of the film, however, the image of the chessboard will be doubled by another virtual inventory of social realities, the *danse macabre*, which collapses or renders absurd the feudal distinctions that order both medieval society and the game of chess.

Jöns the squire in his stubborn Sancho-like physicality repeatedly threatens to render quixotic the knight's existential quest. The squire hails a monk — a real one sitting against a stone, unlike Death who later masquerades as a monk. Receiving no reply, Jöns turns him forcibly by the shoulders only to discover a decomposing face beneath the cowl. This is actual death, the other side of the virtual personification, played with sinister tranquility by Bengt Ekerot. Jöns reports to Block that the monk was "most eloquent." The reference to Shakespeare's Danish tragedy is laconically apt, because the monk indeed has informed him of the plague's arrival in Sweden. Silence in the film is often eloquent, though terrifyingly so. In Bergman's theatrical play from which the screenplay derives, the knight was himself a mute, his tongue having been cut out by a "Saracen."[2] In the film it is God himself who remains horribly silent, and Death, if indeed he knows anything about transcendent realities, isn't telling. For Lacan, death is the Real, that which exists absolutely independent of our ideas about it. In the film Block repeatedly explores the possibility that Death has another, virtual side, one that leads to God. But if God is on the other side of Death, it is a side of himself Death has never seen. As Jöns philosophizes, "wherever you turn, your backside's still behind you." The same is true of the witch supposed to have brought the plague in league with the devil. She invites Block to look for the devil in her eyes — true in a way perhaps because her blank stare is a window onto nothingness. Put in more orthodox terms, earthly knowledge of the divine is always a blurry confusion of the actual and virtual, the limpid and opaque, the crystal image Deleuze dubs a "hyalosign" from the Greek word for glass: *per speculum in aenigmate.*

The supreme crystalline image of the film is the parallel sequence in the church, where Jöns converses with a fresco painter and Block with a "priest." Essential to the ironies of the film is the actualization of traditional representations in medieval literature and the plastic arts. The knight literally plays chess with death and here in a chapel adjoining the church Jöns sees a fresco depicting the danse macabre and the flagellants, both of which are incarnated later in the film. The lack of realism in the fresco leaves Jöns unimpressed

Death (Bengst Ekerot) and Knight Antonius Block (Max von Sydow) begin their chess match in Ingmar Bergman's *The Seventh Seal* (1957).

until the painter begins describing in more *graphic* detail the symptoms of plague victims screaming and tearing open their veins. Freud decided late in his career in *Civilization and Its Discontents* that, as an organic drive, sex comes in a late second to death. Bergman's painter agrees: "a skull is more interesting than a naked woman." Jöns's visit to the chapel is certainly an extended pause in the sensory-motor schema. He goes there to rest and refresh himself and is confronted by a pure optical and sound situation. The tracks are at first distinct and of different force: the pictures crude, the impromptu sermon riveting, until they intersect when Jöns is prompted to take another look. The audience follows this double take and we "see" with Jöns through the scaffolding and shoddy craftsmanship a terror all the more arresting for its primitive realism.

The parallel scene with Block at the church's main altar rhymes with this earlier one but also progresses from representations of death to those depicting judgment. Block prays beneath a fresco that depicts angels and demons contending for a human soul, tugging at the corpse on either side. The mise-en-scène positions the knight in the middle between these contending forces and directly beneath the quilting point of the buttresses that join at the summit of the ceiling. He stares up at a large crucifix, the face of Christ illuminated by sunlight. Then his attention is drawn to movement on his left side and he interrupts his prayers for the second time in the film. The monk he glimpses behind the wooden screen is not immediately sinister but the opaque cowl that hides his face as he turns away is in direct opposition to the sunlit face of Christ who seems to turn toward the penitent. The pattern of sunlight and shadow on the large crucifix above the altar is duplicated exactly on the smaller copy behind the screen when the monk turns away and casts his shadow across it. The shot also rhymes significantly with the dead monk behind the cowl Jöns encountered earlier, though here the *méconnaissance* is drawn out into an extended interval. Block's confession to this figure is his sole lapse of judgment in the film. Masters play chess virtually, in the mind, and Block begins outlining his strategy to Death-as-Confessor through the wooden screen, which itself exactly duplicates the pattern of a chessboard. Block's confession is a litany of postwar existential emptiness: "my heart is a void, the void is a mirror, I look at myself and feel loathing and terror." The mise-en-scène replicates the mirror structures of medieval *memento mori*, on the other side of the mirror-screen is the void of death into which the knight pours his deepest fears and in which he finally sees the image of his own future change from opaque to limpid as Death turns to face him. Block has lived among ghosts and dreams, his "life has been a meaningless search" and he hopes only to accomplish "one significant action" before dying. Death perhaps rightly asks what such aspirations have to do with playing chess but in his dogged literalism fails to understand in Deleuzian terms how new actualities are born out of the virtual. The game will ultimately become a screen behind which the knight conceals his real intentions and through which he is able to accomplish this "one significant act." The envelop-pattern of the sequence concludes with a return to Jöns, who in carnivalesque parody mocks the existential image of the mirror as void. He paints a self-portrait that depicts him laughing at Death, but in the shot's *mise-en-abyme* Jöns holds a painting of Jöns holding a painting and the image and reality mirror one another. Jöns too sees nothing, his void is his own narcissistic disbelief, and the ironic texture of word and image here again emphasizes the specular ironies of *memento mori* doubling.

For Deleuze the characteristic spaces of the crystalline image are "any-place-whatever" through which people wander aimlessly. In *Images: My Life in Film*, Bergman emphasizes precisely this characteristic of *The Seventh Seal*: "What attracted me was the whole idea of people traveling through the downfall of civilization and culture ... it became a kind of 'road movie,' traveling without constraint in time and space" (p. 232). In the bombed-out city-slates of Italian neo-realism, this notably passive aimlessness is punctuated by furtiveness and attempts to escape — an effect Bergman translates powerfully into the no-exit world of *The Seventh Seal*. The plague has emptied the landscape and isolated its few remaining inhabitants: Families are disbanded, buildings reclaimed by the natural world, and human relationships are transient, determined by chance encounters, selfishness, and sadism. A key exception and the most important encounter in the film is that between the knight and the troop of actors. Ultimately Jof and Mia (diminutives of Joseph and Maria), along with their infant son, are a potential that escapes the closure of the time-image into a future of renewed possibility. As an actor/acrobat Jof is not accomplished, but his "daydreams" are superior works of art. His insistence that his vision of the Virgin and the infant Jesus "was quite real ... not the reality you see, but another kind" locates the image not in the Lacanian Imaginary but in the Deleuzian virtual from which new actualities can emerge. Jof wants for his son, to become the greatest juggler of all time (one could even say a juggler of time), to perform the impossible trick of making a ball stand still in the air. Both Deleuze's notion of the time-image and the example of Christ suggest that, at least potentially, this is not impossible.

Depth of field is particularly congenial to the crystal image: when such shots are "wholly necessary" they occur "in connection with memory" (Deleuze 1989, p. 109). The calm before the apocalyptical storm comes in *The Seventh Seal* when Block and Jöns sit down with Jof, Mia, and the infant

Mickael for a picnic of wild strawberries and milk. What had been essential to Block, his quest for meaning in life, becomes "unreal" in this context. He vows to protect the peace and humanity of this moment as a "memory." When Block wanders away from the picnic he appears to be trying to do just that, to fix the memory in his mind. Soon he again encounters the ubiquitous Death, and, as the chess match resumes, actual/virtual and limpid/opaque interchanges radiate through the depth of field in the shot. There are four rather distinct planes: (1) the chess match in the foreground, (2) the picnic, (3) the wagon of the actors upon which hangs the death mask like the anamorphic stain in Holbein's "The Ambassadors," and (4) the knight's horse deep in the background, nervously pacing from side to side. In Deleuze's terms, actual memories are composed in peaks of the present from virtual sheets of time. If the knight is to successfully protect this "memory" of the family of actors from Death, he must transform the game into a diversion. Block's strategy puts Death's king in jeopardy by sacrificing his own knight — a strategy that will ultimately lose him the match, but Block is no longer playing for

Deep focus in Bergman's *The Seventh Seal* (1957) as the significance of the chess match between the knight (von Sydow) and Death (Ekerot) grows ever more complex.

his own life. He has himself become the virtual image of Christ the Knight who conquers death by his self-sacrifice. The game itself has become virtual, containing a secret hope not represented on the chessboard and hence momentarily hidden from Death's mortal gaze. The present for Deleuze (following Bergson) is always splitting in two, one stream arcing to the past and the other racing forward to an undetermined future in the process of becoming. The forking paths of the travelers in the storm — Block and his party return to his castle while Jof and his family take another road — duplicates this structure exactly. As William Paden insightfully remarks: "Their (the actors') escape is the release from closure for them and for the viewer, and corresponds to the continuation of history beyond all successive endings predicted by medieval fears of the apocalypse" (p. 296). We might add that the victory of Christ, his sacrifice, and the new dispensation it brings have once again been realized in human form. Just as in the flight into Egypt, the survival of Jof's family allows new beginnings.

Andrei Rublev

The transcendence of an interval that threatens to stifle the future also helps to parse the complex structure of Andrei Tarkovsky's *Andrei Rublev* (1966)), a film that in a number of ways responds to Bergman's *Seventh Seal.* In Bergman two chief sources of the cinematic image are juxtaposed, namely, painting and the theater. Virtual, artistic images such as those of the flagellants, the *danse macabre,* and the personification of Death are actualized within the diegesis. Only the family of actors survives as a movement-image, an image not circumscribed by the entropic pull of death-as-Real. In Tarkovsky this process is essentially reversed, the epilogue that screens Rublev's religious icons represents the final actualization in the present (and in "living" color) of the film's virtual, black-and-white biography of the painter. This apocalyptic structure is divided by intertitles into seven parts — seven seals as it were — that in their revelations yield the new heaven and new earth of Rublev's art. In effect, Tarkovsky's ending produces a perception-image (the icons) informed and rendered transcendent by an extended interval of physical and spiritual dangers from which it ultimately emerges and from which in retrospect it seems to have been composed. The relations between this virtual background and the actual icons it produces are discontinuous, lacunary, and indistinct, much like the relation of figure and ground within the paintings themselves and further highlighted in Tarkovsky's impressionistic segmentation of the icons in the epilogue. In the final shots rain streams down the walls, washing away the pigments, and four horses stand waiting for their riders in the rain. The film highlights the ravages of time upon the icons (cracks, spots, and faded colors) even before the rain begins to fall into the ruined church. The change to color and the initial state of the icons leads us to suspect the camera eye has entered a modern perspective, but in the last shot through the door we see back into the black-and-white world of Tarkovsky's Middle Ages, which perhaps we have never left. The apocalyptic four horses still await their riders and the icons suffer the very ravages of time, which necessitated the series of over-paintings we know they underwent, but it is no longer possible to discern in these final images if we are in the diegetic past of the early fifteenth century, the actual present of the mid–1960s Soviet Union, or somewhere in between.

The film's prologue flaunts the conventions of epic cinema by launching into a blatantly anachronistic action-image of a chase and escape, which, absent any historical or narrative context, negates the possibility of identification or tension. The Icarus figure struggles with the logistics of the hot-air balloon as well as the superstitious peasants, who try desperately to prevent him from taking off. The first successful balloon flight was reportedly some four centuries later on November 21, 1783, in Paris by Pilâtre de Rozier and the Marquis d'Arlandes — though Soviet documents (subsequently revealed as forgeries) sought to bestow that honor on a Russian.[3] Of course, it is difficult to know how many unrecorded failures preceded the authentic French flight. In the early sixteenth century William Dunbar wrote a brilliant, bathetic poem on the failed flight of the Abbot of Tungland.[4] So Tarkovsky's image perhaps suggests something about the undocumented interstices of history being the virtual spaces occupied by his imaginary biography of Andrei Rublev — what Deleuze calls "the powers of the false." The camera eye like that of the magician-scientist obtains a perspective unavailable to people in fifteenth-century Russia. The latter-day Andrei (Tarkovsky) not only finds his double in the struggles of his namesake to transcend the material world, but he also projects his own characteristic visual style (the slow pan over objects moving across the frame to the right) through the perspective of a giddy, bathetic fellow traveler.

Tarkovsky called his imaginary biography of Rublev "a film of the earth" and it is through the irrational sequencing and cuts that we begin to understand to what this enigmatic designation might refer. When the balloon falls precipitously back to earth, the frame is frozen momentarily a meter from the ground, out of sync with the audio track, which crashes *before the balloon*. The interval opened between the two tracks thus creates a brief space, which includes, however improbably, the possibility of transcendence. The next shot records its grotesque failure as the remaining carbon dioxide from the balloon is expelled (farted) into a stream. A common scientific metaphor in the Middle Ages compared sound waves to ripples in water (e.g., Chaucer's *House of Fame*). Tarkovsky uses this rather erudite "dirty" joke to emphasize the energy inherent in the interval between sight and sound images. The balloon prologue in this way rhymes with the final episode, which follows the construction of the bell. The only extended period of suspense in the film occurs between the completion of the bell and its ringing, an interval that seems interminable because the life of Boriska — the boy posing as a master bell-maker — is also at stake. This "film of the earth" thus situates itself in the extended interval between these two acts of making: a fatal attempt to escape the world by rising above it and a redemptive leap of faith that quite literally refashions the earth from within. The bell tolls for Rublev in particular: He cradles the emotionally shattered boy at the foot of a pole, unconsciously composing a pietà with their bodies, and promises to unite their efforts in Moscow, where "you can make bells and I'll paint icons." This final companionship of what Deleuze calls "opsigns" and "sonsigns" (optical and sonic images) sensibly heals the wound between tracks, between people, and between the artist and his vocation that the film has opened in the imaginary life of Andrei.

Though Deleuze does not discuss *Andrei Rublev*, the time image of the film as a whole is composed of what he calls "*series of time*, which brings together the before and the after in a becoming, instead of separating them; its paradox is to introduce an enduring interval in the moment itself" (1989, p. 155). Tarkovsky's film never reverts to simple causal linkages, which would gloss elements in Rublev's paintings by rendering them autobiographical, nor does he lapse into allegory. Yet the film, I would insist, is consistently figural both in its internal juxtapositions and in its references to the modern world. What Deleuze would call "sheets of the past" compose a logic of figures achieving realization beneath the discontinuous and apparently irrational diegesis. The famous shot of the horse rolling on its back and then righting itself, which follows the crash of the balloon, obviously has a logic inseparable from the earlier shot, though there is no narrative continuity between the two. Later we move from a close-up of a dead bird to a high-angle shot assuming the perspective of a bird in flight, hence reversing, even redeeming, the balloonist's failed transcendence. One experiences images engaged in something vastly more complex than the dialectical montage pioneered by Eisenstein, something like contemplative thought.

Siegfried Kracauer collapses fantasy and historical film as deviations from cinema's métier in "physical reality." For Kracauer period films exhibit "staginess."

Tomorrow will be a great day

The boy bell maker Boriska (Nikolai Burleyayev, center) surveys his handiwork in Andrei Tarkovsky's *Andrei Rublev* (1966).

> They obstruct the affinity of the medium for endlessness. As the reproduction of a bygone era, the world they show is an artificial creation radically shut off from the space-time continuum of the living, a closed cosmos which does not admit of extensions. Looking at such a film, the spectator is likely to suffer from claustrophobia. He realizes that his potential field of vision strictly coincides with the actual one and that accordingly he cannot by a hair's breath transcend the confines of the latter [1960, p. 78].

He goes on to cite with approval the admonition: "Now the cinema must ... feature the inexhaustible by sustaining the impression that the place photographed is a random place, that one could have selected another as well, and that the camera eye might, with no damage done move about in all directions."[5] *Andrei Rublev* is perhaps the most thoroughgoing reply in cinémedievalism to the claustrophobia of the costume drama, but Tarkovsky's surpassing of these limitations is most immediately evident in the first and most claustrophobic episode in the film: "The Jester, Summer 1400." The Jester's lewd song about a beardless Boyar, misrecognized butts in widow frames, and the latent homosexuality of clerics sounds quite like a Russian analogue to Chaucer's *The Miller's Tale*. Bakhtin completed the book that would become known in the West as *Rabelais and His World* in 1940, though it was not published in Russian until 1965 — only a year before *Rublev's* premiere. Still, the carnivalesque upheavals of peasant culture, as well as the class-tensions genres like the fabliau reveal, are masterfully explored by

Tarkovsky through a camera-eye that both literally and figuratively moves in all directions. As the song begins we see the three monks approaching the tavern in the pouring rain through a thin rectangular window, but they do not enter until just as the song is concluding. This temporal discontinuity is important but its significance is only revealed obliquely. As the Jester accompanies himself on a large tambourine and performs tumbling acts to punctuate highpoints in his narrative, the camera follows him in a counter-clockwise 360 degree pan, recording the reactions of his audience. His final trick is a handstand, displaying his naked buttocks, painted like a face. It is this Bakhtinian vertical smile that greets the late-arriving monks. The Jester further mocks them by placing a cup atop his head in imitation of their cowls. He offers them some beer and when the stern Kirill demurs, the Jester replies that monks "don't play around with women either." The joke is devastating considering that the conclusion of the Jester's fabliau had a priest pulling the beardless Boyar into the bushes. Kirill retorts, "God sent the priests, the Devil sent the jesters." The mood in the tavern quickly alters from raucous to somber as the camera again pans 360 degrees, though this time in a clockwise direction. The pan includes a temporally disruptive shot of snow falling outside, which just as quickly disappears as we come full circle. Kirill has also vanished during the strangely indeterminate interval of the pan. Four Boyars arrive on horseback; they smash the Jester's head into a tree before taking him away, in a poetically just repetition of a bit of business from his earlier performance. It seems someone has reported details of the fabliau to the Boyars, who take their revenge by making real the concussion the Jester had earlier simulated. The Jester's counter-clockwise fabliau clearly represented a form of resistance to the domination of the Boyars, just as the clockwise pan brings in time's revenges. That Kirill has informed on the Jester is perhaps not clear to the peasants collected in the room nor to the film audience at this point, but the danger the monks pose to those in the tavern is palpable from the moment of their entrance, from the moment the second, clockwise pan begins. Tarkovsky presents an enclosed space from every possible angle, but that which is outside the frame also maintains a continuity with the inside of the frame, whether the audience sees what happens "outside" or not. The "extension" into space outside the frame is emphasized by the shot of the Jester being knocked unconscious and carried away, filmed from a perspective inside the tavern and through the internal frame of the doorway. The implication that the monks are somehow in league with the Boyars or at least equally dangerous to the peasants is confirmed in the final shot of the episode. Here, as is typical of Tarkovsky, relationships are expressed not through montage but rather by parallel movement (or "internal montage") within a single shot. The

Boyars with their prisoner in the background parallel the journey of the monks in the foreground, both parties travel in the same direction, separated by a reflective pool of water.

As initial audiences were quick to point out, the extended interval of the film itself in which Andrei renounces painting figures the long intervals between the modern Andrei's own films and his difficulties with Soviet censorship. Rublev is also an orthodox saint, canonized largely for his having produced artistic objects themselves worthy of veneration. However his life, as represented by Tarkovsky, is hardly miraculous and the only vow he keeps within the film is his resolution never to paint again. Without the color epilogue of the icons at the end of the film Tarkovsky's Rublev would be the first example of a saint-voyeur (he does little besides observe others), though the icons redeem his gaze, as well as the episodic structure of the film itself, as a *bildungsroman* of spiritual perspective. When Rublev does act in the film, it almost always represents a self-betrayal. He kills a Tartar to save the "holy fool" Durochka from being raped, but she soon sells herself to one of their leaders for horsemeat, only to reappear at the end of the film, richly clothed and accompanied by her child. As *figurae*, these sheets of the past neither determine the future nor are they simply repetitions. Instead, the icons that complete and fulfill incidents in the life render the virtual significance of these incidents retroactively. A clear instance of this is the parallel between the trio of monks and the icon, *The Old Testament Trinity*. The film's structure is circular: at the beginning Danill, Kirill, and Andrei are "leaving the Trinity" monastery. Subsequent episodes trace the separation of the trio up to Andrei's decision to return to the Trinity Chapel and to painting at the end of the film. The apparent disconnection of the seven episodes is rendered teleological by "the poetic logic of the need for Rublyov to paint his celebrated *Trinity*" (Tarkovsky, p. 35). Of course the story of the visitation of the three angels in the Old Testament is itself a *figura* of the Holy Trinity, but Tarkovsky's film makes the friendship of the three monks another link in this figural chain. The icon, in Tarkovsky's entailment of it, actualizes and renders transparent the profound spiritual love of the three monks that their petty squabbles had clouded.[6]

The genre of the saint's life often includes meditations on and imitations of Christ's passion. In the second sequence, "The Passion according to Andrei," the painter's spiritual crisis does not so much mirror Christ's suffering as alternately inflict and deny it. Here the cuts are only apparently "irrational," an effect caused by the ontological confusion of actual and virtual worlds. As Andrei bitterly condemns Russian women for collaborating with the Tartars, Theophanes tries to calm him, urging sympathy. While their dialogue continues in voice-over, we cut to a crucifixion scene being carried out on a stark, snow-covered landscape. The *via crucis* is a direct, even savage parody of the *danse macabre* shot at the end of Bergman's *Seventh Seal*. Here, as in Bergman, a line of people follow a leader across a distant ridge, but in Tarkovsky's version their leader is dressed in white and walking in the opposite direction, from left to right. The snow-clad hill has begun to melt, leaving streaks of mud running down its sides, as if the hill itself were soaked in blood. The painterly shot suggests not only Brueghel's use of space but also his situation of tragedies within the wider context of a world focused on other matters. It is impossible to tell whether this vision of the *via crucis* represents a spiritual reality or a reenactment, though for the faithful perhaps this would be something of a false distinction. Whether the image is deemed supernatural or ritualistic, it fails to capture the attention of many of the peasants. Bergman was an acknowledged admirer of Tarkovsky, calling him at one point the greatest living filmmaker, yet it's hard to imagine a more devastating rejoinder to the existential doubt of Bergman's film — particularly because in its context the *via crucis* occurs in parallel with Andrei's growing cruelty and despair. Embedding the crucifixion scene within Andrei's bitter lack of charity at this point in the film seems to recall the late medieval belief that sin renewed or exacerbated Christ's suffering. Soon thereafter Andrei himself gets a chance to be martyred by pagans who have caught him spying

The Bruegelesque passion play in Andrei Tarkovsky's *Andrei Rublev* (1966), with Mary Magdalene (Irina Miroshnichenko) in the foreground.

on their orgiastic rites; they mockingly "crucify" him and he accepts a kiss and a lecture on love from a naked woman, before asking her to set him free. She complies, but we don't see the monk again until the next morning. The interval leads us to suspect that, like the Christ of Nikos Kazantzakis, he has perhaps succumbed to a "last temptation."[7] Andrei's imitation of Christ then emphasizes his very human frailties but his encounter with the pagans also sacrifices once and for all his sense of superiority over his fellow human beings. Unlike the fresco painter in Bergman's film, Andrei finally refuses to paint images of death and torment such as the Last Judgment because he doesn't want to frighten people and the images sicken him. Though this denial is negated by the survival into the modern world of the very scenes Rublev here determines *not* to paint. The strategy reverses the film cliché of finding sources for images in the life of the artist, but it also urges us to look again at the iconostasis in Vladimir Cathedral for traces of Andrei's reluctance. In one sense, Rublev is the perfect Deleuzian hero, a wanderer so overwhelmed by the brutality and chaos of the world that all he can do is witness it from a distance. In another more complete sense he is like Bergman's Antonius Block, whose "significant act" crystallizes the sublime.

Ugetsu Monogatari

In Kenji Mizoguchi's *Ugetsu* (1953) the present is gendered feminine. The two wives in the film, Miyagi and Ohama, struggle desperately to turn their husbands' attention back to the dangerous and demanding world in which they live. For the forward-looking men, Genjuro and Tobei, the present exists only as an impediment to their dreams of social position and military glory. In the film's ruthless economy the wayward husbands unwittingly purchase their dreams at the expense of their wives. The opening title sequence establishes the place and time of the film with some precision ("Early Spring, 16th Century, A Period of Civil War / Lake Biwa in Omi Province"), but it also casts the film as a "new refashioning" of the "fantasies" in Akinari Ueda's eighteenth-century *Ugetsu Monogatari* (*Tales of Moonlight and Rain*), from which the film takes its title. The screenplay in fact derives from a telling combination of Japanese "gothic" medievalism and modern Western realism. Two of Akinari's stories, "The House Amid the Thickets" (set in the mid-fifteenth century) and "The Lust of the White Serpent (set in the Heian period, tenth to twelfth centuries), are interwoven with Guy de Maupassant's curtly satirical story "How He Got the Legion of Honor." The relationship between these sources in Mizoguchi's *Ugetsu* is complex: in one subplot the desire for feudal honors is channeled through ruthless capital transactions and in the other middle-class initiative tumbles catastrophically into delusions of aristocratic grandeur. Mizoguchi's medieval Japan is designed to reflect the reality of modern, post-war Japan in which the virtual past and future serve to alienate the present from itself.

The film begins its transformation from movement-image to time-image in the voyage across Lake Biwa, which is also the last scene until the very end of the film when the two families are together. Their boat itself first appears a ghostly apparition, slowly assuming solid form as it floats toward us. In Deleuze's terms this image represents the seed of an increasingly faceted crystallization of time. Significantly, in a film in which only women possess a sense of direction and a connection to present realities, Ohama pilots the boat and worries along with Miyagi about the war that can be heard raging on shore. The men focus not on the dangers of the moment but on their future prospects: Tobei, "I swear by the god of war, I'm tired of being poor" and Genjuro, "War is good for business!" Their reckless materialism of course also satirizes mid-twentieth century Japan. They soon glimpse a mirror image floating directly toward them — a boat of the same size and shape though a smoldering wreck and seemingly unmanned. The actual boat of the farmers has run into its virtual double, which Tobei calls a "ghost ship." This apparition had been heralded earlier in the scene when a nondiegetic song told of "death at the rudder": Music in the film typically lags behind or jumps ahead of the visuals it accompanies, allowing pasts and futures a ghostly presence. One badly wounded survivor assures them that he is not a ghost but if they continue on in the same direction they will surely be destroyed. Hence, time here begins to be represented prismatically: The ghost ship offers the prospect of a virtual future. At this point the group begins to split up, Genjuro sets his wife Miyagi and their child Genichi ashore so that they can return home in safety while he, Tobei, and Ohama (the only one capable of piloting the boat!) continue on their journey to the market. This group splinters completely upon their arrival, Tobei running off to join the samurais and Ohama getting lost in her attempt to find him.[8] The film here also seems to lose all sense of consecutive time; episodes featuring the four main characters are juxtaposed but the men enter what Bakhtin would call an adventure chronotope, itself characteristic of premodern narrative forms, while the women are stranded in an extremely perilous real world (Bakhtin 1981). The montage of these characters' four stories is anything but "parallel" in a temporal sense; indeed, it is impossible to reconcile the diegetic time of any particular episode with that of any other. Time exists only within particular episodes and from individual perspectives. In wrenching parallels between the masculine

The two families together in Kenji Mizoguchi's *Ugetsu* (1953).

chronotope of fortune and the feminine chronotope of actual suffering, Mizoguchi forges the greatest supernatural melodrama in film history.

The virtual world of men seemingly has consequences only in the actual world of women, and fantasy fulfillment rigorously exacts its toll on their bodies. Tobei pays the armorer three coins for three pieces of equipment so that he can become a samurai; a roving band of samurai gang rape his wife in a Buddhist temple. The last rapist throws three coins on the floor, casting her in the role of the prostitute she later assumes. Tobei spears a lieutenant who has just beheaded his defeated general, while in a later sequence Miyagi is speared by the hunger-maddened troops of this same general. The general's head wins Tobei a rich reward; he turns homeward in a triumphal procession, flanked by a new retinue of retainers who parrot his praises. The band stops to celebrate his triumph in a whorehouse, where Tobei sees Ohama forcibly extracting a payment of three coins from a customer who had tried to steal away without paying. In this film nothing is gained but what is paid for, and time ultimately brings in its revenges.

The Maupassant plot of prostituting one's wife to gain "honors" is also shadowed by the Akinari plot of supernatural exchanges. Again nothing is gained without payment in kind. Sometime (it is impossible tell when) during Genjuro's sojourn at Kutsuki mansion, in thrall to the ghost of Lady Wakasa, his wife is senselessly murdered. As he leaves for the mansion Genjuro stops to shop for a kimono for his wife. Though she is far away and perhaps already dead, the back of the shop opens to reveal Genjuro's backyard, where the shadow of Miyagi is shelving his pottery. Seen first in silhouette, she seems to take on real existence as she walks to the front of the shop to try on a kimono and model it demurely for her husband. The desire inherent in this daydream is later exposed when Genjuro buys kimonos for Lady Wakasa: showering one's wife with splendid clothing = changing one's wife. Kutsuki mansion is Genjuro's isle of the Lotus-Eaters and in it the discrete realities of time and space are elided. As he enters the gates the mansion is obviously a deserted ruin, though the tracking camera follows his passage through increasingly opulent spaces slowly coming to life with candles and servants. Mizoguchi's supernatural is filmed naturally with a camera that maintains an objective distance, yet in spite or perhaps because of that distance his fantastic world contains nuances and resonance that few such films possess. Lady Wakasa's Nôh theater make-up recalls the self-consciousness of Western *mise-en-abyme* films; but when she begins to sing a Nôh ballad about faithful love, the mannequin clothed in the armor of her dead father sings along. The Lady's reaction to the armor's bass intoning makes it clear that, though a ghost herself, she is also haunted by the spirit of her father. Genjuro's fall into a dazed sexual obsession is covered in an extended tracking shot assembled by hidden cuts that follow he and the Lady from the house to the bath to the shore, including one superb symbolic dissolve wherein a garden of raked sand is blown by the wind, thereby obscuring the cut. The sand thus images both the passage of time and its erasure, registering the disappearance of Genjuro's past from his memory. This transitional shot yields a Genjuro literally weak-kneed and repeatedly collapsing in drowsy surfeits of erotic bliss.

With the help of a priest, he is finally able to break free of the deadly spell that the Lady has cast. However, his disenchantment does not reveal her to be a monstrous serpent — as in Akinari — but rather the tragic victim of Genjuro's faithlessness: His abandonment destroys her just as it has his first wife. When he wakes the following morning the house is significantly more decrepit than the ruin it first appeared, now only a few charred sticks remain, though the gifts the Lady had given him are still in mint condition. The spirit world has borrowed priceless heirlooms from a museum — a detail that helps to cast Kutsuki manor not only as a complex time-image of virtual and actual presents but also as a satire on nostalgia itself. The Lady's song about how all things will fade to dust should Genjuro forsake her is replayed in voice-over

Genjuro's sojourn at the palace of Lady Wakasa in Kenji Mizoguchi's *Ugetsu* **(1953).**

as Genjuro surveys the waste his betrayal has wrought. This ruin also rhymes with the decrepit state of Genjuro's cottage upon his return home. The cottage is deserted and has been ransacked; Genjuro enters through the front door and exits through a side door as the camera tracks him in a 180-degree pan from right to left. The camera thus seems bound by the 180-degree rule for the simulation of naturalistic perspective. As Genjuro circles back around the outside of the cottage only to come in where he had first entered, the camera pans in reverse the same 180-degree arc from within the cottage, magically restoring not only the interior but also his wife and child. The hidden cut is revealing: Physical and spiritual realities inhabit the same space and both are equally "real." Obviously the shot rhymes significantly with Genjuro's entrance to a revivified Kutsuki manor, and this supernatural space goes some way to restoring what he lost in his adventure. There follows a scene of almost perfect domestic bliss, complete with a contrite husband, a patient wife, and a docile child, though Miyagi, like Lady Wakasa, is a ghost. The film's final use of dissonance between visual and aural tracks also works to make good Genjuro's loss: though he discovers his wife is long dead, his son survives and Miyagi's spirit continues to speak to him, assuring him of her presence there beside him as he faces the future. In the optimism of these final scenes Mizoguchi insists that history is nightmare from which we can awaken, though the quietist politics of the film makes us infer that this is only possible by knowing one's place — and staying there.

Harakiri

Ugetsu presents an advanced stage in the debasement of the Bushido Code of the samurai during the Sengoku period, a debasement seen from the perspective of the peasant class for whom samurai represent both threat and opportunity. In *Harakiri* (d. Masaki Kobayashi 1962) and *Kagemusha* (d. Akira Kurosawa 1981) the samurai class is viewed from the perspective of loser history — defeated clans and their ronin — wherein we are encouraged to reflect with some sadness on what has been lost in the rise of the nation-state that brought domestic peace as well as narcissistic isolation. *Harakiri* is set early in the Edo period (1619–1630) when civil war gave way to national rule under the Tokugawa Shogunate (1603–1868). For Kobayashi this feudal autocracy had invented a style of authoritarian rule, cloaked in the prestige of the very samurai class it deposed and debased, that promoted the maintenance of order over the Bushido Code — with disastrous consequences for modern Japan. Perhaps not surprisingly he puts at the center of his film the ultimate personal sacrifice this code requires, *seppuku* or *harakiri*. Here though ritual suicide is commodified, co-opted first by ronin who extort money by threatening to kill themselves, and then by the powerful Iyi clan who attempt to discourage this scam by sadistically forcing the ronin to carry out their threats.

Harakiri is indebted to Kurosawa's *Rashomon* (1950) for its frame of flashbacks told from competing perspectives to create a multivalent past, but Kobayashi's film is more concerned with the silences of official history than with individual perspectives. Like Dreyer's *The Passion of Joan of Arc* it begins with hands turning the pages of an official transcription of events, yet it does this not to authorize the film that follows, as in Dreyer, but rather to position the film's diegesis as counter-memory, situated between the lines of official records. Indeed, the end of the film shows the powers that be erasing all traces of the tragedy the diegesis slowly reveals, sanitizing some acts of *seppuku* with political spin and compelling or concealing others, but eviscerating all these acts of their real meaning. This erasure works to render the screenplay's imaginary narrative virtual even as it casts doubt on the status of the actual record. Given a closed society and a centralized government keen on order and the preservation of respected traditions, had something like what happens in the film actually occurred in 1630 it would surely have been suppressed and/or rewritten in terms favorable to the ruling elite. This is the opposition James Scott draws between "public" and "hidden" transcripts. Reading Benjamin's *Theses of History,* Žižek suggests that such hidden transcripts create a truly dialectical history because they "highlight the fundamental asymmetry" in their "capacity to *arrest*, to *immobilize* historical movement and to isolate the detail from its historical totality" (1989, p. 139). The details of *Harakiri*— many seen as flashbacks — are precisely those things that cannot be seamlessly accommodated within the grand narratives about the bureaucratization of the samurai class in the modernization of feudal Japan.[9]

The fearsome specter of an armored samurai amidst the smoke of battle serves as the initial, emblematic shot of the film. As the smoke is dispelled, the figure is more easily recognized as an armored mannequin taking up its honored place in a domestic shrine. This shift from utility to ornament provides a metonymy for the central problem of the whole film, the transition from a feudal to a bureaucratic state. The mannequin plays both a symbolic as well as a physical role in what follows. Early in the film an officer in charge during his lord's absence asks its forgiveness for the sadistic ordeal he plans to orchestrate. The scene oddly combines ancient beliefs in animism and what sociologists of modern Japan have called "*kagemusha* polycentrism," that is, the deliberate concealment of power behind ceremonial heads. This iconic form of ancestor worship is trumped later when the hero Tsugumo takes the mannequin hostage to ward off the house guards. He employs the armor as a shield (one is tempted to say "human shield" given the anthropomorphizing of the figure), and the guards draw back. The mannequin seems to be the embodiment of a symbolic mandate that interpellates everyone in Iyi mansion. In the climactic fight at the end Tsugumo succumbs to overwhelming odds but not before "killing" the mannequin and a score of Iyi's automaton-retainers. Once the battle is ended the clan begins cleaning up: The mannequin is repaired and restored to its place of honor and the campaign of disinformation about what has actually transpired begins with a vengeance.

That the mannequin embodies the symbolic mandate of the Iyi clan is evident not only in the psycho-spiritual hold it has over the mansion's inhabitants but also in the clan's cynical adherence to "pure tradition." They repeatedly insist on following ceremony and protocol to the letter, though their rituals are as hollow as the mannequin they serve. In the opening sequence an extended series of pans and tracking shots explores the empty palace. These vacant rooms and corridors confirm Kobayashi's view that environment in the modern world pre-exists individuals and produces their subjectivity. Yet the camera, in tracking across interiors partitioned by posts and walls, also seems to suggest the artificiality inherent in the distinct frames of motion picture photography. In fact the camera work recalls the self-conscious reference to the apparatus in the opening sequence of Hitchcock's *Rear Window* (1954), though in Kobayashi the contiguous frames are not teeming with life, they contain enormous zoomorphic murals but no human beings. Once men do begin appearing within this empty space they seem spawned by the mansion itself, virtual human beings whose power derives from their context — an effect intensified at the end of the film when scores of retainers hidden behind sliding panels rush forth to surround the hero. The first to hear Tsugumo's petition is a low-ranking bureaucrat sitting in the Seiza position, but backed by a mural of a crouching tiger. The shot does more than simply register the menace behind the little placeman, it helps to identify the mansion itself as Tsugumo's antagonist. A textbook example of Althusser's Ideological State Apparatus, the house also represents in the Lacanian sense the supra-personal aggression of the vacuous Real. Its armor mannequin is the seed of this environment, its kernel, from which the many cunning passages of the house exfoliate. Within this environment human beings are only the automata of a structure of power that actualizes itself through them. The house is the kind of place where not only the samurai but also history itself goes to die.

Lacan maintained that suicide is the only successful act because it is outside the symbolic, performative matrix in which all other human activities take place. In its elaborate, ceremonial rituals *seppuku* would seem an exceptional case in which suicide is carefully orchestrated to produce meaning and to determine one's place in the Symbolic order. Indeed, in Kobayashi's film, the most despicable machinations of the ruling elite are all directed at controlling the act and its significance, thereby rendering it unsuccessful in this sense. For Žižek (1999, p. 170), there are two deaths, death in the Symbolic and death in the Real; the space between these two deaths is the realm of ghosts and spirits. Those dead in the Real, like Hamlet's father, can persist until the ghost is laid by paying its symbolic debts. In Aeschylus' *Antigone* the struggle of the heroine is to restore her dead brother's place in the Symbolic order by performing the funeral rites that the tyrant Creon has forbidden. Thus the responsibility to fix death in the Symbolic often falls upon family, as it does in *Harakiri* as well. Like Hamlet and Antigone, Tsugumo sacrifices himself to pay the symbolic debt of his son-in-law, though in the cynical politics of the film not even this sacrifice is sufficient to dispel the dark con of the Iyi propaganda machine.

The whole of the film takes place within the extended interval between Tsugumo's arrival at Iyi manor, asking permission to commit ritual suicide, and his final act of *harakiri*. Outside Iyi manor we witness in flashback or

Tatsuya Nakadai (as Hanshiro Tsugumo, screen right) takes his long awaited revenge in Masaki Kobayashi's *Harakiri* (1962).

hear reported three examples of *harikari*, including the special form of *tsui-fuku*, which Tsugumo's close friend Jinnai performs to accompany their disinherited lord into the afterlife. Tsugumo is asked by his friend to absent himself from this felicity awhile in order to raise his own daughter and to foster his friend's son, Montome. The Iyi clan force this young man — and six months later his foster-father Tsugumo — to commit "suicide" under such despicable circumstances that the clan's cynical manipulation of tradition is exposed as pure commodity fetishism, whereby honoring ritual masks a simple unwillingness to share economic resources. Virtual and actual interchanges determine the film's exploration of honor and face-saving cowardice. When the destitute Montome presents himself at the manor asking to commit ritual suicide, the functionaries insist on taking him at his word rather than offering him money or a place, as other clans had done with such desperate suppliants in the past. When he begs a short respite, this confirms their belief that he is a cheap extortionist. Discovering his two swords are only bamboo, they compel him to commit *harakiri* with the shorter of the two, thereby transforming the simulacrum into the real. Of course, this faux sword has no edge or sharp point so that Motome's "suicide" becomes an obscene and extended ordeal, a kind of self-mutilating parody of *harakiri* in which death is at first feared, then desperately sought, but found only when the young man bites off his own tongue. For the Iyi clan "the sword is the soul of the samurai" and Motome's bamboo blades mark him as a fake and a cheat. The ranking officer in the house recounts the story in flashback to Tsugumo as an object lesson against presuming to trifle with him. Asked repeatedly about his "intentions" Tsugumo assures him that both his blade and his desire to die are quite real. True insofar as it goes, yet the full scope of his intentions emerges only as he narrates his tale of the last eleven years, leading up to that moment six months before the present when Motome tried to extort money by asking permission to kill himself.

The background to that moment, offered in a series of flashbacks narrated by Tsugumo, allows the clan as well as the audience to see Motome in a very different light, not as a deceitful opportunist but rather as a husband and father desperately trying to provide for his sick and starving family (his wife and child die of a fever when he fails to return). Tsugumo's revenge on the three high-ranking samurai who conspired to compel Motome's "suicide" is not simply to kill them but rather to expose their cowardice before the whole clan. He seeks each out in turn, defeats them in a duel, and cuts off their top knots — the distinctive sign of their membership in the samurai class. One by one Tsugumo throws these knots onto the ground of the courtyard within Iyi mansion, giving the lie to the sick notes sent to explain the absence of these men from their duties. Such a physical mark of dishonor is too long lasting and all are forced to commit suicide themselves. In surviving Tsugumo's haircut the three have already died in the Symbolic but lived on to their eternal shame. The scandal of their symbolic castration and its very public revelation leave them no choice but to perform a ritual they themselves have emptied of all honor and significance.

Kagemusha

In 1971 Akira Kurosawa survived a nearly fatal attempt at suicide by razorblade. When he finally began production on *Kagemusha* (1980) he had not made a film in Japan for nearly ten years. Throughout the late seventies it looked as though *Kagemusha* would never be produced, until the timely intervention of Francis Ford Coppola and George Lucas convinced Twentieth Century-Fox to purchase the international rights to the film. In the long delay, Kurosawa painted more than a thousand pictures of the film he had in his head. This was not mere storyboarding but rather an elaborate realization of his vision in still pictures of the moving picture he thought he would never be allowed to make. Thus the film entitled *Kagemusha* (*The Shadow Warrior*) spawned its own virtual double, a shadow film that, when funding for the actual film finally became available, determined to an almost unprecedented degree the form it took (Yoshimoto, p. 354). Movement in the film is typically frenzied, without apparent purpose, and often self-destructive; stillness is an abiding virtue both of the mise-en-scène and of the plot as well. In realizing his paintings on film, Kurosawa created a painterly style in which movement is allied to the destructive forces of time.

Further shadows stalked the film. After his suicide attempt, Kurosawa's work grows darker and appears to slip its moorings to humanism and heroic individuality. In the last half of the seventies he was at work on three projects, along with *Kagemusha* he was also developing *Ran* (*Chaos*) as well as a never filmed version of Poe's "Masque of the Red Death." If we ask ourselves what kind of projects would interest a director who had become a shadow of his former self, we would probably imagine ironic, apocalyptic stories like these. *Kagemusha* is rife with quotations from his earlier works, such that Kurosawa seems to be self-consciously making a Kurosawa film. On the first day of shooting another shadow was cast across the project, when the famous comic actor Shinaro Katsu arrived on the set with television cameras in order to record his performance. When Kurosawa refused to allow this shadow film to be made alongside his own, Katsu was replaced by Tatsuya Nakadai (who had played Tsugumo in *Harakiri*). The script had been written with Katsu especially in mind and his loss is evident throughout, where intended comic touches fall awkwardly flat. In my first chapter, I detailed the odd interplay between the imaginary and the real in the making of Annaud's *Name of the Rose*; here I would claim that virtual films similarly overshadow the version of *Kagemusha* actually produced — to such an extent that the film becomes its own pale imitation.

In Garcia Marquez's *The Autumn of the Patriarch* (1975), as well as in the recent film *The Last King of Scotland* (2007), doubles convey the seeming immortality of totalitarian rule; but Shingen's death early in *Kagemusha* allows Kurosawa to focus on the waning shadow of feudalism itself. The opening scene emphasizes the virtue of stillness as well as the attenuations of the virtual. An extended long-take (6 minutes and 55 seconds), filmed with a stationary camera, explores in a leisurely fashion the virtual nature of identity and rule. At the upper center of the shot is a decorative wooden flower with four petals meeting at a central stamen from which radiate veins to the middle of each leaf. The petals at the eastern and western points are fully developed, those at the northern and southern points are half-sized. This pattern of reflection and distinction is duplicated by the human figures: Takeda

Shingen is seated in the exact center of the frame, screen left is occupied by his brother Nobukado, screen right by the "thief," and between Shingen and his brother, reflected above and behind them on the wall, is the shadow of the shogun — only he and his sword cast a shadow within the frame.

In the complicated parallelism of this shot, Shingen and Nobukado occupy the place of the developed petals, Shingen's shadow and his would-be shadow the thief, those of the truncated petals. The image is also subtly complicated by gradations of height. Shingen sits on a raised platform on the dais, Nobukado on the dais, and the thief on the floor — subtly reflecting differences in status — but the Shingen's shadow is highest of all. The three human figures are clothed identically and seated in similar postures. A split screen allows the actor playing both Shingen and his *kagemusha* to appear together in what seems the same frame, while both gestures and language serve to isolate the thief in the foreground and to distinguish him from the three figures in the background. As Nobukado remarks on the uncanny resemblance achieved by dressing the shogun and the thief in the same clothes, Shingen replies that the thief is too morally corrupt to serve as the double of his august self. He punctuates the remark by lifting his arms and readjusting his robe — a gesture aped not only by his shadow on the wall but also by his brother. The thief turns down and away from the dais in apparent deference, though his verbal response is anything but deferential: "I stole only a few coins. I'm a petty thief. A man who's killed hundreds and robbed whole domains is hardly the one ... (turning toward Shingen and becoming tongue-tied) is hardly the one to call ..." (at this point he turns in silence away from Shingen). As the thief collapses in frustration, Shingen picks up the case against himself, playing the role of thief, but sliding into a self-justification that denies the similarities he has just admitted: "I am wicked, as you say. I am a scoundrel. I banished my own father and killed my own son. I will do anything to rule this country. War is everywhere. Unless somebody unifies the nation and reigns over us, we will see more rivers of blood and mountains of the dead." Yet having established their differences, Shingen reverts again to their similarities: the thief has demonstrated by his boldness that he may well make a worthy double. Only when Shingen rises to leave does he appear vulnerable; he complains of an old wound and follows his shadow out of the room.[10]

The next scene is in direct counterpoint. The long take emphasized power as a function of stasis, but frenetic movement presaging a loss of control, a coming chaos, follows it. The messenger's broken-field dash down the stairs wakes the sleeping soldiers into confused attention — a dash tragically echoed at the end of the film when the double seeks his own death by running through a battlefield strewn with the corpses of Shingen's army. Hidden cuts follow the messenger down the winding stairs through the three squadrons —fire, wind, and forest —but his message is trivial and the accompanying music makes the whole scene comically portentous. Movement is weakness, panic, vulnerability; power resides in restraint, which Shingen alone seems to possess in his rural hide-away, while the *kagemusha* takes his place near the frontlines. In fact the shogun is restless himself and longs to join his men and to hear the flute that plays in the night from the besieged castle. He obsesses over troop movements and strategy for which an old advisor heatedly berates him: "People gather and scatter. They go left and right, following their interests. You know that very well, yet you lose yourself in anger.... A man of such small mind cannot dream of ruling.... You are a mountain monkey. You should be gathering nuts in the mountains of Kai!" The "mountain monkey" epithet is used by friends and foes alike and refers not only to Shingen's ancestral holdings but also to the heraldic and strategic structure of his army. This fourfold structure is evident in the mise-en-scène of the opening long take, and it is ubiquitous throughout the film in the army's banners on which four diamond shapes compose a larger diamond. "Swift as the wind, quiet as a forest, fierce as fire, immovable as a mountain," reads the lord's banner. But Shingen does not stay put; he goes to listen to the flute and is fatally wounded by a miraculous shot in the dark. Predictably, he dies during a journey —his fevered brain mistaking the road all must travel for a march on the capital city Kyoto, which he has spent his whole life waiting to make. He orders his flags flown in the capital and completes in his imagination the conquest denied him in reality. The interval opened by this moment occupies most of the rest of the film, the interval between Shingen's death in the Real and his death in the Symbolic. Shingen himself mandates the interval, leaving instructions that his death be kept secret for three years and exhorting his followers: "Guard our domain, never move from it." Just as their ruler's life seemed to depend upon immobility, so it seems does the survival of the Takeda clan itself.

No one informs the thief that he has become a shadow with no actual counterpart. In fact, the shadow is now the appropriate general for an army whose destruction is at this point only virtual but nonetheless assured. We have seen in *Seventh Seal* and *Andrei Rublev* how movement on a higher plain juxtaposes spiritual and physical realities. Kurosawa's spectacular shot of Shingen's army in retreat from the castle rewards comparison. In the foreground soldiers sit in the dark and gossip about the retreat and the rumor that their lord has been shot; in the background the army marches across a ridge, bathed in the flickering red light of the setting sun. Though "Shingen's" appearance on the ridge quashes these rumors and the lethargy of the soldiers is dispelled, it is only appearance. Here pictures speak louder than words: the doomed soldiers are in a valley of shadows, cast by an illusion.

Blue is the color of Shingen's death. In a mise-en-scène already saturated with primary colors every object associated with the mystery of his death is suffused with blue light, which is projected onto these objects via lens and lighting filters. On the night of Shingen's fatal wounding, the castle seen from below is bathed in blue. Significantly, the filtered light also turns the green (forest) banners brown. As news of his possible wounding spreads, a shutter in a dark room is opened to reveal a snow-covered landscape saturated with blue light, which even shines into the dark room. Shingen's palanquin is shot through a blue filter and blue light glints off the armor of his double. Blue light suffuses councils and meetings where the late Shingen's influence is manifest. In the performance of Nôh theater, supposed to dispel rumors of Shingen's death, his whole army watches the spectacle soaked in the sickly blue light. The enormous earthenware jar in which Shingen's body is stored is wrapped in blue cloth, its color sometimes super-saturated by filtered blue light as well. When the thief breaks open the jar to steal the treasures he imagines hidden within, he discovers instead that he has become the shadow of a dead man. As the opaque jar reveals the limpid reflection of his own face, the thief is scared silly by the *memento mori* image. Like the animism inherent in the armor mannequins of *Ugetsu* and *Harakiri*, Shingen's corpse, dressed in armor and painted green, seems to suggest an immortal power based in equal parts on illusion and loyalty. Yet the thief will finally come to accept, even to covet, his role of inspiring loyalty to an illusion.

The *kagemusha* can never completely inhabit nor fully escape the role of Shingen. Once Shingen's shadow, now he occupies the actual place of the ruler, though he himself is stalked in one scene by a shadow many times his size, which threatens to overwhelm him. He fools "his heir" the grandchild, and even the son Katsuyori, who knows of the ruse, transfers his Oedipal resentments to the double, claiming he is robbed of glory because the personage all imagine to be his father stands behind him in battle. In the double's dream Shingen cracks the urn like an egg and emerges as a fearsome specter in full armor standing against a painted sky, almost as if the moving image had emerged from one of Kurosawa's paintings. Though dead, the lord remains a virtual force that returns like the repressed to threaten the present. The double's reactions are revealing: He first flees, then pursues his alter-ego until he finds himself alone, seemingly trapped in a painting. The painting is bordered by an actual shore, along which he runs looking for a way out, but finds only his own reflection in the water. As he splashes the water, he seems to be trying to dispel this hyperrealization of resemblance but the volume of the splash is out of all proportion so that it sounds as though he were stirring enormous surging waves. He wakes drowning in the raging sea of a mural painted on the wall of his bedchamber. The crystalline structure of the dream confirms the extent to which virtual and actual components are no longer distinguishable.

Perhaps the supreme time-image in the film is the sequence representing the Battle of Nagashino in 1575, in which past and future do battle for possession of the present. As Steven Prince remarks: "For Kurosawa, the Battle of Nagashino embodied a contest between the older cultural heritage and the currents of modernization and Westernization that would prove so decisive" (p. 274). Firearms play a significant role in Kurosawa's *jidai-geki* and are always in a sense the technological border between medieval and modern. In *Seven Samurai* (1954), the three samurai who die are all killed by guns. The only truly dangerous rival of the hero in *Jojimbo* (1961) is a gunslinger. Shingen himself is killed by a sniper's bullet and the event is reenacted and debated so exhaustively that Kurosawa invites comparisons with the magic bullet of the Kennedy assassination. The Battle of Nagashino is not so much a battle as a systematic annihilation of Shingen's Takeda clan, when one

Tasuya Nakadai (as Shingen Takeda and his *kagemusha,* or double) in the painterly dreamscape of Akira Kurosawa's *Kagemusha* (1980).

squadron after another rides to their death in the breach. In the mise-en-scène, the victorious side is hardly seen: They hide behind barriers that obscure all but the business end of their rifles, which they fire with such unimaginable coordination and speed that their volleys mimic the automatic weaponry of contemporary warfare. The double can only, like a true Deleuzian hero, sit and watch the waves of carnage crash. Kurosawa stages a battle between past and future, and there is little doubt about where his sympathies lie. This is to reference more than the horrible beauty of the past spending its final fury on the shores of history, it is to insist upon the grotesque dishonor of superior firepower, regardless of the cause in which it is deployed. The atomic bomb is such a technology and all arguments about the just use of such overwhelming force are a despicable obscenity. As Tolkien himself insinuates, supreme force is inherently evil, debasing all who employ it. Shingen's double runs to meet his death, dashing across a field strewn with the remnants of wind, forest, and fire. His suicide does not imitate Shingen, but rather fulfills, virtually, Kurosawa's.

Excalibur

Released a year after *Kagemusha*, John Boorman's *Excalibur* (1981) shares a number of surprising similarities with Kurosawa's film. First, it seems to have been greatly influenced by a virtual film, which Boorman struggled to produce for over a decade but was never able to make, *The Lord of the Rings*. Yet the influence of Tolkien is everywhere apparent in the film he did complete: in the sword (not ring) of power that is magically reforged, in situating the narrative at the twilight of supernatural creatures on the brink of the rule of men, in its ecological supernaturalism, in its casting of the savior Perceval as a nondescript though willing hobbit-like peasant, and finally (though the list could be extended) in conceiving the final battle as a "return of the king." Boorman has graciously preferred Peter Jackson's *Lord of the Rings* trilogy (2001–03) to the film he envisioned, in which children would have been cast as hobbits, but the technological resources available twenty years hence dwarf those to which Boorman had access in the Britain of the late 1970s. Still, Boorman's "lord of the sword" epic in many ways actualizes his unrealized dream of a Tolkien film. In fact, for Boorman the Arthurian material is a return to a fundamental myth that underlays both his own prior work as well as Tolkien's novel.

Another obvious similarity between Kurosawa's film and Boorman's *Excalibur* is the ubiquitous use of tinted light to saturate the image. Kurosawa's

Merlin (Nicol Williamson) and Morgana (Helen Mirren) among the mossy green forests of John Boorman's *Excalibur* (1981).

deep blue light casts a deathly pallor over the interval between Shingen's deaths in the Real and the Symbolic. Boorman's green light suggests a natural supernaturalism, a virtual life that invests inanimate objects with an aura of magical power. Using high-intensity lamps, green filters, and mirrors to throw green light onto reflective surfaces like swords and armor created the effect.

> It is dark in these woods. I told my cameraman, Alex Thompson, not to consider them as exteriors. I wanted to light them as though we were inside a building. We used green filters on the lamps. We pumped green light on to green moss to make it luminous. We shone emerald light at the oaks and on to swords and armour, to enhance the mystical sense of the forest as a palpable living thing [Boorman, p. 241].

This gilding of the lily can be blatant at times (and would become more so in later films, as I will discuss), yet the very artificiality of this movie magic is strangely in tune with the film's bumbling and bombastic magician. Indeed, Nicol Williamson's Merlin steals the show, as he was meant to, because part of the charm of his making, like Boorman's, is the ersatz excess of his powers.

The time-image of the film is not merely crystalline in the metaphorical sense of Deleuze's image typology but literally a "crystal cave," an image borrowed from Mary Stewart's Merlin trilogy the first of which is entitled, *The Crystal Cave*. Here the action-image is for an extended and disastrous interval trapped within a time-image. The screenplay conflates the Malorian use of prophetic dreams with the interlace structures of romance to create a world in which dreams have immediate, physical consequences in reality. A sequence of interwoven scenes in the latter half of the film produces an extended interval that sees a freeze-dried Merlin re-entombed in the crystalline womb that bore him, the onset of the wasteland, and the birth of Mordred. For Boorman the film encapsulates the history of mankind: "man pulling himself up from the swamp, the progress of civilization and the wasteland." The return of the action-image at the end of the film as Arthur rides again with his knights is obviously beyond this pattern: It represents the virtual nature of a once and future king who might potentially heal the modern wasteland.

In the extended interval that creates the wasteland, time and space, dream and reality lose all distinction. These realms begin to fall together in Lancelot's dream, where his ideal self, dressed in his armor and wielding his sword, attacks Lancelot. He defeats his armored doppelgänger only to discover its emptiness, like the armor mannequins in the Japanese films discussed above. But he discovers as well that he has been badly wounded by this figment with his own sword. The wound is both physical and metaphysical, a love wound that will never heal. The psychomachic battle in the forest is soon replayed in actuality when Guinevere meets Lancelot there, but he and his sword are no match for her. Their nakedness in the lush green landscape suggests another fall of man, an effect cinched when the lovers wake to find Excalibur stuck in the ground between their naked bodies and react with shame and despair. In the parallel scene, Merlin takes Morgana into the crystal cave on the pretext that she will finally become his apprentice:

> (Merlin): "Here I was born, here all things are possible and all things meet their opposites." (Morgana): "The future?" (Merlin): "And the past." (Morgana): "Desire." (Merlin): "And regret." (Morgana): "Knowledge?" (Merlin): "And oblivion." (Morgana): "Love?" (Merlin): "Yes, love."

The crystals of the cave, we are told, are the bowels of the dragon, yet that monster is both ubiquitous and invisible. Early on, Merlin lulls Arthur to sleep and suggests that he dream in the arms of the dragon. The precocious Arthur discovers that Excalibur too is part of the dragon, forged as Merlin tells him before time began. Merlin is also immortal and part of the dragon, perhaps its head. Fog is its breath. A riddle seems to be posed, which the film itself never answers explicitly, though, the answer is clear enough: The dragon is time itself. Time, as Deleuze never tires of reminding us, is not in us, we are in time. Past, present, and future are screened within the crystal cave like so many movies in a Cineplex or so many reflections in a house of mirrors: Uther embraces Igrayne, Lancelot Guinevere — their bodies nestled in the green stalagmites of the crystal — and Morgana hatches a plan to take on the form of Guinevere to seduce Arthur, just as Uther had deceived Igrayne. When Arthur drives Excalibur into the ground between the two sleeping lovers, it simultaneously plunges through Merlin's body and into the spine of the dragon. Only a moment before the magician was about to consign Morgana to oblivion, now she weaves the same smoke of lust around him that he had used to aid Uther, crystallizing him in a kind of suspended animation. Merlin thus becomes an essential example of the Deleuzian hero, frozen in time and doomed to watch the tragedy of history unfold like a dream.

Time and space continue to collapse, once the sword has cut into the spine of the dragon. Paganism, everywhere referred to but nowhere seen, begins to wane. Morgana conceives Mordred in one scene and gives birth to him in the next amidst all the trappings of a satanic rite, complete with chanting, black robes, and a lightning storm. Parallel with this is the film's sole depiction of Christianity: in a church Arthur is about to receive the Eucharist beneath a stained glass window depicting a cross. A lightning bolt strikes him, simultaneously with the moment of Mordred's birth, a blow that makes him the film's "Fisher King" and also looks forward to the death-wound he receives from his "son" at the end. The grail quest takes place on both physical and spiritual planes, though there are numerous interchanges and indeterminacies. Bodies of the knights whose quests have failed hang from a tree, while their spirits serve Morgana, who enchants them with "many cups from which to drink." Perceval hangs on the tree with the other strange fruit of the grail quest, but when a spur slowly frays his noose he falls back into the real world, where Lancelot — who has become a kind of messianic scourge of Camelot — leads a band of peasants who try to kill him. Perceval tumbles into a stream and, so baptized, emerges for a second time into the supernatural realm of the grail castle, where he is at last prepared with the answer that redeems Arthur — that he and the land are one.

The extended interval of Merlin's internment and the quest for the grail thus becomes, as is increasingly typical of movie medievalism, a period of stasis from which the action-image must be liberated. Perhaps not surprisingly this interval is gendered feminine. The rise of Morgana not only entombs Merlin in the fog of his unfulfilled desire and lays waste Arthur and the land, but it also disrupts the natural flow of time. Morgana herself doesn't age, Arthur and his knights wither quickly, Merlin remains frozen in time, and Mordred grows like a weed — a jump-cut ages him ten years from a boy to a strapping young man as his mother oils his naked body, making him an immortal god like Achilles, though vulnerable not in one spot but only to one weapon. Merlin's return, comparable to that of Gandolf the White in *The Lord of the Rings*, is pure virtuality. He no longer has a physical presence in the world of the film but rather inhabits the spirit-world of dreams and nightmares, though his influence is no less palpable for that. Throughout the film, fog signifies the mythic potential of medieval fantasy, an integral component of a virtual, latent reality that can be actualized by magic. Uther rides across a chasm borne aloft by the fog to sleep with Igrayne, Morgana entraps Merlin by crystallizing the dragon's breath, and later Merlin uses the power of subconscious suggestion to trick Morgana into serving as its withering vent, which "will stand against" her son in battle.

Merlin's transformation of Morgana's sleeping body into a fog machine is but one of many condensations of medieval and movie magic in *Excalibur*. Indeed, it is not a condemnation to say that Boorman's film is a landmark in the smoke and mirrors approach to the "Dark Ages." After the Technicolor costume dramas of the fifties, one welcomes the misty gloom of Boorman's film, its psychological and mythic complexities. This complexity is achieved by a condensation of Malory's *Morte D'Arthur* that attempts to recover the meaning of the myth for modern audiences who know Eliot's *The Wasteland*

and the anthropological readings of the grail legend by the popular works of scholars such as Jessie Weston and Roger Sherman Loomis. Hence, Morgana subsumes three of Malory's heroines; Perceval, not Galahad, successfully fulfills the grail quest; and Bedivere is nowhere in sight when Perceval throws the sword into the sea. Long before the appearance of *Holy Blood, Holy Grail* and its fictional incarnation *The Da Vinci Code*, Boorman suggests that the grail is a person, merging the grail and Arthur through a lap-dissolve. He collapses too Arthur and the Fisher King and reverses the final duel so that Arthur pulls the spear through his body in order to save the world from Mordred. Still, these condensations, displacements, and reversals are in the service of recovering the spiritual meaning of the myth for modern audiences.

Yet the influence of Boorman's film has been largely poisonous. The smoke and mirrors Middle Ages to which the film helped give birth has increasingly deployed the virtual to license an imaginary with little interest in the Middle Ages except as pretext. A clear example of this is the derivative *Sword of the Valiant* (1984) in which the green light is there with a sickening abundance but serves no diegetic function other than atmosphere. Dreams dilate the perfect plot of *Sir Gawain and the Green Knight* and serve as pretext for the introduction of "magical" and soft-core porn elements. In *Merlin* (1998) the spirit world has been colonized by CGI and magic exists only to showcase special effects extraneous to what little of the Arthur story is preserved by the plot. Mists too become an imaginary pretext for parallel, virtual worlds. The Neanderthals in *The Thirteenth Warrior* are creatures of the mist, appearing from the mists of an imagined time. And mist is both barrier and pretext in the made for TV mini-series, *Mists of Avalon* (2001), for the counter-memory that reimagines the myth from the perspective of its women. In the deluge of sword and sorcery films that follow *Excalibur*, there is more smoke than light. The virtual becomes less a realm from which new actualities can emerge than a hyperreal space of virtual simulations with no particular interest in and nothing particularly interesting to say about their putative sources in medieval history and legend.

Timeline

The morbidity of the Deleuzian time-image is perhaps most fully complete in the recent *Timeline* (d. Richard Donner 2003). In many of the films we have examined above, the medieval serves to screen specific modern anxieties, but here it is reduced to an empty form of "just gaming" in the hyperreality of an imagined virtual space. Amusement parks, participatory tourism, role-playing games, and anachronistic societies are its closest analogues. The actors themselves take their roles with a large grain of salt, overacting and under-emoting by turns — just the sort of self-conscious casualness we see in role-playing games. Tension in the film is almost completely lacking because of this sense of a second-order illusion, of watching actors play a role in a game — a role even they are not taking seriously. The whole thing has the feel of Disney "attraction" composed in equal parts of Wells's *The Time Machine*, Twain's *A Connecticut Yankee in King Arthur's Court*, and the strange over-investment in historical detail that Americans seem to like in their fantasy experiences. In fact one thinks of the scene in Mike Figgis' recent *Time Code* in which studio execs are pitched a film called *Time Toilet* through which the present can "send its shit" back to the past.

In the film a team of archaeologists and historians passes through a wormhole into the year 1357. They rematerialize on the day of a supposedly pivotal battle in the Hundred Years' War fought in Castlegard, France. The Star Trek teleportation (their bodies are "faxed" into the past) allows this regrettable film to touch upon many themes taken up in this book: the use of modern experts and their medieval doubles as determiners in the play of historical continuities and differences; the conflation of medievalism with futurism; the construction of the Middle Ages as by turns nostalgic preserve and death trap; troubled parent-child relationships that calque the conflicted relationship of the present with the past; the use of cinema techniques like montage, fade-dissolve, or time lapse photography to create time machines; and the reduction of historical complexities to a fundamental Manichaeism of spirit versus flesh, light versus darkness that continues unabated into the modern world. The taglines used in pre-release publicity for *Timeline* suggest that the past includes both a road to redemption ("They had to travel into the past to save the future") and a trap for the present ("In six hours they'll be history"). The plot stages the rescue of a beloved father and mentor from the clutches of a violent and superstitious world he adored. His rescue by his wayward son and a team of experts serves as a narrative calque on the loving recovery of the past by archaeologists and historians.[11] The fourteenth century is re-created as a virtual past, an amusement park, in which analogy and continuity are rendered retrospectively. At the end of the film, the historians' resourceful colleague Andre Marek is "discovered" atop a medieval sarcophagus holding hands with his wife, Lady Claire, a woman whose history he had rewritten by saving her from the early death history itself had seemed to demand. As the camera pans up from the sarcophagus, it finds the hands of Chris and his beloved Kate locking together in an identical way. The matching pan shot, whose sources perhaps include both the Zales jewelry commercial and John Donne's "The Ecstasy," suggests not only the truism that love conquers time (familiar from the classic historical cinema of Griffith and DeMille), it also renders essential an ideal of romantic love that finds its source in the Middle Ages.

In H. G. Wells's *The Time Machine*, the reactions of the Time Traveler's dinner guests to his initial demonstration bespeak the skepticism characteristic of our own encounters with the contradictions of historical cinema: "its odd potentialities ... its plausibility, that is, its practical incredibleness, the curious possibilities of anachronism and of the utter confusion it suggested" (p. 11). From magic lanterns and Edison's kinescope through the magic of Lumière and Méliès "the odd potentialities" of anachronism and alternate realities are a major part of the early cinema's attraction. Perhaps not surprisingly the ever-prescient Wells describes time travel in cinematographic terms. The Traveler's journey begins as a kind of fast forward, as he watches his cleaning lady streak across his workshop in record time, though he, like a movie audience is invisible to her. As the machine picks up speed, he experiences quick flashes of light and dark: "night followed day like the flapping of a black wing" (p. 16). Then, with the increasing speed of the machine, the persistence of vision effect takes over, and the time traveler sees a continuous, though accelerated reality, akin to time-lapse photography: "I saw trees growing and changing like puffs of vapour, now brown, now green; they grew, spread, shivered, and passed away" (p. 16). Perhaps even more presciently, Wells understood that the past could not be witnessed without effecting it: "'It would be remarkably convenient for the historian,' the Psychologist suggested. 'One might travel back and verify the accepted account of the Battle of Hastings, for instance!' 'Don't you think you would attract attention?' said the Medical Man. 'Our ancestors had no great tolerance for anachronisms'" (p. 6). Like Twain's Connecticut Yankee, Wells's Time Traveler gets caught up in the events he observes, just as both authors themselves recognize their thorough implication in the worlds they construct. For Wells, technology allows us a glimpse at a distant future in which the inequalities of industrial capitalism have, after eons, been inscribed by natural selection upon the evolution of the human species. Evolution has finally resolved (or perhaps returned) to a basic Manichaeism of spirit versus flesh and light versus darkness — the Eloi and the Morlocks. Both species are "degenerate," the upper world Eloi have shrunk in size, strength, and intelligence; the Morlocks live below ground, have regressed to cannibalism, and fear the light. In the recent movie version the Eloi live in elaborate tree cities (reminiscent of the dwellings of the elves in *The Lord of the Rings*) and fear the earth, while the Morlocks venture forth from underground lairs to exact their tribute of human flesh.

Michael Crichton is certainly the most popular twentieth-century heir to Wells in using science to justify historical and futurist fantasies, and he also shares Wells's fascination with technology and his suspicion of capitalism. The moderns' determination not to change the future falls quickly by the wayside: "the Professor" saves his own life by claiming to be a "magister" (again with echoes of Twain's Connecticut Yankee) and is forced to invent Greek fire. And Andre Marek, the hero of the piece, helps to win the battle, saves and marries the fair Lady Claire (whom history had told us was murdered by the English and hung from the walls), and takes his place as part of the history his colleagues return to uncover in the present. I would draw the following conclusions from the interesting premises of this boring film. First, the Heisenberg effect is much in evidence, repeatedly the historians discover traces they themselves have left in the past, which at least gestures in the direction of postmodern historiography. Second, the past is both romantic preserve and death trap: as the title caption has it, "In six hours they'll be history." The fear of the medieval as trap — or repetition compulsion — is a dominant feature of much medievalism; just as the hero Marek's seamless translation into the past calques modern nostalgia, role playing, and anachronistic societies. Third, the grand narrative of a genealogical discourse, which connects past and present, is calqued in the microcosm of the film's father and son: at the beginning of the film, the two barely know one another and the son Chris shows no interest in the past, but by the end he has awakened both to the value of his father and to the value of the past his father represents. As Chris is told portentously early in the film: "Your father is in the fourteenth century." Finally, time travel constructs the other world as a Manichean contest between good and evil. The Hundred Years' War becomes a conflict between darkness and light or the greedy flesh versus the transcendent soul. The English knight, Sir Oliver de Vannes, whom Crichton describes in the novel's historical paratext as a ruler of "honest dignity ... nobility and character," is in the movie an impassive little sadist. While Arnaut de Cervole, the victorious Frenchman, whom Crichton notes was a defrocked monk (called "the Archpriest"), is tall, blond, courteous, and cuts a dashing figure in his powder-blue tunic. This Anglo-French dualism extends to the modern characters as well: The auld alliance is much in evidence: Frenchmen, like the victim Françoise, and Scots, like the heroic Marek and the father-figure Edward Johnson, revere the past, while the English, like the film's Doniger and De Kere, are cold-blooded capitalists.

Deleuze's theory of the time-image grows out of his recognition that the cinema is itself a kind of time machine, an analogy already apparent in Wells's description of time travel (see Rodowick). But *Timeline* does not deploy a car (like the film versions of Wells or the *Back to the Future* series of films), nor does it seem to derive its version of the mechanism from Crichton's novel. Rather, its time machine is borrowed from one of Deleuze's most celebrated time-images, the funhouse of mirrors in Orson Welles's *The Lady from Shanghai*. The large contraption of glass and mirrors reproduces the sense of a prismatic or crystalline reality and the actors within the machine are shot from a variety of angles, which (though to a lesser degree than in Welles) emphasize the exchange and indiscernibility of actual and virtual images, limpid and opaque planes. Time travel is represented cinematographically as a lap-dissolve replete with the noise, wind, pain, and screams of birth. In both films, the time-image is destroyed, in Welles by bullets and in Donner's film by a concussion grenade. Yet here too arises a significant difference. In Welles the destruction of the funhouse is the climax of the film: there is literally nothing left for the lone survivor of the love triangle, his life and the world he inhabits have fragmented beyond all redemption. In Deleuze's terms the destruction of the time-image precludes the possibility of any further, meaningful action on his part. Donner's deployment of this time-image, though,

Clockwise from top, Neal McDonogh, Gerald Butler, Rossif Sutherland, Mike Chute, Patrick Sabongui, Paul Walker and Frances O'Connor ready themselves to be faxed to fourteenth century France via Richard Donner's time machine in *Timeline* **(2003).**

is thoroughly postmodern not only in the conventional sense of a quotation out of context, playful and without depth, but also in its reintegration of the time-image within the sensory-motor schema of the movement-image. More specifically, the Donner funhouse of mirrors explodes near the beginning of the film, trapping its time travelers in the past, but the race to repair the machine parallels and is in concert with action sequences occurring in the oddly synchronous fourteenth-century France. Like the many other barriers and thresholds, which the time travelers are forever breeching in order to escape or rescue one another, the film's time machine serves as an obstacle that the movement-image of action cinema must surpass. As I said earlier, should we care to trace the time-image from modern auteur cinema through to its cooptation in popular films, we could do worse than follow the trajectory from *Shanghai* to *Timeline*.

PART TWO

The Imaginary
Middle Ages

3

The Waywardness of Cinematic Pastiche in *First Knight* and *A Knight's Tale*

If they met aboard some unidentified flying object near Montaillou, would Darth Vader, Jacques Fournier, and Parsifal speak the same language? If so, would it be a galactic pidgin or the Latin of the Gospel according to St. Luke Skywalker? — Umberto Eco, "Dreaming of the Middle Ages" in *Faith in Fakes*

An art not systematic but additive and compositive, ours and that of the Middle Ages. — Umberto Eco, "Living in the New Middle Ages" in *Faith in Fakes*

That medieval style offends me, it is all artifice. What is it that you painters say? Pasticcio. It is all pasticcio.... "It must be real," she went on. "What is the reason for the imitation of an imitation? — Peter Ackroyd, *Chatterton*

This chapter explores certain broad analogies in the American medievalism of popular cinema, focusing primarily on *First Knight* (d. Jerry Zucker 1995) and *A Knight's Tale* (d. Brian Helgeland 2001). Both movies flaunt their anachronisms and are designed not to render faithfully their respective sources in Malory and Chaucer, but rather to appeal to a medieval imaginary, composed of bits and pieces drawn from film history and popular culture. The postmodern call to revisit the past with a mixture of nostalgia and irony is answered in such films by deploying the "prior textualization"[1] of the cinematic history of the "Middle Ages" as pastiche. *First Knight* re-imagines Arthurian courtly romance as an amalgam of feudal horse opera and Hollywood melodrama; *A Knight's Tale* simulates a fourteenth century England as a Debordian society of the spectacle where jousting is an X-treme sport.[2]

What is by turns engaging and infuriating about both films is their postmodern ontology: Exactly what worlds are these?[3] The two quotes by Umberto

Eco above reflect our mixed emotions about the medievalism-by-collage of such movies. We distrust the depthlessness of pastiche and yet recognize that the anachronistic, agglutinative representation of the past in Helgeland's *A Knight's Tale* may be closer to the poetics of Chaucer's "The Knight's Tale" than we would comfortably admit.[4] Likewise, the nostalgic eclecticism of *First Knight* is, mutatis mutandis, a salient feature of many medieval romances. Yet if both films flaunt the conglomerations of postmodernism, they do not share its suspicion of meta-narratives. *First Knight* rewrites the Day of Doom as a Hollywood happy ending, a smooth *translatio imperii* in which Camelot never falls and Excalibur passes from the notably British Connery to the notably American Gere. Likewise, *A Knight's Tale* traces democratic pluralism and Horatio Alger stories back to Chaucer's England.

First Knight

Despite its considerable commercial success in theatrical release and subsequent enduring popularity, *First Knight* has met with a cool and (I think) hasty critical reception.[5] Both film reviewers and medievalists have panned the film as a seemingly chaotic hodgepodge that distorts the Arthurian material nearly beyond recognition. Kevin Harty's authoritative guide, *The Reel Middle Ages*, represents the mainstream opinion:

> Given that there is no one version of the tale of Arthur, Lancelot and Guenevere, filmmakers can be granted some license in their interpretation of that legend. But nothing here quite works. Clearly, Zucker intends his film to be an Arthuriad for the 1990s, but it fails to capture the spirit of the original legend or to make a case for its contemporary translation of an oft-told story [p. 97].

The passage enlists a number of cross-media metaphors that might well repay a closer look. Despite a nod toward the variety of the medieval Arthurian materials, the verdict is primarily derived from assumptions about fidelity to written sources. The vocabulary hints at a methodology widespread in the analysis of films about the Middle Ages. Filmmaking is seen as being analogous to a scholar's "interpretation" of written sources. The director is like an author who "intends" his version as a response to a literary tradition, and expects it to be understood and evaluated in terms of that tradition. Alternately, he is like a translator who ideally should strive to be faithful to the "spirit" of his "original" and to make his new translation timely. These metaphors of scholarship, authorship, and translation are a convenient but misleading shorthand, common to a good deal of academic criticism of films about the Middle Ages. That the roles of medieval scholars and Hollywood directors are in any but the most frivolous ways similar is almost too ridiculous to merit serious consideration were the assumption not so persistent.[6] In any event, the analogy between filmmaking and scholarly interpretation is misleading. It automatically privileges what need not be the most essential component in a film: the validity or creativity of its "interpretation" of a medieval text, legend, figure, or historical period. While such an approach has its place, contemporary films about the Middle Ages made within the Hollywood system are best approached as products of that system rather than as attempts to approximate the interpretations of professional medievalists.

The metaphor of authorship is vastly more problematical. To analyze a movie chiefly as the product of a director's intentions, based on the analogy of authorship as the controlling intelligence of a work, ignores the realities of the movie industry in which the cinematographer, screenwriters, producers, actors, and others, all have an influential role to play.[7] Auteurist approaches, however, have an esteemed history in the analysis of film. The director/author analogy underwrote the professionalization of film theory and the incorporation of film study within the academy.[8] Despite the numerous theoretical challenges leveled at auteur theories, a large number of book-length studies of particular directors like Eisenstein, Ford, Hitchcock, Scorsese, and Kubrick continue to be published each year. Yet herein lies an especial crux for medievalism. While many studies of medieval films are conducted according to the director/author analogy, little of this work addresses the auteur's complete oeuvre; rather, it tends to focus almost exclusively on a single movie or on a selection of movies about the Middle Ages, directed by different people. In the case of Jerry Zucker's *First Knight*, the film's sentimental romanticism, its melodramatic reconstruction of the love triangle, and the self-conscious fetishizing of the kiss cry out for comparison with Zucker's most commercially successful film, *Ghost* (1990). Likewise, many of the wild anachronisms and the introduction of themes from genres like the western and science fiction may begin to appear to be less a product of unthinking popular cinema and more the result of a deliberate authorial tendency toward parody when we compare *First Knight* with more obvious film parodies produced by the Zucker/Abrahams/Zucker team such as: *Airplane* (1980), *The Naked Gun: From the Files of Police Squad* (1988), and *The Naked Gun 2 ½: The Smell of Fear* (1991).[9]

The final term in this triad of metaphors by which medieval films are conventionally judged, "translation," is the most prevalent and the most difficult to dislodge. It proceeds from the assumption that Hollywood's forays into the past should be governed by fidelity to an original text or group of texts according to the far from complimentary aims of translation to "get it right" and "make it new." Even if one relaxes these imperatives from literal fidelity to a prior text to a requirement that filmmakers be faithful to its "spirit," one still runs the risk of introducing misleading comparisons. In the case of *First Knight*, the often implied source that the film is supposed to mistranslate is Malory's *Le Morte D'Arthur*. Rebecca and Samuel Umland have cautioned against "template matching, in other words, discerning the degree of one-to-one correspondence between a film and its (apparent) narrative source; determinations of the film's merit follow as a consequence" (p. xiii). *First Knight* also suffers from implicit comparisons to John Boorman's modernist *Excalibur* (1981), a respectful but revisionist film that follows Malory's story *ab ovo ad mortem*. While Zucker's film has no definitive medieval source, it is in fact a much more elegant "translation" of Malory's work than many critics have surmised. The screenplay adapts the story of Mellyagraunce's kidnapping of Guinevere and her rescue by Lancelot, narrated in Malory's "The Knight of the Cart" episode of the "Book of Lancelot and Guinevere." The film fashions this story into a sort of microcosm of the Mordred plot of kidnapping and invasion that it replaces.[10] However, in doing so the film is faithful neither to the truth of a medieval source nor to the spirit of any medieval legend. It draws instead on a cinematic imaginary about the story of Arthur, Lancelot, and Guinevere, a swirl of patriotic and heroic images of what we might call a cinematic unconscious and its dreams of the Middle Ages. The "spirit" at the center of the film is derived not from Malory per se but from the trans-historical, transnational ideal of Camelot (*quondam civitas et civitas futura*) that is an essential part of the cinematic inheritance. In the words of Connery's Arthur: "That is the very heart of Camelot. Not these stones, timbers, towers, palaces — burn them all and Camelot lives on because it lives in us, it's a belief we hold in our hearts." Or in the more melodious version of Lerner and Lowe's lyrics, there could be no locale more pleasant for "happily ever-afterings" than the eternal city of Camelot. The question of the film's sources will be examined in more detail below, but first I want to discuss how two central themes, violence and the gaze, link *First Knight* with the postmodern anxieties of a number of historical films produced recently.

Violence and the Gaze

The last decade has seen a surge of big-budget, historical epics garner a large share of American audiences. I am thinking in particular of films such as *The Messenger: The Story of Joan of Arc* (d. Luc Besson 1999), *Braveheart* (d. Mel Gibson 1995), *The Patriot* (d. Mel Gibson 2001), *Gladiator* (d. Ridley Scott

King Arthur (Sean Connery, third from left) presides over the Round Table's eternal flame in Jerry Zucker's *First Knight* (1995).

2000), and *Kingdom of Heaven* (d. Ridley Scott 2005). These films all share an abiding concern with the construction of national identities in the face of colonialism or imperialism. Historical accuracy is seldom a consistent feature. They are probably best categorized by Linda Hutcheon's (1998) term "historiographic metafiction" where the past is revisited through cunning appropriations and additions that address contemporary concerns and foreground their status as motivated remediations of history. Such works investigate the constructedness of received history and project contemporary desires into the past. Still, whether we choose to view the historiography of recent popular cinema as revisionist or opportunistic, it is difficult to ignore the similarity of their appeals to patriotism and national identity. One could argue, for instance, that *Braveheart* and *The Patriot* are in almost every important way the same movie, and that the resemblance is far from nugatory. American patriotism has gone back in time to colonize the patriotic struggles of the past. Contemporary American audiences are interpellated into wars for liberation, national identity, and democracy with which they only too readily identify.[11] Remote, complicated historical processes become distant but clear approximations of American democratic freedoms. And the English, identically sadistic, tyrannical oppressors in thirteenth-century Scotland, fifteenth-century France, and eighteenth-century North America, are made to bear the whole historical burden of colonialism. Americans in the past (*The Patriot*) and in the future (e.g., *Independence Day*, d. Roland Emmerich 1996) are heroic resisters of colonial domination whose current privilege as the sole remaining superpower exists only to promote freedom (and free trade) throughout the world.

Such films thrive on ecstatic carnage and the supernatural invincibility of pious rage, a rage that remains sympathetic because of the particularly grisly way it is born. Both *Braveheart* and *The Messenger* provide a back story of disgusting savagery to explain their heroes' zealousness in battle as adults. In *Braveheart*, Blind Hary's fictional Barns of Ayr story is transposed to an episode that Wallace experiences as a boy, where he rushes into the barn only to be trapped and traumatized by a harvest of swinging corpses that includes his father and brother.[12] Luc Besson's *The Messenger* has the young girl Joan witness her sister's rape and murder from inside a cupboard. The violence in such scenes strikes an audience with particular immediacy because our gaze is sutured to that of a child and also justifies our sympathy with his or her pious carnage later in the movie. Like Joan of Arc and William Wallace, *First Knight*'s Lancelot is a child victim, and like them this status seems to confer on him supernatural abilities as a warrior.[13] As Guinevere herself concludes, "it made you what you are." However, the back story of the murder of Lancelot's family has none of the visceral or visual immediacy of the examples mentioned above. It consists of two brief flashbacks of a burning church in which the camera, in relatively objective mid-shot, shows only the anguish of the boy watching outside, not the suffering of those inside. While being burned alive is surely a gruesome way to die, we do not really watch it happening — and neither does Lancelot, who sees only smoke and stained glass. The distinct lack of carnage in the scene is not an isolated reticence. Despite a screenplay thickly crowded with violence of all sorts (pitched battles, sneak attacks, and hundreds of deaths) only the scarcest hint of blood is ever seen on screen. Arthur receives three bolts directly in the chest and Malagant is sliced wide open by an Excalibur-wielding Lancelot, but neither shed a drop. Death is stylized, in the manner of the classic style of the Hollywood western and melodrama — genres to which the film's mise-en-scène and worldview are deeply indebted. And just as *First Knight* is remarkably bloodless, it is also remarkably sexless. Not only is there no depiction of sexual intercourse, there is never any implication that any sexual exchange other than a kiss ever occurs! But if the film does seem to frustrate the voyeuristic appetites of its audience, it remains deeply invested in celebrity, the gaze, and spectatorship.

It would be difficult to imagine a film more focused on the visual, although this focus is embedded within a style that refuses to call attention to itself in the manner of more self-consciously scopophilic films like Hitchcock's *Rear Window* (1954) and its legion of imitations. The dialogue is packed with references to looking, eyes, and seeing. Indeed, in the movie's reimagining of the adultery-plot, Guinevere's sole crime is having gazed passionately at Lancelot. Connery's Arthur jealously rages at her: "Then look at me as you looked on him!" Gere's celebrity is constantly evoked in a screenplay that seems structured around recurrent public spectacles. The defining characteristic of Gere's Lancelot is performance: in carnival displays of swordsmanship and agility, in repeated scenes in which he receives enthusiastic applause for his exploits (including a round of applause from Arthur and the knights of the Round Table), and finally when he stands on trial in the public square watched by the assembled population of Camelot. In a nighttime battle with Malagant's army, Gere takes off his helmet and shakes his long hair loose like a shampoo model before flying into battle bare-headed.[14] At the end of this battle he is greeted by admiring stares from the other knights. Gere's performance gives us Lancelot as movie star and sex symbol. Conversely, it is difficult to imagine a contemporary treatment of the Arthurian material with a Guinevere more high-principled and chaste than Julia Ormond's.

Perhaps the most influential essay in film studies in the last thirty years is Laura Mulvey's "Visual Pleasure and Narrative Cinema" (1975). Mulvey showed how traditional cinema genders the viewer's gaze as male and thereby reproduces and confirms in cinematic discourse the patriarchal objectification of women. Mulvey (1989) eventually had occasion to modify the determinism of this thesis somewhat in order to leave more room for oppositional readings of the dominant visual strategies by women themselves. However, the mise-en-scène of *First Knight* seems determined to invert the very strategies Mulvey describes. Gere is continually the object of shots designed to maximize not only his sex appeal and virility but also his vulnerability. This curious reversal of roles is also a fundamental feature of the film's dialogue. Arthur's demand that Guinevere look at him as she had at Lancelot follows an earlier scene in the forest in which Lancelot's confident come-on ("I can tell when a woman wants me, I can see it in her eyes") is unconvincingly rebuffed by Guinevere's embarrassed "Not in my eyes." In this film men solicit the passionate female gaze and a woman is embarrassed when caught in the act of sexually objectifying a man. This reversal may simply be a concession to political correctness or a way of capitalizing on Gere's sex appeal, but it also suits well with Zucker's reimagining of medieval romance as a modern romance or sentimental melodrama. The interpellated look that the film invariably solicits is a feminine, not a masculine, gaze and the melodramatic plot attempts to appeal directly to a feminine audience.

This strategy entails not only a solicitation of the feminine gaze but also a chastening of the male gaze. I want to explore briefly three examples of the chastened gaze, first in the movie's advertising poster and then in two scenes in which sex and jealousy, respectively, rear their ugly heads. The movie poster, reproduced for the cover of videotape and DVD releases, is an iconographically complex piece of cover art. Reading down from the upper right hand corner to the bottom left, it includes a half shot of Connery in the background staring straight out at the viewer and dressed in armor, with a reflection of Camelot emblazoned across his chest. The middle of the poster is transected by the sword, Excalibur, which contains a full-shot image of Ormond's Guinevere with the top half of her body in focus, while her lower half blurs into the sword. She stares down intently at Lancelot, pictured in the foreground bottom right, whose shoulder and biceps cover Guinevere's torso. Lancelot, like Arthur, directs his gaze out of the frame toward the viewer. The poster archly quotes a famous scene from *Excalibur* where Arthur finds the two lovers asleep in a forest, embracing naked under a tree. He plunges Excalibur into the ground between their bodies and ultimately into the back of the world serpent, waking the day of doom. In a tour de force of modernist syncretism Boorman's film substitutes the apocalyptic serpent of Norse myth for Malory's dragon. *Excalibur*'s exploration of Malory's love triangle is also deeply indebted to classical tragedy and its psychoanalytic supplements, representing sexual desire as a force that ultimately obliterates all it touches. *First Knight*, though, draws rather on sentimental, distinctly modern notions of romance. The poster's quotation of this image is thoroughly de-eroticized. Guinevere alone retains the power of the gaze as she looks over and down on Lancelot. One could argue that the image of her contained within the sword represents a woman trapped within the constraints of a feudal system designed to contain feminine desires. Yet the movie repeatedly emphasizes her agency and strong will. The purpose of this homage to *Excalibur* is to address sensibilities shaped by melodrama and the soap-opera, those appealed to in the poster's riding caption: "Their greatest battle would be for her love." The story of Arthur is thus reimagined as a melodrama in which no one is at fault and no one sins: It is simply the tragic way of the world that bad things happen to good people.

My second example occurs early in the film, during Lancelot's first rescue of Guinevere. The scene is worth recalling in detail. It begins with Guinevere fleeing through the forest from Malagant's men when she is pounced upon by Lancelot in a thick scrub of brush. He pulls her underneath his body,

In one of many versions of this design publicizing Jerry Zucker's *First Knight* (1995), Richard Gere's Lancelot (left) and Sean Connery's King Arthur (right) compete for Julia Ormond's Guinevere.

covering her mouth — a posture that out of context would suggest assault rather than protection, and fear of this is certainly present in Guinevere's eyes at this point. Two villains arrive and Lancelot makes short and showy work of killing them, watched from the bush by Guinevere in wide-eyed fascination. When she stands up, a third assailant grabs her from behind in a chokehold and, with his other arm, trains a crossbow on Lancelot. Guinevere is held with her back to her attacker, both face Lancelot. The following exchange ensues.

> BAD GUY: You, drop the sword.
> LANCELOT: All right, but can I have her when you're done with her?
> BAD GUY: You were after the woman?
> LANCELOT: Of course, of course. You ever see anything so beautiful in your whole life?
> BAD GUY: I don't know about that.
> LANCELOT: Ah, don't tell me you don't want her. Soft skin, sweet lips, young, firm body.
> BAD GUY: I have my orders.
> LANCELOT: So? Who's to know?
> BAD GUY: I should take her back.
> LANCELOT: How 'bout I hold her for you, you hold her for me? It won't take long.
> BAD GUY: I don't want any trouble.
> LANCELOT: This one's no trouble. No, look at her, she wants it alright.
> BAD GUY: What's she doing?
> (All this while Guinevere has been fumbling with her hands held below her waist out of the shot. Now we cut to a very tight shot that reveals her fingering the trigger of a very phallic crossbow.)
> LANCELOT: See for yourself, turn her around, look in her eyes. See what she's got for you.
> (The bad guy turns her around, pressing her against his body.)
> BAD GUY: Oh, pretty!, pretty! Now what have you got for me then?
> (We hear the clink of the crossbow trigger and Guinevere's would-be rapist drops to his knees, staring bug-eyed up at her. He then falls flat on his back with the black bolt jutting perversely from his groin. Guinevere's eyes dart fearfully back to Lancelot and she receives an admiring nod of approval.)

Lancelot's trick cleverly solicits the objectifying male gaze of her attacker as well as the masculine gaze of the audience who watch her held squirming against his chest and fumbling with her hands beneath her waist. This object lesson in the perversity and impotence of the voyeuristic gaze climaxes with a soft groan from Guinevere as the bolt strikes its target in his lower abdomen. The broad phallic joke as he lies prostrate on the ground with a fatal erection punishes with death and ridicule his attempt to look at Guinevere as a sexual object.[15] Perversion has itself been perverted in a very literal sense. The scene presents in physical form the etymology of the word: the Latin *perversus* (lit., facing the wrong way round, reversed) from the verb *pervertere* (1. To overturn, knock down; 2. To cause the downfall of a person, subvert; 3. To cause to face the opposite way; 4. To distort, misrepresent, divert to an improper use).[16] What she "has for him" is a hidden phallus: he's been had. As we will see in later chapters, rape and the threat of rape have a disturbing and significant ubiquity in movie medievalism. Often too, as in this case, rape serves ultimately to endow its victims such as Besson's Joan of Arc and the eponymous heroine of *Pope Joan* (d. Michael Anderson 1972) with the phallus. The plot of Zucker's film, however, eventually replaces the lustful male gaze with a mixture of sentimentalism and Augustinian *caritas*, as I hope to show in my final example of the chastened gaze.

The classic Hollywood style produces a movie to be looked through, not at. Film editing, shot protocols, music, lighting, and dialogue propel viewers through the story without calling attention to its construction, thereby rendering the simple joys of escapist fantasy through a coherent and uninterrupted diegesis (see, for instance, Bordwell, Staiger, and Thompson 1985). Zucker's film seldom deviates from such a style. One notable exception occurs at the point of crisis in the melodramatic plot when Arthur discovers Lancelot and Guinevere kissing in her room. Radical montage — which Sergei Eisenstein saw as the art of cinema and the chief sign of auteurism — occurs in Zucker's film only this once. The camera zooms in for an extreme close-up of Arthur's jealous eye, glaring at a penitent Lancelot. Then an associative montage, connected by a lap-dissolve, links his eye to the next shot of a burning cauldron.[17] The lap-dissolve expresses the vertiginous collapse of Arthur's world, much like the eye-as-vortex shots that open Hitchcock's *Vertigo* (1958) from which Zucker's image is derived. Next, the camera tracks outward from the central image of the burning eye/cauldron to take in the Round Table itself and Arthur's knights being told of the scandal. In a following scene, Arthur widens the circle of the spectacle even further by throwing open the city gates and allowing everyone to watch Lancelot and Guinevere's trial for treason. The sequence in its widening scope thus mirrors the ripple effect of Arthur's jealousy. Perhaps unsurprisingly, those watching the scandalous trial are themselves under surveillance. Malagant's army springs a surprise attack immediately upon Arthur's tragic recognition that the trial and his jealousy are proud folly. (Of course, the idea that a spectacular sex scandal and show-trial could destroy a popular leader and plunge a society from its peak of prosperity is a far-fetched idea.) However, the film's continued insistence on the pleasures and moral probity of democratic spectacles is subsequently reaffirmed when all the inhabitants of Camelot (king and commoner, knights, women and children) unite to repel the invasion. The democratic implications of the scene bear a strong similarity to the conventional platitudes of Western democracies about terrorism: A free and open democratic society exposes its leaders to both scandal and assassination and places its citizens at greater risk — but it is the only kind of society worth defending. I explore in more detail the significance of public spectacles in medievalized projections of American society in my discussion of *A Knight's Tale* below. *First Knight's* political allegories receive a fuller consideration later as well, under the rubric "Malagant and the Pax Americana." But let us return briefly to the final sequences of the film, which stage the chastening and final sublimation of Arthur's jealous eye.

From the instant Arthur sees Lancelot and Guinevere passionately kissing, the plot moves with Aristotelian precision. Jealousy overcomes Arthur's compassion and he pridefully insists on a public trial in which he makes threats with the self-righteous indignation of a classical tyrant: "the law will judge you." In the next scene, Arthur, gazing down from the dais at a kneeling Lancelot who offers to give up his life for the good of Camelot, finally recognizes his folly, averts his eyes, and mutters, "may God forgive me." When Malagant and his army take control of the city, Arthur is commanded to kneel in submission before Malagant or die. He appears to obey, bowing down, but then, in his last act as king, he raises Excalibur and commands his people to "fight, fight!" At this moment he turns from classical tyrant to Christian martyr, and his willingness to sacrifice his own life (mirroring Lancelot's own willingness to die in the service of Camelot) saves the city. Later, on his deathbed, Arthur lovingly strokes Lancelot's hand as he gives him Excalibur, and then gazes adoringly at Guinevere. All passion spent, his final words are "I can see it now my love — the sunlight in your eyes." As he dies his eyes remain open, averted slightly from Guinevere to the heavens. The melodrama here is deeply invested with an Augustinian *caritas* toward which the film's chastening of the gaze has been moving all along. The ship-burial at sea with which it ends is clichéd and anticlimatic in the extreme, but also thoroughly in keeping with the almost obsessive derivativeness of Zucker's film. However, it does allow him a chance to close the circle of the theme of the fiery gaze. The last shot shows Arthur's burning boat encircled by the dark sea. Quite clearly, this is designed as a visual echo of the shot that began the sequence of the burning cauldron in the middle of the Round Table within the dark hall. The symbol of an eternal flame is an unabashed evocation of sublimity, the sign of an eternal Camelot and the transcendent love it represents. As Arthur says earlier in speaking of the physical city, "burn it all, and Camelot lives, because it lives in us, it's a belief we hold in our hearts." Sublime and sentimental surely, but, I would argue, deliberately and adroitly so. Still, it would be difficult to find any romance from the historical Middle Ages more faithful to the spirit of Augustine's theological distinctions between cupidinous and charitable love on the one hand, and between the city of man and the city of God on the other. In this restricted sense Zucker is perhaps more "medieval" than Malory himself. The combination of nostalgia and pastiche that results from Zucker's melodramatic Augustinianism is explored next.

Going to Pieces

It may be that a director's tendency to think visually, in terms of the shot, is perpetually at odds with the narrative constraints of popular cinema. The transparency of the classic Hollywood style is certainly at odds with heavy-handed auteur cinema that calls attention away from the story and toward the artifice of its construction. Idiosyncratic montage and distinctive mise-en-scène play an important role in foregrounding the director as the creator of a film. Other signs of authorship, such as a director's appearance in his own movie or the ironic quotation of other films, also play a part. The transparent (*metteur en scène*) style of Zucker's *First Knight* leaves few clear traces of authorship. Its hodgepodge of neutral quotations from the archive of popular film would seem to leave it open to the charge of "blank or blind parody" leveled by Jameson at postmodern pastiche. Even more relevant is Jean Baudrillard's critique of postmodern images, which he sees as controlled by the logic of late capitalism, namely, simulation. For Baudrillard the final, postmodern, phase of the image comes when copies no longer bear any meaningful relationship to their originals or to any reality whatsoever. When the image becomes its own pure simulacrum, it erases any connection to history or to the real, becoming "hyperreal." It could be argued that Zucker's film makes of the legend of Camelot just such an image, a sourceless story in a timeless world that reflects only the Plato's cave of popular culture: a kingdom of shreds and patches — a hyperreal Camelot set somewhere between medieval England, the American frontier, and Deep Space Nine, where no one commits adultery, where Camelot never falls, and room is left at the end for a sequel! However, some of the film's parodies are more than empty shadows playing on a wall. There are distinct signs of authorial irony and political burlesque beneath its postmodern superficiality. Still, the profusion of pastiched quotation deserves to be surveyed before we try to pick up the pieces in search of patterns of irony or allegory.

Like Zucker's early credits in more obvious parodies such as *Airplane*, *Top Secret*, or *The Naked Gun*, *First Knight* is at least in part a send-up of the genre picture. The title seems roughly "medieval" but it clearly recalls big-budget, patriotic action films such as *First Blood* (d. Ted Kotcheff 1982) and *Top Gun* (d. Tony Scott 1986). Indeed, as Arthur's first blade, Lancelot goes through a process of maturation similar to Tom Cruise's Maverick in *Top Gun*. He begins the film as a fatherless, self-obsessed outsider whose fearlessness grows out of alienation and spiritual emptiness. Through an older man's guidance and the love of a powerful woman who tempers his selfishness, Lancelot, like Maverick, finds a new family in the army and takes his rightful place as their leader at the end. Lancelot's character (like Maverick's) is drawn almost whole cloth from the gun-for-hire exile of American westerns (see, for instance, *Shane* [d. George Stevens 1953] or *Angel and the Badman* [d. James Edward Grant 1946]). He rides a small, sleek pony saddled with a bedroll which comes trotting to its master whenever he whistles. He foils stagecoach robberies, tracks villains to their hideout, and magically disarms antagonists without hurting them. At the end of the pre-credits sequence in which he demonstrates how well he can handle a sword, the hero rides off, iconically, into the sunset. Just as more recent Academy Award–winning movies such as Costner's *Dances with Wolves* (1990) and Eastwood's *Unforgiven* (1992) excoriate the stereotypes of conventional westerns, so these stereotypes return with a vengeance in medievalized westerns such as *First Knight* or Costner's own *Robin Hood: Prince of Thieves* (1991). And just as Baz Luhrmann's street gangs in *William Shakespeare's Romeo and Juliet* (1996) tote silver-plated automatic pistols engraved with the words "sword" or even "Excalibur," so too must Lancelot sling his sword like a gun. To emphasize further the blurred boundary between the western and medieval romance, Zucker arms his villains with miniature crossbows, which they fire like Colt 45s.

Richard Gere's Lancelot also follows a number of action-hero stereotypes. The film employs countless quotations of famous action sequences, specifically recalling shots from *Die Hard* (1988), *Lethal Weapon* (1987), *Romancing the Stone* (1984), and the early James Bond. In the second chase sequence, Gere begins by diving à la Errol Flynn's Robin Hood from the castle ramparts into a moat. Then in a shot quoting Connery's own stint as James Bond (*Goldfinger*, d. Guy Hamilton 1964), he latches onto rope and body skis behind a boat towed with such speed that it leaves the distinctive wake of an outboard motor. Later, he and Guinevere make their escape from Malagant's castle by plunging headlong through a subterranean stream and over a waterfall — shots that specifically echo *Raiders of the Lost Arc* (d. Steven Spielberg 1981) and *Romancing the Stone* (d. Robert Zemeckis 1984), respectively. The same sequence of shots is employed to exit Beowulf and his company from the

Thunder Caves in the recent *Thirteenth Warrior* (d. John McTiernan 1999) — the game continues. Closer to the tradition of Arthurian cinema, the film's oft-repeated Round Table oath ("Brother to brother, yours in life and death") is in homage to Robert Thorpe's Technicolor *Knights of the Round Table* (1953). Examples could easily be multiplied, but it would serve no particular end. Recognizing these echoes does not tell us much of anything of importance about *First Knight*, it merely confirms our worst suspicions about the promiscuity of popular cinema. It is blank parody, a simulation in movieland: a style born of film schools and home video, clever perhaps, but as cluttered as a back lot warehouse.

The suspicion of a derivative, facile imitation is doubly encouraged by the fact that all three of the major stars are cast so rigidly to type. Connery, as the reigning king of medieval movies, reprises earlier roles such as those in *The Name of the Rose* or *Robin Hood: Prince of Thieves* in which he serves as the familiar embodiment of a benign paternalism who oversees a younger man's transition into full adulthood. Gere reprises the role of the cold-hearted individualist — narcissistic but technically brilliant — that he has made a career of playing. Just as in the 1990 film *Pretty Woman*, in *First Knight* he is delivered from ruthless selfishness by a woman's love and the respect of a surrogate father. Ormond's Guinevere is also the result of typecasting. In *Legends of the Fall* (Edward Zwick 1994), she again plays the melodramatic role of a strong woman torn between the love of two good men, one whom she deeply respects and the other a wandering individualist whom she deeply desires. As the head of the production company Indican Pictures, associated with Fox Searchlight Pictures, she seems perfectly typecast as a career woman who rules a small empire in her own right. The screen personas of major stars have an enormous influence on the kinds of films they make. Screenwriters or directors — and occasionally even actors themselves — can construct roles contrary to audience expectations, but there has been no attempt to do this in *First Knight*. Indeed, the film could be adequately described in terms of the Hollywood jargon mocked in movies such as *The Player*: "*Legends of the Fall* meets *Pretty Woman* in *Camelot!*"

First Knight is certainly a star vehicle, but it also bears traces of its director's personal style and attitudes. The first hint of this occurs at the end of the film's title sequence. An establishing shot of the pastoral Lyonesse concludes with the final credit "Directed by Jerry Zucker." In the background on a hillside, behind Zucker's name, a windmill revolves in the breeze and sheep graze beneath it. The image quietly suggests the quixotic anachronism of any director engaging in medievalism — tilting (one's camera) at windmills imitates the madness of Don Quixote's quest to re-create the Middle Ages in the modern world. Movie medievalism is here not only quixotic but possibly idiotic as well: in the last instant the music of the sound track ceases to be replaced by the noisy "bah" of the sheep. The effect is relatively subtle but it is all of a piece with the humor of Zucker's earlier film parodies. His shot parodies are also not always as neutral as those outlined above. In a film that seems to respond to contemporary anxieties about violence in popular Hollywood movies, Zucker quotes a scene emblematic of indomitable masculinity, but he quotes it backwards and with irony. The first invasion of Lyonesse culminates with a shot of the villain Malagant on a rearing horse, internally framed by the burning threshold of a barn door. Inside the barn, from the perspective of the frightened inhabitants of Lyonesse, the audience sees this icon of power and domination from the point of view of those oppressed. The framing of this shot quotes Kenneth Branagh's *Henry V* (1989). In Branagh's film, though, the fiery arch of the gate of Harfleur behind him frames the young king. The audience views the indomitable power of Henry from the point of view of his beleaguered soldiers. Henry's two subsequent speeches are perhaps the most stirring calls to patriotic bloodlust in the English language, exhorting "once more unto breech, dear friends, once more/ or close the wall up with our English dead" and next threatening the inhabitants of Harfleur with the murder of old men, the rape of their daughters, and "your naked infants spitted upon pikes." Zucker's quotation of this shot criticizes the might makes right mentality of Malagant and the idea of war fought for personal glory. In contrast to Malagant's pursuit of personal heroism, Arthur wishes only for peace and Lancelot chiefly excels in the rescue and defense of the oppressed.

Perhaps the most distinctive sign of authorship in the movie, as I have been maintaining throughout, is its complete sentimentalization of erotic love. Here that most enduring of Hollywood images, the kiss, plays the central role. Guinevere kisses Lancelot and Arthur each three times, and, in the fairy tale rhythm we expect in romance, the third in each series makes a significant change. Guinevere treats Lancelot's first two kisses as unwelcome advances, and after the second she makes him promise never to do it again. Their final kiss in her chamber is one she asks for, the only really passionate kiss in the film. It is interrupted by the arrival of Arthur. The lovers' reaction to being caught in the act is shot through heavy filters and in slow motion — the close-ups savor of Adam and Eve caught between shame and despair. The final kiss between Arthur and Guinevere occurs on his deathbed. The result of this kiss, as discussed above, is the opposite of eyes downcast in shame, an image of love without jealousy, in which Arthur finds at last "the sunlight in your eyes." The organization of a plot around the kiss is a staple of classic Hollywood filmmaking. The final scene in Zucker's *Ghost*, of course, includes the ultimate transcendental kiss. Patrick Swayze's ghost at last becomes visible to his wife and she kisses an angelic vision of him bated in heavenly light. His parting words are "You take it with you, Moll, the love you feel inside." Just as in *Ghost*, the kiss in *First Knight* becomes a sign of love transcending death and is offered as an alternative to the selfishness and jealousy of cupidity. One could argue that this sentimentalized vision of love, composed of equal parts of Hollywood nostalgia and the Christian doctrine of charity, is a distinct sign of Zucker's authorship.[18]

Colonizing Myth: Malagant and the Pax Americana

Zucker's film is not, however, simply sentimental, it is also a highly nationalistic political allegory, albeit one tinged with provocative satire. Louis Althusser famously insisted that ideology "represents the imaginary relationship of individuals to their real condition of existence." The peculiarity of the American imaginary relationship to imperialism and colonialism has been outlined by Edward Said.

> Even if we were to allow, as many have, that the United States foreign policy is principally altruistic and dedicated to such unimpeachable goals as freedom and democracy, there is considerable room for skepticism.... Are we not as a nation repeating what France and Britain, Spain and Portugal, Holland and Germany, did before us? And yet do we not tend to regard ourselves as somehow exempt from the more sordid imperial adventures that preceded ours? Besides, is there not an unquestioned assumption on our part that our destiny is to rule and lead the world, a destiny that we assigned ourselves as part of our errand into the wilderness? [Said 1993, p. 55].

Such assumptions about the purity of American motives and the certainty of its destiny underwrite much of America's foreign policy, as well as popular cinema's colonization of the Middle Ages, as we have seen. In our medieval imaginary, distant historical struggles become dim approximations of America's globalization of democracy and freedom. Zucker's deployment of this imaginary not only plays to American patriotism but also seems to chide it. The director has a great deal of fun with the official ideology of George H.W. Bush's years (1989–1993) in the White House. At first sight in the film Camelot appears only as a "thousand points of light." Elizabeth Chadwick's novelization of the screenplay makes this connection explicitly:

> On the far bank, Guinevere could see many moving points of light like giant fireflies.... Rising out of the water on the far side the towers of the city of Camelot glimmered with the light of a thousand torches. Reflected in the lake, the city seemed to float in mid-air, as if transported from the mythical land of Faery [Chadwick, p. 75–76].

In the film, as the camera pans downward, the city becomes more easily identifiable as the island of Manhattan.

The film is also distinctly colored with the black-and-white patriotism of the first Gulf War. In this view a peace-loving Camelot/America is drawn into war because of its need to protect weaker nations against old allies who have become rogue nations. Such leaders are less heads of state than warlords, never pictured out of their uniforms. David Zucker's *Naked Gun 33 ⅓*, released the year before *First Knight*, begins with a long running gag about an incredibly "smart bomb," which, after many twists and turns, finally reaches its target: Saddam Hussein sitting on a commode. Though Saddam was in fact ultimately discovered in scarcely less heroic circumstances, the example is useful because it shows how such satire can be double-edged, mocking not only foreign despots but also the absurd hyperboles of wartime propaganda — witness the subsequent though no less absurd attempt to target bin Laden with cruise missiles. The character of Malagant is a particularly interesting creation in this regard. Substituting Malagant for Mordred produces a version of the Arthur legend sanitized of incest and adultery but tightly packed with political implications. It is worth noting that Mellyagaunce's motive for kidnapping Guinevere in Malory's "Knight of the Cart" episode is strictly personal: "And thys knyght sir Mellyagaunce loved passyngly well quene Gwenyver, and so he had done longe and many yerys. And the boke seyth he had layn in awayte for to stele away the queen" (Vinaver, p. 1132). Yet *First Knight*'s Malagant demonstrates no sexual interest in Guinevere at all. She is merely a hostage taken as a bargaining chip, which Malagant hopes will make Arthur "more reasonable" about Lyonesse. If Gere gives us Lancelot as movie star, Ben Cross plays Malagant as Middle Eastern despot — his complexion noticeably darkened to encourage the inference. His crimes include terrorist attacks on noncombatants, hijacking, political kidnapping and ransom demands, border raids, intimidation, and so forth. He is as cruel to his own troops as he is to his enemies and he is willing to sacrifice as many of his own men as necessary in order to win. He raids border towns on the false pretext that he is countering aggression and bringing law and order to a chaotic border: "Last night, men from this village crossed the border and murdered three of my people. In reprisal, I have destroyed your village. The borderlands have been lawless long enough. Know now that I am the law." However, Malagant's real motive, like all Middle Eastern tyrants, is not simply to annex small kingdoms, but rather to bring the superpower Camelot to its knees. In the allegory Lyonesse seems to be both Kuwait and Jerusalem — a kind proto-Israel (Zionesse?) ruled by Guinevere with her spiritual advisor Jacob at her side. The special relationship between Camelot and Lyonesse is not susceptible to change by any temporal condition, nor is it dependent upon what Guinevere does; rather, it is absolute. Beneath the fable is an allegory, part nationalistic and part parodic, of the United States's "special relationship" with Israel and the ideology that underpins American interventions in the Middle East.

At the United Nations Round Table in Camelot, the chair of the rogue Malagant remains empty. When he returns to negotiate with Arthur, Malagant offers to trade peace for land. His political solution is the partitioning of Lyonesse, but Camelot does not negotiate with terrorists. Malagant's criticisms of Arthur's Camelot are based on a suspicion of globalization in medieval form, and Arthur's reply is an appeal to universal democratic principles.

> MALAGANT: Come on Arthur. I'm here to settle this business. We both know Lionesse is too weak to stand alone. Let's say half each. The lesser gives way to the greater, and what could be greater than Camelot: the land of justice and the hope of mankind....
>
> ARTHUR: You know the law we live by. And where is it written that beyond Camelot live lesser people — too weak to defend themselves — let them die.
>
> MALAGANT: Other people live by other laws, Arthur. Or is the law of Camelot to rule the entire world?
>
> ARTHUR: There are laws that enslave men and laws that set them free. Either what we hold to be right and good and true, is right and good and true for all mankind, under God, or we're just another robber tribe.

Their exchange seems a medievalized rendition of the Gulf War propaganda issuing from Iraq and the United States.[19] (Though Malagant's suggestion about the partitioning of Lyonesse also evokes proposed solutions to the "Palestinian problem.") Surely Malagant's suspicions about the motives behind Camelot's interventionist foreign policy are an unfounded pretense, yet the law to which Arthur refers sounds suspiciously like the American Pledge of Allegiance: "One nation, under God, with liberty and justice for *all*." This is not quite Jameson's "blind parody" nor is it simply blind patriotism: Zucker is clearly winking at his audience here. That the Malagants of the world must be resisted at all costs is never questioned in *First Knight*, but exactly how much less tyrannical is Arthur's one law for all than is Malagant's "I am the law" remains an open question.

Perhaps the most radical change to the Arthurian legend is the film's happy ending — more latterly imitated in Antoine Fuqua's *King Arthur* (2005). Hollywood's against-all-odds recourse to happy endings has been a recurrent figure of ridicule in the many *mise en abyme* parodies of the industry (e.g., *The Player*, d. Robert Altman 1992 and *State and Main*, d. David Mamet 2001). Throughout my discussion of *First Knight*'s politics, I have been moving toward the notion of a carefully negotiated balance between patriotism and parody. This is nowhere more evident than in the film's handling of King Arthur's happy death. A central, even defining, theme in medieval romance itself is the notion of *translatio imperii*. Zucker makes of the ending of the Arthur story not a cyclical prophecy of rebirth but a tale of continuity, a peaceful, loving transition as from father to son. Excalibur passes from the British Connery to the American Gere, but the idea of Camelot, transhistorical and transnational, lives on. "Arthur's dream," as Malagant had contemptuously called it, becomes the American dream of a benign superpower that will spread its "one law" across the face of the earth. Umberto Eco claims we are all "dreaming of the Middle Ages," but Zucker suggests they may be dreaming of us as well. King Arthur dreams not of dragons but of America.

A Knight's Tale

If *First Knight* marks a sentimental, nostalgic return to the classic Hollywood style, Brian Helgeland's *A Knight's Tale* heralds the onset of an MTV Middle Ages. And if *First Knight* is in some sense a strange mixture of melodramas like *Ghost* and parodies, such as *Airplane*, *A Knight's Tale* is certainly, in the Hollywood jargon of our time, *Gladiator* meets *Shakespeare in Love*. Such amalgams are increasingly a feature of popular films crafted to appeal not only to established cinema appetites but also to the growing film literacy of audiences who can appreciate cinematic pastiche. I want to focus in turn on two particular discourses engaged in the film: the therapeutics of democratic spectacle and Helgeland's self-conscious addition to the Chaucerian apocrypha.

Democratizing Spectacles and the Thatcherite Knight

In their celebration of spectacle, *Gladiator* (d. Ridley Scott 2000) and *A Knight's Tale* participate in popular cinema's ongoing rehabilitation of the gaze. Through analogies with modern sporting events and other examples of spectator culture, ancient and medieval arenas become sites of democratic freedom in which Debord's anxieties about "the society of spectacle" are ultimately assuaged by a more Bakhtinian view of public space as a carnivalized, dialogized forum of social justice. Spectacle in *Gladiator* appears at first to be doctrinaire Debord. The Roman Coliseum is a monument to empire, a confined and policed space where slaves die only after professing undying allegiance to their emperor. The games also attempt to portray an official

version of Roman history in obscene masquerades. Worst of all, the spectacle is instituted by a proto–Machiavellian dictator as a replacement for real
democracy: open the Coliseum and you can close the Senate. Yet the plot
ultimately fails because Commodus the tyrant, who had sought to manipu-
late the spectacle, is finally drawn into it himself. At the mercy of the celebrity
spectacle manufactures, he finds that he has opened a forum for defiance.
Commodus is first forced to bow to popular opinion, then despairs as the
games make a slave more powerful than the emperor, and finally dies in the
arena as the villain in a public drama into which he has been ineluctably
drawn.

In contemporary movies such as *Gladiator* and *A Knight's Tale* spectacle
restores democracy, despite cynical attempts by those in power to manipu-
late it or use it as a narcotic. It is implosive, drawing into its center and under
its scrutiny people and ideas that the spectacle itself was supposed to fix in
power. The democratized gaze offers a cinematic experience that answers
Debord and other critics of postmodernism with Bakhtin. Popular media can
be a therapeutic carnival that works to dethrone the powerful and question
accepted ideologies — that it may be designed to do the opposite makes little difference. Such a reply to the critics of popular cinema and mass media
has the benefit of offering a way out of the no-exit approach to postmodernity, but it meets their doctrinaire dismissal with an equally doctrinaire acceptance. That popular cinema can be subversive does not mean that it often is.
The implicit exaltation of modern spectator sports and celebrity as the site
of democratic leveling panders to the contemporary obsession with sports
stars as symbols of Western society's pursuit of excellence and its vaunted
progress toward social justice.

A shared devotion to public spectacles is the only abiding similarity
between Chaucer's "The Knight's Tale" and Helgeland's version. Both exalt
spectacles as the supreme expression of civilization. In Chaucer the ideals of
feudalism are undermined by fate (and perhaps by irony as well), whereas in
Helgeland's film they are toppled by an emergent democracy. The film gives
us a view of chivalric hierarchy as it might be represented by the Wife of
Bath, in which real nobility ("gentilesse") is based on worth, not birth.[20] Susan
Aronstein and Nancy Coiner, in their analysis of Disney and Las Vegas versions of the Middle Ages, make an important addition to Eco's celebrated ten
little medievalisms, which they dub "a peculiarly American Middle Ages, the
Middle Ages of Democratic Possibility" (p. 213). Helgeland's story of William's
rise from a thatcher's son to international jousting star certainly qualifies.
After successfully pretending to be a knight, he is ultimately dubbed a knight
in reality by Edward, the Black Prince of Wales, because he so completely

embodies the chivalric ideal (one thinks of British actors such as Sir Laurence Olivier, Sir Alec Guinness, and Sir Sean Connery himself, as well as the many sports stars so honored). The film's remarkable revisioning of the medieval tournament is propelled by the analogies it draws between knights and professional athletes, producing something akin to a medieval aristocracy of sports celebrity.

If *First Knight* embeds anachronism and satire within the seamless diegesis of the classic Hollywood style, Helgeland's *A Knight's Tale* brings the medieval and postmodern worlds into violent collision — like two riders in the lists intent on unhorsing one another. A key characteristic of postmodernist fiction, according to Brian McHale, is its troubled ontology. The villain Adhemar taunts William by asking, "in what world could you have beaten me?" After defeating him William wryly observes: "Welcome to the new world." Our sense of an upstart from a "new world" displacing the old world of privilege is also conveyed in the film by setting Adhemar's (Rufus Sewell) British accent against the distinctly Australian accent of the peasant William (Heath Ledger). This new world is a decidedly capitalistic one in which athletic prowess confers nobility, but the film makes no attempt to hide the preposterousness of such an assertion. The sound track is almost never extra-diegetic: Queen's "We Will Rock You"— the anthem of contemporary sports spectatorship — is heard within the diegesis by fourteenth-century spectators at the joust, who respond, like their modern counterparts, by singing along and stamping their feet to the beat.[21] They also take off their shirts to flaunt their potbellies, do the wave, jostle to catch flying helmets as modern fans do baseballs, and clamor for autographs. The tournaments in the film are arranged on a schedule that forms a "season," ending in London with "The World Championships." The jousts are filmed like modern football (English or American) in which decisive moments within a panopticon are dissected from different angles, close-ups, and multiple replays.

The hero, William, is a boy whose athletic prowess has raised him, like the prototypical American basketball superstar or English soccer player, from poverty in Cheapside to the world stage. In a shot that recalls a number of advertisements featuring athletes like Michael Jordan's spot for Coca Cola, William momentarily glimpses himself as a boy in the adoring face of a young fan. Even though trophies are presented to him on an Olympic-like dais, he materialistically pawns them for ready cash. His final triumph is attended by his poor, adoring father. Like most contemporary sports stars William is a privately held corporation. His squires, Roland and Wat, have a share in the proceeds of his victories equal to the percentage of their earlier investments. William also signs a sweet endorsement deal with Ur-Nike — a female blacksmith whose ingenious armor gives him a competitive advantage. Umberto Eco's list of the "ten little Middle Ages" could, of course, be extended *ad absurdum* but William's lighter, tighter-fitting armor made of tempered steel and marked with a double Nike swoosh suggests a Middle Ages of Trademark Capitalism. These techniques are calculated to sustain disbelief in audiences and to foreground the constructedness of this image of medieval chivalry. Its analogies — between Chaucer's pluralism and ours, between medieval and modern notions of "gentilesse," and between athletic spectacles then and now — are designed for audiences who enjoy the play of continuity and anachronism. This sense of continuity within historical differences is also a distinct part of the love story. In one exchange Jocelyn describes William as a hunter tracking a fox — a characterization he endorses by replying: "You are a fox." The pun, perhaps suggested by Chaucer's own pun in the *Book of the Duchess* on "hert-huntyng," plunges the audience from medieval love allegory to modern singles' bar slang in an instant.[22] Later, with the crispness of a D.J. changing records, the ordered symmetry of "medieval" music and dance gives way in mid-beat to the dance club strains of David Bowie's "Golden Years" and everyone in contemporary fashion begins finding their own groove.

What world is this? Well, it is certainly one created by pastiche and deeply indebted to the virtual reality of fantasy sports. The jousting pitch becomes a field of dreams or a hall of fame where the shades of tournament champions like Edward, the Black Prince of Wales (1330–1372), William Marshall (ca. 1146–1219), and the flamboyant Ulrich von Lichtenstein (fl. mid–thirteenth century) can break a lance or two. While there certainly is no medieval source for Helgeland's screenplay, there is a modern one that he follows religiously and from which almost every major plot element derives: Maurice Keen's *Chivalry* (1984). Helgeland's use of the book as a source is confined mainly to three chapters: "The Rise of the Tournament" (pp. 83–101), "Heraldry and Heralds" (pp. 125–42), and "Arms, Nobility and Honour" (pp. 162–79). In fact, most major plot twists in the screenplay derive directly from two brief passages in Keen's book (pp. 89–92 and 135–39). On page 89 Keen discusses William Marshall's use of the tournament as a road to riches and international celebrity. Then Keen goes on to recall the passage from *Historie de Guillaume le Maréchal* in which William and the Countess of Joigni pass the time at a tournament dancing to one of William's songs (p. 91) and which in turn leads to a mention of the episode's source in Chrétien's *Lancelot* in which the hero is commanded to demonstrate his love by intentionally losing a tournament (p. 91). This is followed in Keen's book by an extended discussion of Ulrich von Lichtenstein's prodigious career as a jouster and his love of disguise and masquerade (pp. 92–93). Likewise, Keen's treatment of

Heath Ledger's William and Shannyn Sossamon's Lady Jocelyn get their groove on in Brian Helgeland's *A Knight's Tale* (2001).

"Heraldry and Heralds" (pp. 135–39) provides most of the core plot elements for Chaucer's role as William's herald in the movie, including William Marshall's herald grossly inflating his knight's accomplishments (p. 135), the integral role played by heralds in confirming nobility (p. 134), their mastery of the blazon (p. 139), the association of heralds with poetry (p. 139), their use of "letters patent" to confirm noble ancestry (p. 164), and so forth. Indeed, it is perhaps not too great an exaggeration to say that Keen's masterful introduction to chivalry is more the source of Helgeland's screenplay than anything Chaucer wrote. We might also note that Helgeland's reliance on expert modern scholarship does not serve to curb, but rather to thicken and diversify, the film's wonderfully eclectic chronological hodgepodge. Keen's introduction clearly fired Helgeland's imagination — to such an extent that one wonders whether he is not owed a screenwriting credit and a check — but the effect of this collaboration between medieval scholarship and filmmaking is pastiche, not historical accuracy.

Helgeland's stadium abolishes both time and class. It is the site of public masquerade in which Edward the Black Prince and William Thatcher — from opposite ends of the social spectrum — can pretend for awhile to be someone they are not and compete on equal terms. In the film, tournaments are spectacles of the new world of free market capitalism at work, displacing the old order of aristocratic privilege. This is the world that Margaret Thatcher, herself the daughter of a shopkeeper, supposedly played so great a role in creating, a world in which individual initiative and speculation are rewarded. The to-the-manor-born Adhemar represents the hierarchies of the old world — he forfeits a match once he learns a disguised Edward is in the lists but cheats to maintain his sense of an inherent superiority over William. After an early victory, he taunts William with the biblical judgment: "You have been weighed, you have been measured, you have been found wanting." However, for the feudal society Adhemar represents, the writing is always already on the wall: The trio of Roland, Wat, and Chaucer look down on his ruin at the end and repeat the same taunt. We have entered the age of Thatcher.

"The Naked Text in English to Declare"

The rejuvenation of Elizabeth I, Shakespeare and Chaucer is itself worthy of a major study. All three have had a major image overhaul in the last decade. Their famous, oft-reproduced, morphed, and parodied portraits become, in modern visual culture, an equivalent of the increasingly archaic language in which students encounter them. These monuments to English (and, vicariously, American) culture offer the contemporary world quaint mixtures of the authoritative and absurd: the bald and bug-eyed Shakespeare, the peacock Elizabeth, and the pudgy, sententious Chaucer. Shekhar Kapur's *Elizabeth* (1998) excavates the famous icon by offering a prequel to it, showing us the passions and uncertainties of a young woman who, in a sublime act of renunciation and self-fashioning, becomes the distant, powerful goddess of the portrait. In *Shakespeare in Love* (d. John Madden 1998), the bald pate and the big tome it customarily adorns are nowhere in sight; instead, a spendthrift young lover with writer's block takes center stage. These are heroes for a Gen-X culture: successful only after inglorious youths, unsure of themselves and their vocation in life, given to self-parody and self-pity, beautiful and quick-witted, but without direction. The screenplays of these films are made to appeal to a generation in which games of trivia are a defining obsession. These trivial pursuits account for the chief pleasure of watching films in which etiological fables explain the homoeroticism of Shakespeare's sonnets or Chaucer's grudge against pardoners. High culture is repackaged as a game show full of transparent inside jokes — a form of knowledge designed especially to appeal to Gen-X audiences. These audiences can relax: Chaucer and Shakespeare were late bloomers too!

A Knight's Tale, unlike *Shakespeare in Love* or *Elizabeth*, is a film of very few words. Its primary inspiration is not Chaucer's language — the influence of his "The Knight's Tale" is minimal, confined primarily to the tournament spectacles. Rather, it attempts to "translate" directly from the visual culture of the Middle Ages. The manuscript illumination of medieval texts as a way of translating text into image becomes a model for the film's cinematography and mise-en-scène. While the use of illuminations in movies about the Middle Ages is nothing new (Cf., Zeffirelli's use of images from *The Book of Kells* in *Hamlet*, 1990), Helgeland's film animates manuscript illuminations of tournament combats. It also, like *Elizabeth*, offers a rejuvenating prequel to authoritative images through which contemporary culture visualizes the past.

A Knight's Tale takes its cues from the Chaucerian tradition of portraiture and apocryphal continuation, even though it mounts a concerted assault on that tradition. Chaucer is here seen as one of the overgrown kids, a Gen-X rogue, who mocks himself as well as the establishment; directionless, without belief, but fascinated by spectacles; overeducated, talented, poor, and struggling to find a place for himself in the new economy; an amoral wanderer in a shaken world: ambivalent, addicted to gambling, but clubbable — a Chaucer willing to do nude scenes! With some squinting this picture can be viewed as a thoroughgoing reaction against the moral Chaucer of the Victorian Age that witnessed the birth of the modern Chaucer scholarship (see Ellis and David O. Matthews). It is instructive to compare, for example, Robert Bell's reaction to the Hoccleve portrait in *The Poetical Works of Geoffrey Chaucer* (1878) in its mixture of *gravitas* and *suavitas* with the view of Chaucer implied by Helgeland's image. For Bell,

> The mixture of gravity and sweetness in Occleve's portrait conveys the perfect image of a character not the less remarkable for its rare combination of power and sympathy, than for the variety of accomplishments by which it was graced [qtd. in Matthews, p. 15].

Bell's description of the Hoccleve's portrait could easily be rewritten to yield Helgeland's Chaucer:

> The mixture of flippancy and acerbity in Helgeland's portrait conveys the unreliable, self-fashioned image of "a real character" not less unremarkable for its combination of ennui and exuberance, than for the paucity of accomplishments with which it is burdened.

Helgeland's portrait is also a rejoinder to the currently fashionable understanding of Chaucer as a man of the world, confident civil servant, diplomat, and confidant of the rich and powerful. In fact, when the young poet, naked and covered in mud, appears on the road early in the film it is not as a court poet or portly pilgrim, but as Chesterton saw him, a force of nature.

William Thatcher (Heath Ledger) and Geoffrey Chaucer (Paul Bettany) celebrate the triumph of personal initiative in Brian Helgeland's *A Knight's Tale* (2001).

> When I think of Chaucer in this primary and general fashion, I do not think of a court poet receiving a laurel from the king or a flagon from the king's butler, not even of a stout and genial gentleman with a forked beard setting forth from the Tabard upon the Canterbury road; but of some ... elemental and emblematic giant, alive at our beginnings and made out of the very elements of the land [qtd. in Ellis, p. 37].

In the film the poet's portrait develops gradually from an "elemental" to a "social Chaucer,"[23] a Chaucer schooled in the social graces but never completely at home in the world in which he finds himself. Helgeland's Chaucer mixes uneasily with the nobility and with lower characters alike. He is a self-conscious performer who, while dressed in a weathered cloak, can still hold an audience, a coarse but genial observer of all classes who seldom pays his debts but who always settles his grudges, a servant of love's servants — not above a little good-natured pandering.[24]

I want to focus on two instances in which the film seems to respond directly to traditional images of Chaucer. Three manuscript illuminations have had an enormous influence on the modern reception of Chaucer: the Hoccleve portrait (in e.g., British Library MS Harley 4866, f. 88r), the pilgrim portrait in Ellesmere (Huntington Library MS EL 26. C. 9 f. 153v), and the frontispiece to *Troilus and Criseyde* in the Cambridge Corpus Christi

College MS (61, f.1v.54).[25] We first see Helgeland's Chaucer on the road, but gone are the rich mount and dwarfish legs of the Ellesmere portrait and gone too are the moral gravity, quiet mien, and clerkish garb of the Hoccleve portrait. Helgeland's Chaucer can still give directions to the lost — the Hoccleve portrait is often lifted from its context in modern reproductions so that Chaucer seems to be pointing the way to the corner store — but in the film he is unexpectedly young, tall, and thin, and as naked as the day he was born. As I discussed above, the image is more than sheer impertinence, it thoughtfully demystifies traditional constructions of Chaucer as moral exemplar or affluent bureaucrat. It also suggests that a very different image of Chaucer could be gleaned from his works. Debunking the "moral Chaucer," it offers a biographical etiology for Chaucer's "Proverbs:"

> What shul thise clothes thus manyfold,
>   Lo! This hote someres day?
> After greet hete cometh cold;
>   No man caste his pilche away.
>
> Of al this world the large compas
>   Hit wol not in myn armes tweyne,—
> Whoso mochel wol embrace,
>   Litle therof he shal distreyne
>   [ed., Benson 1987].

Helgeland's portrait shows Chaucer naked in both the senses hinted at in these moral epigrams: undressed and destitute. The image may stem as well from the apocryphal Canterbury tale, *The Tale of Beryn*, in which the fool Geffrey and Beryn both suffer like indignities at the hands of Falsetown loan sharks. However, the film's Chaucer is also naked in distinctly modern senses. The popular media continually portrays celebrity character for a scandal-obsessed culture in terms of embarrassing nude photos that undermine (or advance) famous stars' carefully constructed public personae. Candid shots, often taken in sordid circumstances, carnivalize celebrity status, by turns desanctifying and humanizing the public image of famous people. In Helgeland's film, Chaucer is no distanced observer of the carnival world he represents; instead, he is both its hapless victim and the recipient of its leveling graces. His nakedness is also the naked truth behind his most celebrated fictions. The devastating depictions of the Summoner and Pardoner are traced to Chaucer's "real-life" crisis as an inveterate gambler repeatedly at the mercy of this merciless pair. The second time they strip him naked, the loan sharks threaten, in perverse accordance with biblical law, to take in partial payment an especially precious pound of his flesh. Freed by William from the debt, Chaucer threatens the unholy pair with a decidedly Dantesque form of revenge: "I will eviscerate you in fiction: I was naked for a day, you will be naked for all eternity."[26] Later, the stadium, where "all are equal," becomes the genesis of the idea of the pluralistic *Canterbury Tales*, a fictional world that can match the diversity of Chaucer's London. Only Chaucer's tongue-tied, bullying nemesis, Wat (Tyler, I presume), need be excluded from this collection of God's plenty: "All human activity lies within the artist's scope — maybe not yours...." The implication is clear: like the Shakespeare of the recent film, Chaucer requires no mountain of scholarly commentary to explicate his works. At their core, such masterpieces are not simply translations from the Italian but rather mediated reflections of the author's life — an approach currently out of fashion in much of academia though alive and well in a good deal of contemporary fiction and film.

Helgeland's excavation of the famous *Troilus* frontispiece of Chaucer reading his poem outdoors to an assembled crowd is wonderfully imaginative and completely over the top. Here Chaucer is a youthful herald, quickly learning how to win the crowd and inventing a distinctive new style, soon to have its imitators. For modern audiences the style clearly parodies the vowel-belaboring public address announcers of contemporary sports arenas. Chaucer's introductions of William, spoofing the Knight's own hyperbolic press guide in the "General Prologue," whip the crowds into a frenzy. This is no bookish Chaucer standing before a podium but an improvising, oral entertainer who appeals, from his perch standing on the lists, both to the nobility and to those in the cheap seats, "those not sitting on a cushion." Helgeland's Chaucer impishly relishes his place at the center of a pluralistic spectacle. Clearly in love with the sound of his own voice, he begins to conceive of public poetry while coining patently absurd idealizations of Christian knighthood, such as "I give you that seeker after serenity, that protector of Italian virginity, Ulrich von Lichtenstein."

In the film, the historical Chaucer is not unknowable because of a paucity of historical evidence but because his own identity is a rhetorically constructed fiction. The second most celebrated tidbit from the historical record is Chaucer's testimony to establish the authenticity of Sir Richard Scrope's claim to bear the coat of arms "*azure a bend or*" over that of Sir Robert Grosvenor in the High Court of Chivalry in Westminster, on October 15, 1386. The episode is archly evoked in the film. Helgeland's Chaucer is a skilled coiner of false identities, willing — for a price — to draw up forged "patents of nobility" complete with spurious coats of arms. His price is a cloak to cover his nakedness. The search for an historical Chaucer, the film seems to suggest, can uncover only a rhetorical Chaucer, a self fashioned out of economic necessities: "Let no man caste his pilche away." The word "pastiche" in English means not only "assemblage" but also "forgery" (see Rose 1991). Any reconstruction of the past is to some degree pastiched in both senses of the word. Helge-land's images of Chaucer and of the medieval joust do not invite us to meas-ure his vision of the Middle Ages against our own. Instead they encourage us to understand medievalism as the practice and study of pastiche, or rather of generations of pastiche stretching back not to an original but to earlier acts of compositive forgery. That we all of us "justen at a fane" represents what is best in the discipline of medievalism: its arcane proficiencies, its quixotic nos-talgia, and its curiously central place in the postmodern world.

4

Shooting the Messenger: Luc Besson at War with Joan of Arc

A number of recent big-budget, historical films construct symbolic national identities in spite of daunting imperialism, for instance: *Braveheart* (1995), *First Knight* (1995), *The Messenger: The Story of Joan of Arc* (1999), *Gladiator* (2000), *Patriot* (2001), *The Lord of the Rings* (2001–03), *King Arthur* (2004), and *The Kingdom of Heaven* (2004). Historical fidelity is routinely touted in the pre-release blitz and then just as routinely lamented in finger-wagging reviews, but really rather beside the point. Such movies do for us what mutatis mutandis the fanciful Trojan genealogies did for the emerging nation-states in the late Middle Ages; they fabricate the continuities upon which any conception of national or personal identity must rely.[1] Linda Hutcheon's term "historiographic metafiction" perhaps best characterizes these projections, that is, narratives that appropriate the radical alterity of the past while at the same time contriving visions of history and legend that work in the present (Hutcheon 1989 and 1998). Historiographic metafictions are about the play of exotic difference and unlikely affinities. Such works leverage the constructedness of received history in order to screen contemporary desires, conflicts, and anxieties. Pictures are the chief means by which the culture of the image attempts to know itself. Just as an individual assembles a photo album that records memorable events but also establishes the continuity of that individual across a lifespan, just so do movies assemble our cinematic imaginary, a scrapbook that records differences across time within a master narrative of continuity.[2] The technology of moving pictures is crucial in the production of this continuity and overrides the eccentricities of a "cinema of (historical) attractions." The earliest forms of the technology were dubbed

111

"living pictures" and that makes for a presentist art form, even if the material of this art is distant historically — a proviso that scholars of movie medievalism ignore at their peril. Just as the perceptual factors such as "persistence of vision" create the impression of continuous movement from distinct frames of film projected at a sufficient speed, so do the medieval projections of modern cinema produce the illusion of a living Middle Ages, occurring in the present.[3] Historical and ontological confusion, I would argue, is hard-wired in the technology itself.

However, whether we view the historiography of movie medievalism as hard-wired or pandering commercialism, it is difficult to ignore the ubiquity of its appeals to patriotism and national identity.[4] And patriotism in an era of global capitalism is readily commodified. The centrifugal, imperial culture of Hollywood colonizes the patriotic struggles of the past by treating history as a *fons et figura* of America's own original and continuing struggles for freedom at home and abroad.[5] Of course, such appropriations are hardly new. Mark Twain's magnificently discordant novel, *The Personal Recollections of Joan of Arc*, concludes by making the fifteenth-century French teenager the most portable of signs:

> With Joan of Arc love of country was more than a sentiment — it was a passion. She was the Genius of Patriotism — she was patriotism embodied, consecrated, made flesh, and palpable to the touch and visible to the eye. Love, Mercy, Charity, Fortitude, War, Peace, Poetry, Music — these may be symbolized as any shall prefer: by figures of any sex and of any age; but a slender girl in her first young bloom, with the martyr's crown upon her head, and in her hand the sword that severed her country's bonds — shall not this, and no other, stand for PATRIOTISM through all the ages until time shall end? [p. 318].

The dissemination of Joan's patriotism, its de-carnation as an idea which floats free of the Middle Ages and even of France itself has been explored in a number of recent books, such as Ann Astell's *Joan of Arc and Sacrificial Authorship* and Robin Blaetz's *Visions of the Maid*.[6] In what follows I first trace the origin of Joan's calling and character in Luc Besson's film not only as a personification of patriotism but also as the *fons et figura* of the psychopathology of freedom-fighters, gender warfare, and religious extremism. I then look at how the latter portion of the film, which details Joan's heresy trials, interrogates with a contemporary urgency her assurance of a divine calling for jihad. In these episodes not only does a postmodern skepticism enter Joan's prison cell, but also she herself comes to figure (and to stand accused of) the distinctly modern crime of presuming to be God's warrior. Though Besson is a Frenchman with a clear fondness for Joan, his fear of nationalism and terrorism has certainly provoked an uncompromising examination of Joan's conscience. Besson's Joan is a bundle of contradictions, but these contradictions reflect an ambivalence ubiquitous in recent movie medievalism, an ambivalence that couples nostalgia for an age of faith with the fear of religion.

Coming Out of the Closet

The portrayal of Joan of Arc in *The Messenger* initially constructs her character according to traditional conceptions of subjectivity, in both Augustinian and Freudian versions. The first half of the film is in effect a bildungsroman that imagines Joan's formative experiences as an overdetermined mélange of divine vocation and childhood trauma. In the second half of the film, however, certainties about her mission and what she represents are witheringly questioned by the Church as well as by her own conscience. Relentless interrogations undermine the divine sanction for Joan's authority, even as she is scourged in her prison cell by self-doubt that assumes the physical form of a nemesis-like personification. Freud's imperious ego, able to know itself, to understand the processes that have shaped it, is the twentieth century's most influential expression of the Enlightenment *cogito*. Yet under the reign of postmodernism the ego has been dethroned as subjectivity is increasingly seen not as a function of individual enlightenment, but rather as the product of institutions such as the military, government, church, and school through which the individual is rendered subject to society. Anti-essentialists such as Foucault, Lacan, and Althusser have seen in the early modern period a radical development toward societies based on incarceration and surveillance, documentation and classification, and especially the internalization of these forms of control in terms of a punitive and self-monitoring conscience. The torturous examinations of Joan of Arc in her Trial of Condemnation and the postmortem Trail of Rehabilitation have left us with a record about her more detailed and dialogically nuanced than that of any other private person of the late Middle Ages. Yet the verdicts of both these trials, though in direct contradiction, were politically driven, foregone conclusions. Joan's canonization some 500 years after the fact (1920) suggests that medieval subjectivities remain an open, contested space even in the modern age. Perhaps the contingency of Joan's identity as well as the decisive role of the church, the school, and the state in establishing that identity should lead us to nominate her as the first modern subject.[7]

I am arguing, in brief, that *The Messenger* is structured around these two very different ways of understanding the construction of the self: as a process of progressive enlightenment and formative experiences and as the product of repressive social forces. I would argue further that this distinction parallels that between the Church Triumphant and the Church Militant in the film. In the first half Joan's direct apprehension of the will of the Church Triumphant through her "voices" is unquestioned by the saint-in-the-making and by the movie-going audience as well. The Church Militant's *apprehension* of Joan in the second half refocuses our attention on the legitimacy of the messenger herself, just as it forges an uneasy alliance between medieval and modern skepticism. The second half then deconstructs the premises of the first, as the arbitrary nature of the signs that had called Joan to action is exposed by her ruthlessly nominalistic "Conscience." Yet, though the film is clearly about the formation and contingency of a woman's subjectivity, it is also, in Laura Mulvey's (1975) terms, a textbook example of a classic Hollywood narrative whose structure is determined by the male gaze. As a virgin, as a woman, and as a transvestite warrior commanding and at times intimidating men, Besson's Joan is a "bearer of the lack" who provokes fears of castration and blurs gender distinctions in the male psyche. In the second half of the film, just as Mulvey's theory would predict, Joan is subjected to regimes of investigation and demystification that allow men once again to take control of her — not only her judges but also her own conscience, here gendered male. In particular I want to look closely at a number of claustrophobic misesen-scène because it is here, I think, that we are encouraged to identify most intensely with her inner world.

Joan's modern biographers — and they are legion — often attempt to understand how the terrors of English occupation would have impacted her personality. Yet Besson's scene of Joan watching her sister being raped is a wholesale fabrication; there is no evidence for such an episode in the historical record. In fact Joan testifies that she and her family escaped their village before it was attacked. In the scene as "a girl aged about ten" Joan witnesses her sister's murder and subsequent rape from inside a closet. From their vantage point at the dinner table two English soldiers enjoy a pilfered meal as they casually observe their comrade's struggle with Joan's sister. Joan watches the rape through cracks in the door — the space, lighting, and restricted POV are eerily similar to scenes before and after with Joan in the confessional. The soldier, frustrated with his victim "squirming about," impales her on the sword, which lifts her off her feet and plunges, blood-streaked through the door, inches from Joan's face. The lean, black-toothed soldier (dubbed Blackbeard in the screenplay) then quickly finishes, sighs, and calls to his nonplussed comrades, "your turn, now." The violence in such moments strikes an audience with particular immediacy because our gaze is sutured to that of a child. In essence Besson is reading backward from Joan's character at the time of her arrest (the period from which all the evidence about her derives) in order to imagine a childhood that could have given birth to such an adult. Of course such projections into the past bear telling traces of mass-market Freudianism: the symptoms of the adult are rendered explicable by our privileged access to the child's primal scene.[8] Both a fear of sexuality — Freud thought young witnesses likely mistook intercourse for violent assault — and the substitution of *thanatos* for *eros* will define the fault lines of Joan's fractured psyche. The sequence detailing the rape of her sister provides an alternate psychological cause for Joan's mission that supplements and implicitly challenges more metaphysical explanations. It represents not only the defining moment in the development of Joan's identity, but also contains many of the visual strategies that will be variously elaborated as the film continues.

Near the beginning of the sequence a large wolf creeps down a path toward young Joan, who stands frozen with fear as an entire wolf pack storms by her, intent on the carrion-prey awaiting them in the burning village. The shot works to imply Joan's election, her apparently supernatural imperviousness to harm — this Little Red Riding Hood is certainly afraid of the big bad wolves — but they ignore her and her newly found sword in their pell-mell rush to the site of the massacre. Of course, "the beasts of battle" *topos* is formulaic in medieval war poetry: often, personified wolves are heard to anticipate with relish the feast that war is preparing for them.[9] Crosscutting repeatedly juxtaposes the pillaging of the wolves and the English, deftly revealing the point of the *topos*, that war reduces men to animals. The wolves not only herald the invasion, they also symbolize the bestiality of the English forces. Joan has often been portrayed as a shepherdess, whose innocence and good sense were of a piece with nature and country life.[10] Besson though implies that her hatred of the English is as natural, as elemental, as a country girl's animosity for marauding wolves plundering a sheepfold. Later, the English soldiers enter Joan's cottage looking for spoils but find only food and a young woman: "Now that's what I call booty!" The collocation, of course, plays on the pun implicit in the word: in American slang "bootie" refers specifically to the objects of male predatory sexual behavior. Shifting perspectives in the scene work through montage to associate the two soldiers' consumption of food with their comrade's ravenous rape of Joan's sister. The cuts as well as the use of deep focus reinforce this connection. That the English are wolfish is clear from the earlier crosscutting, but the mise-en-scène of the homely cottage disturbingly couples the fundamental taboos of cannibalism and necrophilia. It is just possible in a film centrally concerned with gender boundary transgressions and reinforcements that this collocation goes deeper than simple sensationalism. In *The Savage Mind*, Claude Levi-Strauss speaks of the common "equation of male with the devourer and female with the devoured" as a complementary reaction to man's fears of castration and absorption by the feminine, expressed mythically as the *vagina dentata* (p. 106). Joan's early response to the taboos she has witnessed is her private celebration of a tabooed sacrament, as we see a bit further on.

The sword, which later figures so large not only in Joan's career as a warrior but also in the questions raised at her trial about her status as a noncombatant, is first wielded against the English by her sister. The legends about the miraculous discovery of a sword buried behind the altar of St. Catherine of Fierbois are significantly altered here. Besson's Joan will wield a sword that has been tempered in her sister's belly, not coincidentally also named Catherine. She first discovers the sword lying in an open field. In fact, the sequence begins with an internal montage matching the child's body lying in the tall grass with arms outspread to the latent sword resting as yet undiscovered alongside her. Of course these matching forms are both in the shape of a cross. The relationship of sword and cross is as yet unknown to her, just as she is unaware of her own body's martyr pose, splayed out like that of Christ on the cross. She uses her arms and legs to create the impression of an angel in the tall grass, daydreaming of sanctity. Her first glimpse of the sword beside her makes it look like a snake in the grass, and its discovery signals an end to her innocence. She carries the fateful weapon into the cottage where her sister tries to use it to defend herself, only to be penetrated first by the sword and then by the Englishman. As Joan's tearful confession makes clear, her sister dies because she gave up her hiding place to her younger sibling; she dies in effect as a surrogate or substitute for Joan. The child experiences the rape from her sister's perspective; in fact their perspectives merge and become one — in a very real sense what happens to Catherine happens also to Joan. Our gaze is sutured tightly into this claustrophobic scene, as we see the rapist's face from Joan's POV with all the menace of low-angle photography and tight, masked framing. The suture forces us to look through Joan's eyes and to believe what we see and to sympathize with her "shock and awe." Besson's Joan suffers from survivor's guilt; the sword she wields later to rout the English at Orléans is the same weapon that killed her sister. She, like Catherine, is "a woman with a sword," but the image develops progressively from that of pathetic and risible incongruence into a contradiction with which the English will be quite unable to reckon. In making the sword an instrument of sexual violation, Besson is not subtle. That Joan later uses this sword dressed as a man suggests that she has in a very real sense taken up the phallus and turned it against her attackers.

Her status a *virgo intacta* was supposedly established by physical examination, a detail of the historical record that Besson treats with the grandiose and solemn hilarity that one encounters in many of his films. The elaborate unfurling of a portable examining room of white sheets within a large hall filled with an expectant audience objectively correlates with the unfolding of the private(s) within a very public, political space, comparable to the final love scene in *The Fifth Element* (d. Luc Besson 1997). The stakes of this very public private examination are high: Yolande D'Aragon (Faye Dunaway) predicts that Joan's virginity "will put the fire back in our armies" but "if she's not, I'll kill her myself."[11] Still, the claustrophobia of the rape scene suggests that, psychologically at least, Joan herself is violated along with her sister. Quoting a cliché from horror films, Besson has the blood-streaked sword plunge through the door into Joan's hiding place, in effect destroying her innocence even as it miraculously fails to injure her — yet another example, as her confessor later assures her, that "God is saving you for something." The shot preserves Joan's virginity, even as it allows us to watch at close quarters the rape of her psyche.

A following sequence soon thereafter duplicates these visual strategies. Once again we have Joan viewing a man from a dark, claustrophobic space through a masked frame. The implicit linkage of sexual violence to the sacrament of confession is both daring and impudent, but such blatant juxtapositions are a hallmark of Besson's style. This duplicated mise-en-scène works to link psychological violation and righteous bloodlust. The film will go on to interrogate the association of violence and religion, ultimately undermining Joan's assurance of a divine calling to kill. The confession scene in the church opens with the priest consecrating the Eucharist for mass at the high altar. Interestingly, our view of a prominent crucifix on the wall above and behind him is occluded when the priest turns to focus his attention on Joan's aunt and uncle, who have come to him for advice. The shot physically enacts the Church's role as a mediator between God and the faithful, but it also hints at the institution's opacity, the way its mediacy could frustrate the need for direct and personal connections with God. In a famous shot from Carl Dreyer's *La Passion de Jeanne d'Arc*, Bishop Pierre Cauchon is made to step upon the shadow a cross casts across the white floor as he moves to confront Joan. Many of the challenges to the Church's hegemony in the late Middle Ages and early modern period saw such interruptions as sterile and artificial. Much of thirteenth- to fifteenth-century medieval mysticism, reform efforts within the Church, as well as movements it declared heretical, questioned the Church's abuses of its power as an intermediary between God and man, seeking the intensely private immediacy that is a defining hallmark of much late medieval spirituality. Perhaps Besson's quotation of Dreyer's shot in what appears to be a benign context suggests that the intrusiveness of the Church into personal spirituality is institutional rather than simply a matter of bad priests such as Cauchon.

As the confession scene continues we witness the beginning of Joan's frenzy for revenge. She is told that soon she will be at one with God through the sacraments, able to partake of his flesh and to drink his blood. In effect, the promise of the sacrament is offered as a means of sating Joan's hatred for the cannibalistic English, yet Church law necessitates that she wait until she is older before she can receive this form of grace. Returning home later that day, as her desire for a spiritual union with Christ reaches a fevered pitch, she steals away from her uncle's wagon and back into the empty church. Storm clouds gather and lightning flashes within its now menacing architecture — a startling example of how lighting and sound can transform the meaning of a shot. As Joan approaches the altar, the crucifix looms large above her without obstruction, illuminated by flashes of lightning, and overseeing her wide-eyed hunger "to be at one with You now!" All the atmospherics for a black mass are present. The English would later accuse Joan of being a witch and burn her, just as at the same time they were burning Lollards who questioned the doctrine of transubstantiation. Not unlike Luther more than a century later, the followers of John Wycliffe dared to suggest that communion was akin to cannibalism. And as we have seen that cannibalism figures prominently if only implicitly in the rape scene. Joan celebrates a private mass that is frenzied, even vampiristic. The shot of her lips and chin drenched in the sacrament powerfully evokes a number of recent movie images of devil worship and vampires. In fact it directly quotes a shot from *Interview with the Vampire* (d. Neil Jordan 1994) in which a child soaks her chin and lips in blood and gazes upward in blissful satiety. Both girls, the vampire and the young Joan, drink deep of the life-sustaining blood, and both radiate a truly perverse hunger, born of loss and despair. The girl-vampire remains a child forever, just as Joan remains stunted by her childhood trauma. The next shot performs a radical jump cut, as we see from behind a cloaked and hooded Joan — now a full-grown young woman — riding off to meet Charles: She has become a dark rider. The jump cut passes over a wealth of information about Joan's crusade to meet the man she would make the king of France, but the point of the psychological biography that Besson provides instead is made abundantly clear. This "victim" is no longer (yet eternally) a child. And she herself is now a threat. The rage of this child has given birth to an adult wedded to vengeance. Religious fervor and righteous bloodlust become indistinguishable, revenge takes on a sacramental authority, and the shadowy realm of international politics is invested with the terrible clarity of a divine calling.

Gendered *Bricolage*

In the scenes depicting the siege of Orléans, the stability of gender roles is undermined by a series of reversals that put bodies and objects to unaccustomed usages, reversals I would dub gendered *bricolage*. The episode rings variations on the paradoxical theme of "a woman with a sword," which recurs throughout the film. The scornful taunts of the English commander from the battlements of the Tourelles betray his assurance that power and the technologies of warfare are an extension of male anatomy and as such these privileges are unassailable and irreversible. "She doesn't even know how to use it" sums up his disgust at a woman in command, who has taken up the phallus in a risible attempt to overcome a fortress no less impregnable than gender barriers themselves.

After being wounded in a rash attempt to storm the battlements, Joan has a nightmare that forces her to relive both the horror and the impotence she felt as a child. She is trapped in a dark, wooden tunnel, desperately seeking a way out. The dream is perhaps provoked by wish fulfillment: She is in a subterranean mine of the sort employed in siege warfare to undermine heavily fortified positions such as the English stronghold at Orléans. Her dream though is also a *catabasis* of sorts, a journey to an underworld, wherein Joan confronts her own private vision of hell. Reaching the end of the tunnel, she is forced to watch helplessly yet again the murder and rape of her sister. Less a flashback than a compulsive return to a psychic trauma from which she quite literally cannot escape, Joan is caught in a vicious cycle of remembrance, rigidly circumscribing both who she is and the boundaries of what she can accomplish — boundaries reinforced by her failure to breach the walls earlier that day.[12] Strangely, she wakes from this nightmare miraculously healed in both body and spirit. Journeys to the underworld typically occur at the center of texts, *catabases* force heroes to come to terms with their pasts and, as Virgil put it, to "find another way." Joan does just that; she discovers by remembering and repeating a traumatic event, the gendered nature of warfare, and how it consists of turning one's enemy into a woman — an idea at least as old as Homer's *Iliad*. Certainly, the English had managed quite literally to accomplish that in making the French so desperate that they would allow themselves to be led by a girl. More figuratively speaking, the politically and economically emasculated Charles, played lispingly in the film by John Malkovich, is at the mercy of the English, his own more powerful noblemen, *and* his mother-in-law. The film makes clear that, in donning male clothing, Joan is attempting to reinvigorate the lagging masculinity of the French; yet, her dream suggests that she has remained within her disguise the

Top: Milla Jovovich as Joan of Arc rallies her troops in Luc Besson's 1999 film *The Messenger: The Story of Joan of Arc. Bottom:* Joan of Arc (Milla Jovovich) helps to rear the siege tower in Luc Besson's *The Messenger* (1999).

helpless child who witnessed her sister's death. The change comes when she realizes that rape is not an unfortunate excess of war but rather its very essence.

Joan's clever variation on the Trojan Horse stratagem is an overdetermined bit of gender warfare. It employs the genius of *bricolage* to turn the siege into a battle of the sexes. Cities from the ancient world to the present are repeatedly gendered feminine. Their walls compose a protective womb subject to attack from without by any number of masculine technologies of violation. The situation at Orléans when Joan arrives has the English laying siege to the city. She turns the tables — as well as the gender valences — by forcing the English to scurry back to the supposedly unassailable Tourelles. Then, Joan lays siege to the besiegers. But, of course she's a woman and women don't know how to use *it*. Joan assails the fortress without the help or advice of the French commanders, apparently committing the ridiculous mistake of approaching the walls with the siege engine turned back to front. She is shrill and unbalanced throughout much of the movie, but here her apparent error is profoundly hysterical — in many senses of the word. What the English see is the distinctly unmenacing hollow belly of the device, a womb-like protective enclosure, but one that grows more menacing as it moves closer. From the French point of view, however, the tower looks considerably more formidable, and Joan is twice pictured in the foreground with the rising tower looming behind her. To put perhaps too fine a point on it, the English are confronted with a gigantic vagina, perversely exposed, but one whose threatening character they realize too late. What the French see is a phallus wielded expertly — if unconventionally — by a virgin peasant girl in drag.[13] This phallic effect is cinched when the French are shown using a trebuchet, captured from the English, to hurl two large stone balls into the fortress! In effect, Joan has reversed the gender valences of the apparatus: Its female side now faces the English, its male side stands erect before the resurgent French forces. Her followers tip the colossus in the direction of the fortified gate and it crashes through with a bang, eliciting screams and panicked flight from the men now exposed within. Evidently, she does know how to use *it*.

Joan's phallic assault on the Tourelles is her greatest triumph, symbolically at least she turns the English into women — and it is that insult her military foes in the film are most keen to avenge. A victim of her own success at gendered warfare, Joan is brought in her trials, and more profoundly in her confrontations with her own Conscience, to struggle with the consequences of taking up the phallus. While the Church charges her with having transgressed her gender and status, "Conscience" (in the person of a ridiculously portentous Dustin Hoffman) upbraids her with having usurped God's authority, for having presumed to carry God's messages and to do his work. The battle of the second half of the movie is then the battle for Joan's soul, a *psychomachia* in which Conscience ruthlessly assaults Joan's assurance of God's favor. This blend of medieval allegory and postmodern undecidability, of nominalism and antifoundationalism, of confession and psychoanalysis is bizarrely captivating. The debate with her Conscience does not so much resolve as it does perform our doubts about Joan, her visions, and holy wars. This final violation, this final bit of psychological warfare, witheringly conducted between bouts of physical torture and public examination, cruelly tosses back on us the cruelty of modern skepticism, even as it projects its timelessness.

"Conscience doth make cowards of us all"

The scenes with Mila Jovovich's Joan and Dustin Hoffman's "Conscience" are among the most troubling that Besson has created in his controversial career. In the records of her trial, Joan maintained that the Saints Michael, Catherine, and Margaret continued to visit her throughout her captivity, giving her support and advice — even promising that she would be freed from her prison, although they failed to tell her how.[14] In Besson's film, Joan's voices have deserted her; she invokes them in vain. The saints are replaced by Hoffman, robed in a monk's black cowl: *sed cucullus non facit monachum*. The screenplay calls this figure simply "Man," and a number of scenes featuring him were not preserved in the final cut. In one such scene, Joan's suicidal leap from the ledge outside her prison window is actually precipitated by a shove from the Man. The film credits and DVD scene selections both credit Hoffman with the role of "Conscience." Clearly, Besson has sacrificed the moral ambiguity of the figure in the screenplay and chosen to concentrate instead on the drama of Joan's self-questioning *askesis*. Of course, the figure of a Satanic tempter visiting the cell of a saint facing martyrdom represents a recurring theme in hagiographic literature.[15] One thinks first perhaps of the devil in Cynewulf's *Juliana*, who tries to seduce her in a battle of wits and ends up thoroughly vanquished, confessing the misery of his life in hell. In fact, this is the pattern of most such episodes in *The Golden Legend*, the tempters are unsuccessful, their efforts only serve to demonstrate the unshakable faith of the martyr. Besson's tempter is decidedly more adept, particularly because he seeks not to shake her faith in God but in herself.

A good many late medieval dream visions feature allegorical personifications who visit prison cells to console and chide their charges. Joan's near contemporary James I of Scotland was in prison in the Tower of London until 1423 and he tells in *The Kingis Quair* how the goddess Minerva (Wisdom) upbraided him for his fascination with Venus (Earthly Love), and helped to secure his release. Conscience has an important role to play in late medieval literature as well. All of these figures ultimately descend from the early *Consolatio Philosophiae*, where it is the personified Philosophy's task to chide and console Boethius as he awaits execution. Besson's Conscience certainly participates in the tradition of such figures, Hoffman is by turns hectoring and patient, mocking and sympathetic. However, yet another distinct layer is added to the portrait. Besson's Conscience is obviously in homage to an important *locus classicus* in movie medievalism, the figure of Death in Bergman's *The Seventh Seal*. Like Bengt Ekerot in *The Seventh Seal*, Hoffman is forever peering, white-faced, through his black cowl to confront his antagonist with the inevitable. Both have a way of sneaking up on their opponents, appearing out of nowhere, assuming false identities to baffle and frustrate their targets. Both too have the dogged ubiquity of doppelgängers, the Knight and Joan can no more evade these haunting presences than they can their own shadows. And most crucially, both are trickster-figures, given to role-playing and impersonation, who easily outwit their charges and bring them to self-doubt before they bring them to their deaths. In *The Seventh Seal*, though, Death remains an antagonist, whom the knight fights to the very end. He manages to sidetrack the Grim Reaper long enough to spare the family of actors. Conscience in *The Messenger* cannot be fooled or bargained with, he is more ineluctable than Death itself, yet he also finally performs the sacrament of confession and grants Joan absolution before she dies.

Joan's stalker is part comforter and part scourge. He stands in for postmodern doubt, personifying the presentist skepticism implicit in many reconstructions of medieval spirituality, but his appearance also turns the film from history to metacinema — a cinema that debunks its own and its protagonist's illusions. Conscience gives Joan's self-justifications short shrift, exposing the arbitrary nature of the signs to which she hitched her star:

CONSCIENCE: God asked you to do something?

JEANNE: No, but ... he sent me so many signs!

C: What signs?

J: Like ... the wind ... and the clouds ... and ... the bells ... and what about that sword lying in the field ... that was a sign...!

(At this point we as the audience are remembering uncomfortably how persuasive such things seemed at the time.)

CONSCIENCE RESPONDS: No. That was a sword in a field.

J: But it didn't just get there by itself.

C: True — every event has an infinite number of causes — but why pick one rather than another? There are many ways a sword might find itself in a field....

(At this point a series of possible causes is presented in a montage sequence — all it must be admitted are more probable than the cause Joan (and perhaps we) had imagined.)

CONSCIENCE CONCLUDES: Yet from an infinite number of possibilities, you had to pick this one...

FLASH: A peel of thunder — clouds swirl — a familiar wind stirs the long grass — a fabulous shaft of light illuminates the patch — the sword slowly descends from the heavens and lands gently in the grass. Mission accomplished, the shaft of heavenly light disappears

[Birkin and Besson, screenplay].

This is the Monty Python Middle Ages with a vengeance. One is reminded of the peasant's exasperated quip about the divine right of kings being "based on some farcical aquatic ceremony." The parody though cuts in a number of different directions. First, it is self-parody, which renders preposterous Besson's own carefully constructed illusion. Second, it takes a cut at the tree-hugging, Enya-loving, new age spirituality that plays such an annoying role in postmodern medievalism. But of course we are made to suffer along with Joan; we have believed in her visions just as she has, if only within the context of the film's diegesis, and Joan's Conscience mocks us along with her for being so easily led astray by time-lapse and slow-motion photography. It is as though we are being punished for our willingness to suspend our skepticism, for our sympathies with an age of faith. Besson has smuggled postmodern uncertainties into Joan's prison cell, and we, like Joan, feel abused and manipulated. Hoffman's presence there is as anachronistic as a Connecticut Yankee in King Arthur's court or a group of modern archaeologists playing a crucial role in the Hundred Years' War, but such anachronisms emphasize the labile nature of historical reconstruction. Put in Deleuzian terms, Conscience exposes the virtual nature of the past in screening for Joan and for the audience alternate versions of her memories. Our willing belief is exposed as credulous, but that exposure itself constitutes the dirtiest and most cynical of tricks. However, the film does more than simply debunk Joan's vocation; in fact, there is one more ontological turn of the screw to come.

In the final scenes of the film we alternate between the public interrogations of Joan by various clerics, which she dominates with her good sense and quick wit, and the relentless interiority of her prison cell, a torture chamber with an Inquisitor who knows Joan's weak spots in intimate detail. Here the claustrophobic mise-en-scène of the earlier shots is reproduced; again our gaze is tightly sutured into an editing strategy of shot counter-shot and subjective camera. The cruelest cut, however, comes when an objective long shot pulls us away from this intimacy to reveal Joan alone, kneeling upon the stone floor of her cell, pleading and praying to an empty space. Again, Besson has manipulated our sympathies by encouraging us to assume the truth of her perspective, only to expose that perspective as a figment of her imagination. Audiences of the film have to wait until the credits to have the Hoffman figure identified as Conscience, but this reality effect of objective camera results in desperately isolating Joan within her own troubled mind. The editing strategy is similar to Zeffirelli's shooting of the ghost in the bedroom scene of his *Hamlet* (1990). We see the ghost at the window through Hamlet's eyes, but when he turns to his mother for confirmation of this, we see with her only the "nothing" that is "all there is." But how are we to read this negation of a negation in Besson's version? That is, how are we now to understand Joan's supposedly flawed reading of the signs that nominated her God's messenger when those doubts themselves are revealed to be lacking any substance? Of course, the recent Derrida would surely claim that we must be suspicious of even doubt itself. Uncertainty is just as much a production of the human mind as is faith. And by a curious litotes, doubting doubt is akin to belief. Then, finally, the figure of Conscience, having been exposed as the fleetingly contingent production of Joan's mind, reenters the film undaunted and is again established as an actual presence through objective camera. Effectively bracketed, but no less real, he helps Joan face the flames with courage and resignation. These, it would seem, are an agnostic's Middle Ages.

The Name of the Man

Death appears as Monk, I said. "Or a clown," Bergman replied. —Bragg, p. 25

Andrew Birkin received a scriptwriting credit along with Besson, and, though it is impossible at this stage to be certain about their relative contributions, some tentative conclusions can be drawn from the available evidence. Their names are credited out of alphabetical order, suggesting perhaps that Birkin is responsible for the lion's share of the original screenplay. The movie's ubiquitous concern with signs and their interpretation, with heresy as a semiotic as well as a political problem, and especially the uncompromising nominalism of the Conscience figure suggest an intimate connection with Jean-Jacques Annaud's *The Name of the Rose* (1986), for which Birkin also received a screenwriting credit. Indeed, we find in both Eco's novel and in Annaud's "palimpsest" of it an attitude expressed toward the problem of discerning between sanctity and heresy that could well serve as *The Messenger*'s epigraph: "the step between ecstatic vision and simple frenzy is often very brief." To some degree Eco's work, like *The Messenger*'s version of Joan of Arc, can be read as a contest between Realist and Nominalist theories of the sign. The real nature of Joan's visions and her mission remain without question in the film's early diegetic world, just as they had remained without question in earlier cinematic representations. In the second half of the film, however, signs are cut off from their assured connection to a divine source, their possible significance multiplies, as Joan's mute but impressive visions are apparently reduced to phantoms of her own fevered psyche, in many ways analogous to the signs of the apocalypse in *The Name of the Rose*, which turn out to have been written not by the hand of God but by his self-elected apostle, Jorge de Burgos. Finally Conscience's adherence to logic, physical evidence, and Occam's Razor make him an obvious successor to William of Baskerville.

The publicly available screenplay, which I am attributing primarily to Birkin, includes perhaps the most troubling event in the historical record, Joan's attempted escape/suicide from the tower in Beaurevoir. Vita Sackville-West's biography reflects the positive light in which this leap of faith/despair is often viewed:

> At last she knew for certain that the transaction had been completed, and that she was indeed about to be handed over to the foreigner and the enemy by one who, Burgundian though he was, was yet her own countryman. At this, a kind of frenzy seems to have taken possession of her. On her own showing, she had no desire to commit suicide — she had only the desire to get away. To fall into English hands was the thing she most dreaded. It was in vain that her Voices sought to restrain her. In vain that Saint Catherine assured her that she would not be delivered until she had seen the King of England. She had no desire to see him and said so. Still, the Voices would not authorize her to do as she wished. The argument continued daily for some time, Jeanne beseeching, the Voices refusing their permission. Finally she took the law into her own hands, commended herself to God, and threw herself off the top of the castle tower. The leap from Beaurevoir constitutes one of the most inexplicable and curious episodes in her career. It is assumed that the height cannot have been less than sixty or seventy feet. The Act of Accusation expressly states that she jumped from the top (*a summitate unius turris altae*) [pp. 267–68].

The episode is a fundamental part of the case against Joan, because here on her own testimony, she admits willfully disobeying the very "voices" that had dictated her mandate and mission. Sackville-West goes on to claim, in a whopper of circular reasoning, that in failing to follow her voices Joan "disposes, almost *ipso facto*, of the argument, again so often advanced, that her voices were merely the subjective expression of her own inward desires" (p. 269). Of course Sackville-West's *ipso facto* not only assumes facts not in evidence, but also presupposes quite a dubious view of the unconscious: what kind of world would we live in if "inward desires" could not be resisted? Presumably, that of the modern horror film, one without a superego.

In the screenplay of *The Messenger* Joan's superego makes an unexpected appearance we never see in the film. I quote the scene in its entirety:

EXT. LEDGE-BEAUREVOIR-NIGHT

Jeanne clambers out onto a narrow ledge, high above the frozen moat below.
    Only a fool — or one bent on suicide — would hazard such a leap.

VOICE (OFF-SCREEN): Need some help?

(The Man we saw after Compiègne is once again behind her.)

JEANNE: What are you doing out here?

MAN: I might ask you the same question.

JEANNE: I ... I'm leaving ... I can't take anymore ...

MAN: And what exactly is it that you can't take any more of?

JEANNE: Everything! Prison — humiliation — being abandoned and betrayed by everyone — I can't stand it anymore — I'd rather die!

MAN: You'll be dead soon enough anyway, so why be in such a hurry? Why not face up to your lies? It's your lies you can't stand anymore ...

JEANNE: I ... I never lied.

MAN: If you were true to yourself ... if your faith was firm, you wouldn't need to run away from yourself like this ...

JEANNE: I am true — to my Lord, the King of Heaven. He knows how much I love him — that's all that matters to me ...

MAN: How can you pretend that you love God when you're about to throw away the most precious thing he gave you? Life is a gift, Jeanne — a gift from God. You know what He'd say to you, if He was here? "What are you doing to me Jeanne?"

(Jeanne is lost, exhausted, numbed. She gazes into the void, contemplating the fall ...)

JEANNE: You're right ... I shouldn't do that.

(The man suddenly pushes her so that she nearly falls ...)

MAN: That's too easy. One minute you want to die, the next you want to live ... (again pushes her) Do you think that life is a toy that can be played with and then broken when you don't want it anymore?

JEANNE: No, no ... I'm just so tired, and lost, and ... I didn't realize what I was doing?

(He pushes her again ...)

MAN: Oh? And just because you realize now, everybody else should just forgive you?!

JEANNE: I don't know — I don't care anymore — I just want to be at peace!

MAN: Oh, so you don't want war anymore? You want to be at peace? You want to be able to change your mind anytime you feel like it and expect everyone to go along with it?

JEANNE: I don't understand. What do you want from me?

MAN: I told you already ... I'm here to set you free ...

(Again the Man pushes her! This time she loses her balance, and with a startled

> cry falls from the ledge — plunging down, down — and crashing into the frozen
> moat...! Two castle GUARDS on watch are alerted by the SOUND of the
> splintering ice ... Jeanne is drowning, barely able to cling to the broken ice
> around her. The first Guard to reach the moat tests the surface with his foot ...
> GUARD #2: Don't try — you'll fall through!
> (The First Guard lies flat to spread his weight, then crawls toward Jeanne ...)
> GUARD #1: Good God, it's the prisoner!
> (The second guard glances up at the tower ledge far above ...)
> GUARD #2: If she jumped from up there, she's dead for sure! Forget it ...
> (The first Guard reaches the edge of the hole just as Jeanne disappears beneath
> the water. He plunges in his hand and grabs her hair, pulling her head back
> above the water ...)
> [Birkin and Besson, Screenplay].

Some version of this scene seems to have been filmed: a trailer for the movie
includes a brief glimpse of Joan falling backwards from a high tower. The
decision to delete it and the name change in Joan's hectoring nemesis from
"Man" to "Conscience" severely delimits the figure's semantic play. Another
major scene that is completely cut is that in which Jean d'Aulon attempts a
last minute rescue, offering Joan a continued life of love and marriage, which
she foregoes in favor of martyrdom. This penultimate scene in the screenplay
immediately strikes one as discordant and derivative; it smacks of undigested
references to Cecil B. DeMille's *Joan the Woman* and Martin Scorsese's *The
Last Temptation of Christ*. Yet the excision of the earlier scene quoted at length
above does make quite a difference. Whatever role Besson played in the production of the original script, he certainly would have had the final say about
the character's name (or lack of one), and it would have been his decision to
cut entirely what certainly promised to be a very dramatic scene.

In the original screenplay "Man" is more of an uncanny figure, morally
indeterminate rather than just stern and uncompromising. His domestication
as Conscience to a large degree disambiguates the character. The figure in the
screenplay coheres perfectly, in both his *in bono* and *in malo* aspects, as savior and tempter, confessor and fetch, when compared with C. G. Jung's shape-
shifting tricksters. For Jung, the trickster was a more ancient, accurate
representation of an element in both the collective and individual unconscious than the notion of a conscience, Christ, or the Catholic pantheon of
saints.

> Ability to change his shape seems also to be one of his characteristics.... His
> "approximation to the savior" is an obvious consequence of this, in confirmation
> of the mythological truth that the wounded wounder is the agent of healing, and
> that the sufferer takes away suffering. These mythological features extend even to
> the highest regions of man's spiritual development. If we consider, for example,
> the demoniac features exhibited by Yahweh in the Old Testament, we shall find

not a few reminders of the unpredictable behavior of the trickster, of his sense-less orgies of destruction and his self-imposed sufferings, together with the same gradual development into the savior and his simultaneous humanization. It is just this transformation of the meaningless into the meaningful that reveals the trick-ster's compensatory relation to the "saint" [p. 136].

The substitution of Hoffman's shape-shifter to occupy the place left by the complete absence in the film of Sts. Michael, Margaret, and Catherine seems to reflect the archetypal theory that the role of saints derives from (or compensates for the loss of) the trickster in post-primitive civilizations. For Jung, this archaic figure is born from our common experience of the tension between conscious and unconscious impulses. It represents the "counter-tendencies" of a "sort of second personality," which Jung dubs the "shadow."

> ... the personal shadow is in part descended from a numinous collective figure. This collective figure gradually breaks up under the impact of civilization, leaving traces in folklore which are difficult to recognize. But the main part of him gets personalized and is made an object of personal responsibility [p. 142–43].

Hoffman's designation in the credits of the film as "Conscience" makes strained sense if he is also the source of Joan's earlier visions of the child and the suffering Christ, as his shape shifting back and forth between the three identities of the child, the Christ, and the old man would suggest. Jung's the-ory of the shadow would seem to explain this tripartite figure and its relevance to Joan, because for Jung the shadow "participates in the observer's psyche and appears as its reflection, though it is not recognized as such" (p. 150). In *The Messenger* the aging of the shadow from boy to young man to old monk par-allels Joan's own maturation, the figure is a "reflection" of her own develop-ing psyche. And of course from a feminist perspective the fact that the figure first appears as a male playmate, then as an attractive male god, and finally as a censorious monk reflects the derivation (or obviation) of female subjec-tivity within the patriarchy. In figuring Joan's core self as masculine, Besson perhaps accounts rather back-handedly for her transvestitism, but he also appears to support Lacan's provocative dictum that "Woman does not exist." We note too that these three apposite figures (boy, Christ, and monk) have only one thing in common besides their gender, their putative chastity. That the Man is more of a shadowy trickster-figure than a conscience is also borne out in his sadism and his use of parody to ridicule Joan's most treasured mem-ories. In his final incarnation as an *unheimlich* monk Joan first mistakes him for the devil — "Get thee behind me, Satan" — a characterization he never denies. Instead he rebukes her for presumption: "Who are you to even think you can tell good from evil?" It follows, of course, that if she has indeed mistaken the black-robed figure for Satan, perhaps too she was incorrect in assuming that the young man with the blood dripping down his forehead was Christ. The mind games, the ridicule, the metamorphoses, the ambivalence of good and evil, and especially the character's reflection of Joan's changing age and circumstances seem to confirm Man as Joan's shadow. For Jung, a figure like conscience could only be a sop to civilization, holding the place, impersonating as it were, a figure of much greater psychological depth and complexity, which modern society must repress. "Man" is finally less a figure of medievalism than of psychoanalytic primitivism — which, admittedly, in popular culture is much the same thing.

Freud's theory of the double provides a companionable explanation of the figure's genesis from which Jung's concept of the shadow certainly derives. In the famous essay "The Uncanny," Freud sees the figure developing in consciousness as a by-product of primary narcissism, which, with the passing of this stage, turns aggressively back upon the self.

> Such ideas, however, have sprung from the soil of unbounded self-love, from the primary narcissism which dominates the mind of the child and of primitive man. But when this stage has been surmounted, the "double" reverses its aspect. From having been an assurance of immortality, it becomes the uncanny harbinger of death. The idea of the "double" does not necessarily disappear with the passing of primary narcissism, for it can receive fresh meaning from the latter stages of the ego's development. A special agency is slowly formed there, which is able to stand over against the rest of the ego, which has the function of observing and criticizing the self and of exercising a censorship within the mind, and which we become aware of as our "conscience." In the pathological case of delusions of being watched, this mental agency becomes isolated, dissociated from the ego, and discernable to the physician's eye. The fact that an agency of this kind exists, which is able to treat the rest of the ego as an object — the fact, that is, that man (sic) is capable of self-observation — renders it possible to invest the old idea of a "double" with a new meaning and to ascribe a number of things to it — above all, those things which seem to self-criticism to belong to the old surmounted narcissism of earliest times [2001, p. 940].

The chief importance of Freud's conceptualization of the figure of the double for our purposes is twofold. First, it argues that conscience is a sublimation of something that, with the passing of primary narcissism, becomes much more protean and threatening to the subject than the Pollyanna modern notion of a conscience would suggest. In this Freud anticipates the "othering" of the conscience by later writers like Althusser, Lacan, and Žižek, who would emphasize the figure's role in internalizing the traumatic split within the individual between his drives and society's frustration of those drives (that is, between id and superego), transforming them into mediated desires in the compensatory formation of the ego. Second, Freud's theory of the double explains more thriftily than Jung the reversal that takes place as the individual matures between the double who encourages the narcissistic faith in immortality and the antagonistic "uncanny harbinger of death" who brings home to us our own mortality. Of course, this notion equates powerfully with the development of the figure in *The Messenger*. The early appearances of the "beautiful" boy and later of Christ are profoundly reassuring to Joan, they provoke in her raptures of unbounded joy as she skips through fertile, burgeoning fields and softly burbling streams. Later Dustin Hoffman, reprising Berht Ekerot's role as Death in *The Seventh Seal*, coldly and rationally prepares to lead Joan to the stake, but not before bullying her into spasms of self-doubt in which she is brought to admit the narcissism of her convictions, a narcissism that the figure's earlier incarnations had helped to inspire. In forcing Joan to turn on herself, Man elicits a litany of self-abjection.

> JEANNE: ... So I helped myself ... and I saw signs ... the ones I wanted to see — and I fought, out of revenge and despair. Yes, I was proud, — stubborn — selfish — and cruel ... I was all the things that humans believe they are allowed to be when they're fighting for a cause.

With this litany of deadly sins in a decidedly contemporary idiom, Joan pronounces herself "ready," but in the screenplay Man has a "last temptation" in store to ascertain if she has well and truly turned her back on the selfishness of primary narcissism: a continued existence as the wife of Jean d'Aulon. When Joan dismisses d'Aulon's offer of love and continued life, the work of the Man is complete and he absolves her, as did the priest in the first scene in the movie: "Ego te absolvo, in nomine Patris, et Filii, et Spiritus Sancti, Amen."[16]

A Sign of Contradiction

Besson clearly found the contradictions inherent in Joan's history to be provocative:

> Why did it take this slight 19-year-old woman, officially declared to be a "witch," 500 years to become a "saint"? What torturous paths did human thought have to follow to discover the good hidden in evil? After being an instrument of death for centuries, would faith at last bring us its real message of peace?... She is our ancestor, lost in her time as we are in ours, caught between her beliefs and her ignorance
> [no pagination].

The opening credits of the DVD hammer home this ambiguity, superimposing a series of labels over our first sight of Joan: "Witch, Lunatic, Warrior, Savior, Legend." Of course part of Besson's project, like that in so much of movie medievalism, is to modernize Joan, to make her a sign of the times,

times when religious warfare, churches mixing in temporal matters, the psychopathology of messianic figures, and rampant nationalism are too much with us.[17] Christ spoke enigmatically of himself as a "sign that would be spoken against" or a "sign of contradiction" in Luke 2:34. And John Paul II, in a book that sold over 4 million copies, characterized the contemporary Roman Catholic Church itself as a "sign of contradiction," that is, a Church whose controversial nature, whose very opposition to the secular humanism of the modern world, demonstrated its truth.[18] The phrase has certainly caught on in much recent religious discourse, as any perusal of the Web or religious bookstores will demonstrate. It is particularly frustrating since, at a time when many feel the Church should be responding to its many critics, the phrase acts as a sort of shibboleth, which paradoxically turns any criticism of the Church into a confirmation of its authority.

Certainly Joan of Arc, particularly in Besson's version of her, is also a "sign of contradiction," "a sign which is spoken against." The last frame reminds us in an intertitle against a black screen that it took the Church 500 years to canonize her, analogous to the hundreds of years it took the early Church to reach its position of hegemony in the Western world, the long struggle ending with Constantine, which many, including John Paul II, have felt Christ's words were predicting. Joan certainly has been a sign much spoken against and many have suggested that in creating a postmodern saint's life Besson is speaking against her as well. But speaking against Joan in the film is always followed by defeat. The English speak foully against her in Orléans and are routed, the clerics speak against her, condemn her in Rouen, only to have their decision overturned. The lapsed heretic is belatedly canonized by the Church that had once deemed her anathema. Joan even speaks against herself in signing the formal confession of heresy "for fear of the fire," but she recants her recantation and tries to tear it apart: a sign then fraught with contradictions. Of course her own Conscience also speaks against her throughout her trial and even catechizes her self-condemnations in the final confession scene. As I said earlier, the film begins and ends with a scene in which a priest absolves her. Besson's Joan could be said to have a confession obsession, but the sacrament allows one a sublime self-contradiction, absolving the very sins to which one confesses oneself guilty. Such signs of contradiction, as I contended earlier, imply a faith on the other side of postmodern doubt. In putting our doubts about Joan into her own mouth and by allegorizing modern skepticism in the figure of Joan's own Conscience, postmodernism's seeming contradiction of faith is a perspective allowed full expression, only to find itself co-opted as part of a continuing *askesis* that confirms the truth of the sign. That Joan has been a sign spoken against in her own time, throughout history, and even by Besson's film itself only increases her sanctity. In a word, doubt is very much back to what it used to be, no match for faith — and no bar to it either.

As a final salvo let me confess a deep fondness for Joan, a fondness I hope no less sincere than that of many critics (a director-in-waiting among them) who have found Besson's treatment of her disrespectful.[19] Joan masterfully employed the religious zeal of the Crusades in the cause of her country's liberation. She always maintained, however, that this was but a first step; she hoped to unify the Christian world as a prelude to a renewed invasion of the Holy Land.[20] What would our verdict on her have been, I wonder, had she lived to lead the English and French armies in a new crusade against "the Saracens"?[21]

5

Theaters of War: Paracinematic Returns to the *Kingdom of Heaven*

They forgot how intellectually respectable the Christian theory of holy war once was. —Jonathan Riley-Smith

Even before the general release of what he insisted was an unassuming "movie about a knight" Sir Ridley Scott found himself caught in a mass media crossfire every bit as chaotic as the gauntlet depicted in his earlier film *Black Hawk Down* (2001). Though reactions to this film were not nearly as intense as the storms brewing around the even more controversial films released the year before and after *Kingdom of Heaven*— Mel Gibson's *Passion of the Christ* (2004) and Ron Howard's *The Da Vinci Code* (2006)— the responses to all three films demonstrate how much is at stake within post–9/11 culture in imagining Jerusalem as the once and future center of the world. This chapter begins by tracing the controversies surrounding the release of *Kingdom of Heaven* not in order to arbitrate between opposing positions but rather to demonstrate how the film came to serve as a contested site in an ongoing battle of historiographies.[1] More than an isolated skirmish in George Bush's "War on Terrorism," such disputes are rather one of its most crucial fronts: a battle over our collective memory about the crusades and their continuity with contemporary Western interventions in the Middle East.[2] This battle is no respecter of traditional boundaries between academic discourse and popular culture; it swiftly reveals the political implications of supposedly sober academic judgments about the past as well as emphasizing how quickly scholarly authority is marshaled in the service of mass-mediated demagoguery.[3]

If the paracinematic controversy over *Kingdom of Heaven* exemplifies the persistence of medievalism in contemporary political discourse surrounding wars in the Persian Gulf, successive versions of the film evidence a series of shifting responses to that controversy.[4] The first DVD release (2005) includes a "Pilgrim's Guide" (hereafter PG), which serves as a kind of concurrent palinode, marking the film's many departures from history. This feature creates what I will dub a dialogic *filmtext*—a cognitive overload of audio, image, and text that produces remediated dissonance and exacerbates friction between the reel and the real.[5] The "Director's Cut" of the film released a year later replaces the "Pilgrim's Guide" with an "Engineer's Guide" (hereafter EG), which stresses the continuity of technological problem-solving between the Middle Ages and present reconstructions of it, focusing thereby on fidelity to the material world of the Middle Ages rather than the film's frequent (and frequently derided) lapses from the history of the late twelfth century.

The pre-release controversies sparked by the film as well as its responses to its critics participate in a larger problematic of the filiations between past and present. This problematic is composed of dialectically opposed positions: the absolute alterity of the Middle Ages and the desire for a relevant, usable past. As the multifaceted spaces of paracinema frame as well as transgress the margins of what we might nostalgically call the film itself, we discover that temporal homologies are not simply an inherent quality of these films, but rather a variable in the transnational marketplace of cultural capital in which contending forces vie to value (an attribute values to) movies medievalism's presentist reconstructions of the past. Historical films often do attempt to determine their contemporary resonances, such as when DeMille frames his story of Joan of Arc within the context of a British foxhole in World War I. However, I would maintain that homologous constructions of past and present are — to a great degree — productions of the paracinematic realm.[6] If paracinema contributes to the construction of homologies between the past and the present, this process is anything but orderly or monologic. Instead, the realm of paracinema, particularly with films that screen controversial topics such as imperialism or nationalism, can become a zone of heated contestation not simply over the merits of a film, but over the validity and political valances of its homologies. Discourse ostensibly designed to frame for its audience the film's analogies with, or lines of descent from, the Middle Ages quickly reverses its field and ground, such that the film comes to frame contemporary political debates as well as their attendant historiographies.

Ridley Scott's film relies on spectacle and technical brilliance to produce a cinema of (orientalist) attractions while insisting upon its relevance to and continuity with the contemporary world. In this chapter medievalism and orientalism are treated as opposing though mutually implicated terms: medievalism refers to the perception of continuity between the Middle Ages and the modern world, while orientalism signifies not only the othering of the Middle East but also of the past itself. I would argue that the modern disentangling of Romanticism's amalgam of Gothic with the Oriental has been only partial, and tellingly so (see Fay 2002 and Ganim 2005). Western societies have vested their self-image and self-interests in an ever-widening gulf between modernity and the "medieval" Middle East, while they fear the return of the repressed from Islamic states conceived of as fundamentally static, anachronistic "empires of faith." In this form of orientalism historical "progress" is conceived broadly as a Western phenomenon, while Islamic societies are trapped in a lack of development that makes the continuities between medieval and modern Islam all too apparent.[7] Anachronism becomes in these conservative discourses a malign master trope in which both Islamic fundamentalists and Western liberals are revealingly implicated, because both refuse to leave the medieval Crusades out of the discussion of the contemporary Middle East.

This chapter traces these culture wars across a number of battle fronts, beginning with the pre-release controversies and the version of the film theatrically released and then moving to a consideration of the two subsequent DVD releases, focusing on their remediations of the film through digital paracinematic extras. The chapter concludes with remarks on the prevalent *memento mori* and *danse macabre* imagery in Ridley's Scott's "Director's Cut" as yet a further contribution to the debate over the medieval as a speculum of the modern, one in which reflection threatens to become a inescapable repetition.

Theaters of War: Pre-release Controversies and the Theatrical Cut

Attacks on *Kingdom of Heaven* came from at least three very different directions: Jonathan Riley-Smith, the reigning dean of British crusade historians, who thought the film a politically correct and dangerous distortion of history that would feed the flames of radical Islam; Khaled Abou el-Fadl, professor of Islamic law at the University of California, who judged its portrayal of Muslims stereotypical and likely to provoke hate crimes against Arabs; and James Reston, Jr., the author of a popular history covering the period represented in the film, who sued for copyright infringement. Of course, however improbably, it is just possible to steal from and still widely distort a popular

**The armies of Saladin lay siege to Jerusalem in Ridley Scott's *Kingdom of Heaven*
(2005).**

history, as well as to demonize *both* the "Franj" *and* the "Saracens." Still, these
contradictory reactions tell us more about the already charged environment
into which it was released than they do about the film itself. As has long been
the norm for films on controversial topics, the knives were out for this picture well before anyone knew much of anything about what it would contain.

In the instructive case of Jonathan Riley-Smith, Dixie Professor of Ecclesiastical History at Cambridge University, *Kingdom of Heaven* was judged
fatally ignorant of the new orthodoxy among crusade historians, which takes
seriously the religious inspirations of the Crusaders and tries to respect the
differences between their worldview and that of post–Enlightenment cultures.
The older view, most authoritatively represented by Sir Steven Runciman's
three-volume *A History of the Crusades* (1951–54), broadly characterized crusading as a frenzied, greedy dash for plunder fueled by revenge and religious
hatred. For Riley-Smith this misunderstanding of the Crusades is an invention of nineteenth-century medievalism, exemplified in the works of Sir Walter Scott and Joseph François Michaud. One could argue, however, that both
approaches to the Crusades are abundantly represented throughout the twentieth century, already neatly encapsulated in perhaps the finest movie ever to

explore the ambivalent continuities between the crusading era and modern times, John Huston's *The Maltese Falcon* (1941). In the film Sidney Greenstreet's suavely gross Mr. Gutman lulls the questing detective Sam Spade (Humphrey Bogart) to sleep with a history lesson on the Knights of Malta: "as we know, the Crusades were for them largely a matter of plunder." But Spade does eventually awake from his mickey-laced slumber to mete out punishment according to a code of honor and a sense of justice that take his would-be conspirators by surprise. As he finally admits, "maybe I'm not as corrupt as I'm supposed to be." Spade himself, then, might well serve as the film noir equivalent of the new understanding of crusaders championed by Riley-Smith: He is repeatedly underestimated by a modern society that attempts to project upon him its own moral relativism, greed, and ruthlessness, while he undauntedly pursues a just vengeance according to a sense of duty beyond their understanding.

For Riley-Smith "The Fatman" view of the Crusades is not only a simplistic projection of medievalism, which violates the near-absolute alterity of the crusaders' mentality, but it also presents a very real and present danger in the propaganda wars surrounding the recent Clash of Civilizations. He has waged a long offensive against the popular view of crusaders as plunder-crazed barbarians at the gates of a vastly superior civilization. Some of his frustration perhaps derives from the stubborn persistence of the Fatman view from Sir Walter Scott's *Tales of the Crusaders* trilogy, through Runciman's work in the 1950s, down to the Pythonization of crusade history by Terry Jones.[8] Interviewed by the British newspaper the *Telegraph* in January of 2005 (well before the *Kingdom of Heaven* was released in May), Riley-Smith responded to what he could glean from pre-release publicity with the following: "It's Osama bin Laden's version of history. It will fuel the Islamic fundamentalists."[9] In its shrill tones and paranoia the charge is nothing less than that of giving aid and comfort to the enemy. Ridley Scott's reply was characteristically blunt: "How can a historian say that? That's like me being a specialist telling you you've got (expletive deleted) cancer and I haven't examined you." Riley-Smith's charges represent the degree zero of an academic approach to movies all too common. Not only is discourse on a movie confined to the script or a paraphrase — or even the pre-release buzz — but these materials are thought to be sufficient in themselves, without ever having seen the movie, to launch dismissive judgments like his final verdict, "it's absolute balls, it's rubbish!" Rubbish it may well be but scholars entering the public arena to comment on films and foreign policy with the authority vested in them by major research universities should perhaps more closely follow the same canons of a careful and balanced evaluation of evidence upon which that very authority relies.

The major point to be made here though is that medieval historians almost never do treat movie medievalism with anything like the care they reserve for the past. But the slippage between these different registers is itself revealing. Riley-Smith has forgotten more about the Crusades than most of us will ever know and it is upon his work, as well as that of other contemporary crusade historians such as Jonathan Phillips and Carole Hillenbrand, that this essay relies.[10] However, his attempt to wall off the present from the past and to paint with a single brush all those who draw analogies or trace continuities between medieval and modern invasions of the Middle East not only underestimates the crucial role of medievalism in the production of ideologies (both Eastern and Western) but also misses the chance to tease out similarities and differences in finer detail. In his popular discussions of the crusading movement, not only in reactions to the film but also in a number of articles and presentations between 1995 and 2005, including a lecture given at Old Dominion University entitled "Islam and the Crusades in History and the Imagination, 8 November 1898–11 September 2001" (and one suspects in his reported consultations with FBI and CIA analysts), Riley-Smith has attempted to establish and police a chronological boundary between the Crusades and contemporary military interventions in the Middle East that is unenforceable.[11] In his narrative the Arab world had put the whole matter well behind them until it was suddenly reawakened by Abdul Hamid II who took the idea of modern crusading from "romantic nonsense that had been washing around Europe, where many writers compared contemporary colonialism to crusading."[12] Two points need to be made here. First, that the region lost interest in the West as well as its own history throughout the long "dark ages" of the Ottoman Empire is not to be wondered at, closed societies foster just this kind of forgetting. When the West again began to occupy the Middle East, Arabs did not need to read Walter Scott to see the similarities. Riley-Smith attempts to dissociate things like the writing of history and fiction from the politics of imperialism in ways that should be impossible after Edward Said.[13] Those in the Arab world knew that the triumphalism of the English and French commanders, Allenby and Gouraud, were deliberate evocations of an imperialist vision of history, which traced its spiritual genealogy from the Latin Kingdom and the likes of Godfrey of Bouillon and Richard the Lionheart.[14] And their descendants surely saw a kindred spirit in George Bush in the aftermath of 9/11, especially when on September 16, 2001, he rallied and readied Americans, warning "this crusade, this war on terrorism, is going to take awhile."[15] One cannot un-ring that bell, nor should one try, it tells us a great deal about the fundamental mixture of faith and militarism in the kind of uncompromising commitment Bush was determined to arouse in the Western world.[16]

An insistence upon the alterity of Middle Ages is a defensible and well-represented intellectual position that itself derives from humanism and the Enlightenment. In Riley-Smith's important *The Crusades: A History*, man is indeed the measure of all things, even a phenomenon thought to have endured for more than 700 years. The opening chapter is titled "The Birth of the Crusading Movement" and is followed by "Crusading in Adolescence," "Crusading Comes of Age," "Crusading in Maturity," and "The Old Age and Death of the Crusading Movement." The narrative traces the growth of crusading on the analogy of the development of a human being through phases that roughly correspond to the Ages of Man, an approach of which many medieval thinkers would have doubtless approved (see Burrow). Within this framework Riley-Smith is at pains to demonstrate the maturation and ultimate senescence of an intellectual rationale for crusading within the dizzying, far-flung varieties of the phenomenon. The life cycle metaphor naturalizes and structures variation within a developmental grid. Another organizing metaphor borrowed from the Middle Ages is that of the body as the site of a psychomachia wherein the Church hierarchy and its intellectuals represent the heart and the head, attempting to control the often wayward members of the body. For Riley-Smith the countless atrocities committed in the name of crusading represent "side effects."[17] Were one in search of analogies, one could compare here the responses to the torture at Abu Ghraib and subsequent acts of murder and rape that spawned the near frantic attempts of both politicians and the press to isolate such atrocities as the misguided actions of a few rogue soldiers. More important for our purposes, though, is Riley-Smith's attempt to essentialize the Crusades as ideally having been fought for the possession of "a cave in Jerusalem" and to construct deviations from this target as being out of character, that is to say, aberrations by rogue members of a tired, frustrated body driven on a lifelong pilgrimage toward a just and holy goal. Such allegories structure his master-narrative of the crusades and it is to the theological underpinnings of the movement — not to its regrettable "side effects" — that he refers when making the case for an absolute distinction between modern and medieval adventures in the Middle East. Of course, the Cambridge historian knows better than most that crusading could take a dizzying array of forms, for instance, that "the Spanish Armada of 1588 was an unsuccessful crusade" but it is not to this standard — nor to the cannibalism at Marrat, the bloodbath in Jerusalem (1099), the annihilation of the Cathars, or the sack of Christian Byzantium — but rather to an essentialized, intellectually justified quest that he appeals when accusing Ridley Scott of having adopted "Osama bin Laden's view of history."[18]

One of the many regrettable distortions in this overheated, neoconservative slur is the fact that the view of history the movie champions is most certainly not that past wrongs justify all measures of revenge. Instead the film's "message" calls for toleration and coexistence, though, as we shall see, such a message is not without its own difficulties. Riley-Smith rightly calls out of bounds the film's "Holy Land ... as a kind of early America, a New World welcoming enterprising immigrants from an impoverished and repressive Europe." As we have seen in earlier chapters, the Americanization of the Middle Ages is a constant in many films from Cecil B. DeMille's *Joan the Woman* through Zerry Zucker's *First Knight* and Antoine Fuqua's *King Arthur*. What surprises is his unwillingness to admit the extent to which cooperation and mutual respect were a necessary part of keeping a fragile peace in the Outremer. For Riley-Smith there was "no brotherhood of liberal-minded men," but historical sources, however idealistically, sometimes beg to differ. Usama bin Manqidh's famous *Memoirs of an Arab Gentleman* claims that the Templars are his friends and describes the kind of close personal relationship that perhaps inspired the sort depicted in the "romantic nonsense" of the two Scotts, Walter and Ridley:

> There was in the army of King Fulk son of Fulk a modest knight who had come from their country to go on pilgrimage and return home. He was on friendly terms with me, became my constant companion and used to call me "my brother" and there was between us love and companionship [qtd. in Hillenbrand, p. 55].[19]

Baldwin IV, the leper king, is also celebrated by the Arab chronicler Ibn al-Athir for his generous treatment of Muslim prisoners — a portrait in keeping with the film's characterization. And two contemporary Arab chroniclers, Baha ad-Din and Imad ad-Din, report having interviewed Balian about the Battle of Hattin for their histories.[20] Indeed, in its negative general depiction of the Franks and in its celebration of the chivalry and honor of a few, Monahan's screenplay would seem to derive more directly from Arab than Christian sources. Yet the point to be made about Jonathan Riley-Smith's entrance into the arena of cultural politics concerns more than the validity of his judgments about elements of the film but more crucially the political consequences of his insistence upon an absolute alterity between modern and medieval. If the notion of a continuity or analogies, however qualified, between Western invasions of the Middle East, past and present, is only the ravings of Muslim extremists and their politically correct Hollywood brethren and if peaceful coexistence, however fragile, is little more than wishful thinking, then the United States is essentially freed from any burden of the past in pursuing its ever-widening interventions in the Middle East. Indeed, it is free to cast the conflict — as Bush, Rumsfeld, and others were eager to do — as war not between civilizations but between epochs, a war between medieval barbarism and post–Enlightenment rationalism.

Complaints about the historical inaccuracies of Scott's film were to be addressed if far from resolved by the addition of a "Pilgrim Guide" in the initial DVD release (discussed below), but objections to its unfavorable portrayal of Muslims seemingly provoked a more immediate response. UCLA professor of Islamic law Khaled Abou el-Fadl opined more or less the opposite of Riley-Smith, "I believe this movie teaches people to hate Muslims." The incendiary nature of his rhetoric about a movie he too had not seen is comparable to that of Riley-Smith, though, unlike the Cambridge historian, his repeated insistence in a number of interviews on the dire consequences he predicts seems almost driven to create a self-fulfilling prophecy. I quote at length selections from an interview he gave to Beth Pearson of the *Herald* in March of 2005:

> In my view it is inevitable — I'm willing to risk my reputation on this — that after this movie is released there will be hate crimes committed directly because of it. People will go to see it on a weekend and decide to teach some turbanhead a lesson [....] There is a single (Muslim) character who is human-like — Saladin, he has consciousness and awareness. There's another character who is a mad, ranting, raving, bloodthirsty lunatic, screaming "jihad, jihad, jihad." The rest of the Muslim characters are willing to die without any emotion [....] This movie actually went a step further (in portraying Saladin as conflicted about his Islamic identity), which I found deeply offensive. Despite the savagery of the Crusaders and despite their ability to commit massacres and pillage and rape, Saladin identifies with them and is nearly sympathetic towards them. In one of the most unbelievable scenes, though I don't know if it stayed in the movie, Saladin thanks the Crusaders for teaching the Muslims chivalry [....] I'm not a conspiracy-theory type (sic!), but the timing of this movie is most suspect. The film falls into the category of "it's okay to invade these people, something good will come out of it." Not only that but the fanatics are better off dead because they want to go to heaven. This at a critical time when the logic of the white man's burden is coming back through the invasion of Afghanistan and Iraq and a lot of people are wondering if there is a civilizational (sic) showdown between Islamic and Christian culture.

Abou el-Fadl was responding to an advance copy of the original screenplay sent to him by the *New York Times*. What is most remarkable about these knee-jerk reactions is that many of the objectionable details he cites do not appear in the version of the movie generally released May 6, 2005. While Riley-Smith's charge of supporting terrorism does not seem to have had any appreciable effect whatsoever on the film as it was released, the more threatening tones of Abou el-Fadl did perhaps contribute to Fox Studio's politically correct, *ense rescindendum* approach to editing the film. In any event, the version privately screened in late April 2005 for the Council on American-Islamic

Relations (CAIR) in Los Angeles was lacking many of the elements el-Fadl had found so offensive and it received the organization's unqualified approval: "Our overall impression is that *Kingdom of Heaven* is a balanced and positive depiction of Islamic culture during the Crusades. Muslims are shown as a dignified and proud people whose lives are based on ethics and morality." Having won a small victory in the culture wars, *Kingdom of Heaven* premiered without incident, though violence had been done to Ridley Scott's film by Fox, which released a decidedly inferior cut of the film.[21]

James Reston, Jr.'s *Warriors of God* (2001) is an engaging if sensationalistic history of the period, but the short history of the book's reception is decidedly more engaging. After 9/11 it was one of three books on an understandably short list that Karl Rove suggested George Bush read in order to comprehend the history of East-West conflicts. Bush actually seems to have made his way through it, confessing disarmingly, "at first I was confused by Saladin, but then I enjoyed it." When Ridley Scott and William Monahan began to discuss making the film in the aftermath of 9/11, news of Bush's reading list had just begun to circulate widely, initially in the *New York Times* and subsequently across a broad span of media. It seems unlikely that neither Scott nor Monahan had read the book as they later maintained when Reston sued them for copyright infringement. The merits of Reston's suit or the niceties of "intellectual property" laws are well beyond the competence of this essay, but squarely within our purview is the mass-mediated struggle to *source* the film. The reactions of Scott and Monahan to the lawsuit predictably deny any specific sources whatsoever: Scott blustered "for just this reason I don't read anything at all" and a studio spokesman for Monahan assured that the screenwriter had been a fan of the Crusades since youth and consulted hundreds of books (though none were specified).[22] Indeed, the film's thoroughly re-imagined biographies of *dramatis personae* like Sibylla, Baldwin IV, "Tiberias," Balian, and his supposed father Godfrey would make matching the film's script to any history nearly impossible. What the filmmakers took from Reston's book (if they took anything at all) is the setting of the action in the years before the Third Crusade, as well as perhaps some of Reston's rather elegiac approach to the remnants of the medieval past within the present world.[23]

Riley-Smith's comment that the film's anachronistic medievalism was based on Sir Walter Scott's *The Talisman* was widely taken up by reviewers who went on to assume that Scott's novel was the film's major source. In point of fact the indebtedness is confined almost exclusively to a particular scene early on in which Balian is attacked at a desert oasis by what he is led to suppose is an Arab emir and his bilingual servant. Riley-Smith intended the connection to be a damning indictment of the film's source in nineteenth-century medievalism, but its revision of the opening episode in *The Talisman* reveals significant differences that complicate appreciably our perception of the cultural politics at work in the film. In the opening chapter of the novel, the Scottish crusader, Sir Kenneth, Knight of the Couchant Leopard, approaches a desert watering hole on the back of a huge battle horse, in full body armor, equipped with a shield and sporting an impressive array of weapons, including a sword, battle axe, mace, dagger, and lance. His own size and that of his steed make him tower over his Arab opponent. But his superior size and equipment prove a disadvantage in the sun and sand against a foe who uses agility and speed of horse to fight Kenneth to a draw, whereupon both decide to honor the reigning truce and, despite their vaunted differences, become traveling companions, each ultimately swearing to defend the life of the other. This pledge turns out to be important because Kenneth's new friend is none other than Saladin in disguise, who will protect and serve the beleaguered Scottish knight in a variety of guises throughout the narrative.

The film version of high noon at the oasis preserves none of Sir Walter's sense of a fair fight between equals, however different physically and culturally. The shipwrecked Balian has spent the day wandering through the desert — a refugee in search of a runaway horse, while all his shipmates lay dead on the beach. Two Arabs on costly mounts set upon him; the most belligerent of the two claims to be an emir. He demands through his interpreter that Balian must either fight him or surrender the horse Balian has finally managed to tether at the watering hole. The supposed "emir" insists the horse belongs to him because it is on his land, yet Balian, employing a paradox borrowed from Scott's novel, claims that he "took this horse from the sea."[24] Balian is on foot, dressed in only pants and jerkin, armed only with his father's sword. The "emir" attacks on horseback with the sun behind him, wielding a large javelin above his head like a spear rather than a lance — just as Saladin is said to do in Sir Walter's novel (p. 23). Balian parries the first attack and then shouts "fight me fairly," to which the emir replies that he is not bound to do so since he is a lord and Balian an obvious commoner. Balian replies that he is the "Baron of Ibelin" and when the "emir" demurs, he insists, "I am the new one!" Indeed. This mixture of underdogism and romanticized bastard feudalism is as we have seen in earlier chapters a commonplace of American movie medievalism. The emir finally dismounts to battle Balian on foot, while the presumed servant on horseback pleads with them to stop. The battle looks perhaps more one-sided than intended, since Orlando Bloom is physically more like his Woolfean than his Tassoan namesake — this elf had better stuck to his bow — but despite barely being able to wield the sword and stumbling along behind it with each swing, Balian at last manages to slice through the emir's neck.[25] The movieland splash of blood spooks the other Arab's horse and he is thrown flat on the ground, at the mercy of Balian's heavy sword. Balian spares him and they travel together to Jerusalem where Balian refuses to keep Imad as a slave and gives him the horse, which Imad generously returns at the end when Balian leaves Jerusalem.[26]

Monahan's screenplay thus splits Walter Scott's Arab in two: a good Arab, Imad, who only appears to rank lower than his pretentious servant, and a bad, bloodthirsty Arab bent on defending what, despite his claims, is certainly not "his land." The allegory is palpable. The false "emir's" unwillingness to fight fairly is a strategy one often hears lamented today by Western soldiers and the press alike in referring to terrorist or guerrilla tactics. As is demonstrated in short order, the fake emir can't win on equal terms. The land he defends is not his and his pretence is motivated by greed and religious prejudice. Walter Scott's Saladin repeatedly pretends to be less than he is, Ridley Scott's desert bandit pretends to be a wealthy leader in order to attack someone he thinks unable to fight back and recklessly throws his own life away on a whim. Balian is not a general arriving with an invading force but a lone soldier, lost, at the mercy of the elements, and looking to make friends among the indigenous population in the hopes of recovering a birthright (however dubious) in the Holy Land. He is "a verray, parfit gentil knyght," like Chaucer's Knight, poor and unassuming, a penitent pilgrim in search of forgiveness, who, were it not for his troubling agnosticism, would closely resemble the portrait of crusading chivalry constructed by modern day apologists for the Crusades like Riley-Smith. Tiberias (Jeremy Irons) wonders wistfully if Jerusalem can sustain "anything so rare as a perfect knight" like Balian, in an episode dubbed "The Perfect Knight" in the scene selection menu of the DVD. The core of this perfection is the purity of his mission entrusted to him by his dying father to "protect the people" and renewed by the dying Balwin IV, who makes him promise to "save the people." The figure of Balian allows Monahan and Scott to represent the Crusades as fundamentally neither imperialistic nor religious (these motivations are reserved for the villains in the film). Balian's charge, like that belatedly offered to justify extended engagements in contemporary Afghanistan and Iraq, is to save the indigenous population and to reconstruct a fallen infrastructure.[27] Balian's new Arab friend, Imad, represents an even more disturbing modern equivalent. We first see him up close when he is flat on his back with eyes closed, passively awaiting the death he believes he deserves because of his compatriot's unmotivated attack on Balian. Splashed with the blood of motiveless malignity, he asks Balian to kill him quickly. When Balian spares him, Imad calls himself "your servant, your slave should you wish it." But Balian, who "will neither keep slaves nor suffer any to be kept," sends Imad on his way with the gift of the horse. He has not come to dominate or control, though a stranger in a strange land he has fought a defensive battle for a prize he quickly gives back to a worthy if overmatched native, who comes quickly to admire Balian's restraint and generosity. In short, the scene is an enthusiastic representation of the ideals that support American interventions in the Middle East: a native inhabitant who cannot control the rabid bloodlust of a radical fringe but who gratefully acknowledges Balian's judgment (like that of a "smart bomb") to discern the difference between the just and the wicked, to punish those whose rage cannot be contained, and to set free and supply aid to those who are not a threat. If Ridley Scott's medievalism reveals the liberal Hollywood bias of which he has long stood accused, then it is only the sham liberalism of a Planet Hollywood that, as in dozens of other historical and futurist films, romances audiences with the possibility of benign, honorable, and short-term imperialist ventures. The "real" Balian lived his whole adult life in the Levant and died there in 1193. The "reel" Balian ultimately renounces the lands he has made better — and convinces the "reel" Sibylla to renounce hers as well — in order to return to a stubbornly guarded, peaceful isolation back in the West.

Orientalist claims that Islam is an "imposter religion" are comically evoked in *The Talisman* in Saladin's various disguises and in *Kingdom of Heaven* as well where Imad also plays the role of an underling. Such masquerades participate in orientalist conventions whereby Arabs, despite their assumed disadvantages, come to share and serve Western interests because they admire Western ideals, as well as those invaders whose conduct embodies them. The friendship between crusaders and Arabs in the film screens the possibility of a shared possession of the Holy Land and displaces opposition to colonialism onto a shared disgust among allies for the warmongering tactics of a few evil men on either side: a coalition of the just. Like the Gulf War I fantasy *Three Kings* (d. David O. Russell 1999) with which it deserves to be compared, an heroic few among an invading army are quickly transformed in *Kingdom of Heaven* into a peacekeeping force bent on the protection of the helpless from the horrors of war. The politics of both films openly plays to antiwar sentiments, while screening a much more ambivalent romance of heroes who get their religion back in the Middle East and save the natives in the process. Despite the liberal patina of such films, it becomes a much more menacing question to ask "Why can't we all just live together?" when *we* are for the most part not living *there*. In almost single-handedly inventing the historical novel and with it the notion in fiction of distinct cultures and histories, Sir Walter Scott not only helped to spark fascination with the Middle East but also supported its settlement with British subjects. As he jokes at the beginning of *The Surgeon's Daughter*, he has followed the common practice of sending his fiction (as Britain sends its sons) to India. Sir Ridley Scott sent a film crew to Morocco (which is 90 percent Muslim) and built there at enormous cost a replica of medieval Jerusalem, which he then set about destroying in spectacular fashion, employing thousands of Moroccans as extras to assail its walls. The captivating spectacle of a Technicolor Siege of Jerusalem and the wish for peaceful settlement of/in the Holy Land are not contrary impulses in Scott's film (or for that matter in contemporary American society) but rather integral parts of a postimperial and circular logic of ameliorative pacification.[28]

Attacks on films about the Middle Ages are almost always provoked by their ubiquitous claims to historical accuracy in pre-release publicity, but this is the flimsiest of pegs upon which to hang an increasingly weighty discourse — the equivalent of dissecting a film's claim to be "spectacular" or "awe inspiring." Certainly such movies would do better to employ upfront the equivalent of the Nun's Priest's disclaimer, "this storie is also trewe I undertake,/ As is the book of Launcelot de Lake." Also, there is nothing much wrong with scrutinizing an advertising topos, but one must first recognize that it is a commonplace of movie releases and treat it accordingly. In fact, experience suggests that audiences are not so easily taken in by such claims and that films often inspire their viewers to search out the differences between the "reel" and the "real" history. What we must not do, however, is to continue to erect a discipline based upon false and misleading notions of genre. The publicity sound bites for *Kingdom of Heaven* maintained that "historical accuracy colored every facet of the production" (whatever that means), but the film was wholly conceived and shot within the Hollywood tradition of historical romance — "historical" here signifying little more than that these films are set in the past. Where medieval films such as *Kingdom of Heaven* are concerned, the appropriate generic analogy is not chronicle history but medieval romances themselves. Indeed, Scott's Balian is significantly closer to fictional romance crusaders like Guy of Warwick or Bevis of Hamptoun than he is to the middle-aged, faithfully married Balian of the historical record.[29] Yet, if criticism of movie medievalism in general and of this film in particular has allowed itself to be consistently misled by repeated, "surprising" claims of historical accuracy, it has been even more deaf to the lyre of the history of film. The privileging of written sources over those in other media not only greatly impoverishes our analyses but also specifically distorts our sense of what is new or especially relevant about a film. In the case of *Kingdom of Heaven*, the talismanic, stigmatizing misidentification of *The Talisman* as the film's major source not only tended to obscure significant departures from the one episode imitated in the film, but it also misrecognized elements of agnosticism and pacifism as being particularly contemporary because it failed to account for the film's chief source in Cecil B. DeMille's 1935 film *The Crusades*.

Scott's *Kingdom of Heaven* was first reported in the trade papers as a project entitled *The Crusades*. The change in title obscures the fact that Scott's film is a loose remake as well as a kind of prequel to the DeMille classic. Filmed a year after the imposition of the Hays' Office Production Code (1934), *The Crusades* still manages to seem transgressive, even now, though it contains nothing so delightfully wicked as Cleopatra's (Claudette Colbert) milk bath or Charles Laughlin's camp Nero. That Scott's film and publicity nowhere acknowledged its source in DeMille probably reflects less the director's anxiety of influence than it does the low cultural capital of his precursor's work in contemporary Hollywood, where the name DeMille is synonymous with budget-busting, cast-of-thousands, vacuous spectacle. One suspects that Scott would not relish the comparison. DeMille originally marketed his film as an "interpretation of history" and indeed it champions noninvolvement and peaceful settlement for a 1930s isolationist America. It imagines the Third Crusade as ending in a mutually beneficial stalemate, with the gates of Jerusalem thrown open to all comers, and Richard the Lionheart set to return home to put his own house in order. Indeed, the last scene in *The Crusades* and the penultimate scene in *Kingdom of Heaven* cast Europeans as chastened pilgrims: in the former with the declaration of peace, pilgrims slowly parade through the gates of Jerusalem, which Saladin has opened to them, and in the latter, just as solemnly the Western population of Jerusalem issues forth from the gates to begin its long journey back to Europe, assured by Saladin of safe conduct. The matter of *Kingdom of Heaven* is anterior to *The Crusades* and dovetails with it as a kind of prequel in the overlapping Saracen victory at Jerusalem shown at the beginning of DeMille's film and near the end of Scott's. The two films intersect precisely at a shot of the top of the Dome of the Rock: in DeMille a cross is knocked down from the summit and in Scott's a crescent is reared there in its place. Scott's chosen time frame not only allows metacinematic flourishes — in his last scene Richard quixotically meets a stubborn blacksmith, just as he does at the beginning of DeMille's film — it also significantly positions the final scene in the Holy Land as a solemn withdrawal. Indeed, in both senses of the word the film's *conclusion* is a retreat from empire-building in the East and a perdurable resolve not to go back again. Balian not only denies Richard and the imperialistic wanderlust that figure represents but he also refuses to admit his own noble identity, insisting "I'm the

Blacksmith," thereby denying the land and title he had earlier claimed and perhaps metacinematically as well his connection to the historical Balian. Despite the circularity of the movie's plot, the reel Balian has learned that history need not be a repetition compulsion and refuses to participate in any further Crusades.

Of course casting the hero as an alias Smith or Jones who discovers a hidden aristocratic inheritance savours of both Mark Twain and Walter Scott and is part of the imaginative ties that bind America to Europe's past, but a hero casting a sword and his future in a forge is also the paradigmatic scene in both films. In DeMille's *The Crusades* Richard attempts to help forge his own sword and is rebuffed by the kindly blacksmith with whom he trades a cuff for a cuff. The association of smithies with the diabolic in medieval literature and art is evoked when Richard expresses scorn not only at the prospect of a crusade but for the Church and even faith itself: "Why should I fear and pray for what I don't understand." His treacherous brother Prince John complains: "Why it is an open scandal. He has no faith in God. He is graceless." While Richard boasts he will not join the Third Crusade because he has "no love for monks and shaved pates." In Scott's film the blacksmith scene and the atheism are taken more seriously. Balian too is called to the Holy Land, but, like DeMille's Richard, he is convinced that "my place is here." Balian's pride, unlike Richard's, stems from despair over his wife's suicide: "God does not love me." In both films, the hero is also urged to go on Crusade by a greedy brother who plans to usurp their possessions in their absence. Balian's brother is a priest who buries Balian's wife at the crossroads, has her decapitated as suicide, and yanks a small golden cross from her neck, which he takes for himself. The shot quotes the opening of DeMille's film in which a white women is being sold into slavery after the fall of Jerusalem to Saladin and the cross is snatched from her neck by an Arab auctioneer. The imitation of this shot is instructive: for both the priest and the auctioneer, the small golden cross holds only monetary value and so it makes no sense to sell or bury a woman wearing one. For DeMille this is one shot in a montage sequence of Arabs enslaving Christians and destroying their icons, Bibles and crosses. Arabs, excluding Saladin, are the villains of the film. Scott's villain is really religion itself, in all its various denominations, which, as Balian later says, "makes men mad." Indeed, perhaps the most tellingly contemporary turn in Scott's film is the absolute separation of faith from religion.

Balian kills his brother with a sword hot from the forge and sets his body aflame. As the priest writhes in agony, Balian reaches in to tear his wife's cross from the thieving monk's neck and brands his own palm in the process. Crusaders "took the cross" in elaborate ceremonies conducted by priests to sanctify crusaders as "warriors of God" and wore cloth crosses to signify this obligation. Balian "takes the cross" from a burning priest writhing in agony. In killing the priest he also takes "back" the cross from a malign institution and receives the stigmata of the cross on his palm. The following scene depicts a sneak attack by the bishop's soldiers on Balian, Godfrey, and his multicultural band of crusaders bent on returning to the Holy Land. They suffer a number of casualties but beat back their attackers, and Balian is playfully dubbed by the kindly Hospitaller (David Thewlis), who later replies to Balian's claim that, "I am outside God's grace ... I have lost my religion" with the reassurance:

> I put no stock in religion. By the word "religion" I've seen the lunacy of fanatics of every denomination be called the will of God. Holiness is in right action and courage on behalf of those who cannot defend themselves. And goodness — what God desires — is here (pointing to the head) and here (pointing to the heart). By what you decide to do every day, you will be a good man. Or not.

This speech is the central theme of the film and represents an almost parodic reinterpretation of God's desires as voiced in Pope Urban II's call for a crusade in 1095: "*Deus hoc vult!*" Like Richard, Balian undergoes a long process of suffering, which slowly rekindles his faith in God; however, faith must be won outside of religion. The Kingdom of Heaven is most certainly within him but the Church and its right arm the Templars are its chief foes. The Bishop of Jerusalem's counterpart in *The Crusades* is the Hermit — a mixture of Peter the Hermit and Bernard of Clairvaux — who is martyred for his beliefs rather than be used as hostage against the advance of the Christian armies. Given his chance to die a martyr, the Bishop in *Kingdom of Heaven* is willing to become a Muslim: "convert to Islam now, repent later." Balian too is finally converted but into that distinctly modern sect of Hollywood fideism that believes salvation a matter of personal choice. Back in his smithy at the end of the film, the season has changed from winter to spring and Balian can watch the buds blossom with his new wife, absolved by the screenplay from the doubly mortal sin of having murdered his brother the priest.

Digital Dialogism and the Filmtext: The Pilgrim's Guide

The criticisms of *Kingdom of Heaven*'s departures from history had a more belated, muted effect upon the evolution of the film than the more volatile charges that it was anti–Muslim and likely to provoke hate crimes. The attempt to counter charges of historical inaccuracy and political correctness could not be dealt with by simply removing objectionable scenes, the movie's anachronisms and outright inventions were far too numerous and integral to its structure. Instead, a palinode was added to the first release of the DVD, an enabled track entitled "The Pilgrim's Guide," defined as an "historical reference track" that "provides background information on the real people and true events depicted in the film," and elsewhere more briefly as an "historical text companion." The slippery diction of this description suggests a much closer relationship between real and reel than is actually the case. In *Crusades: The Crescent and the Cross*, an excellent documentary originally aired by The History Channel in 2004, the historian Jonathan Phillips engagingly navigates his way through the sites of contemporary Jerusalem with the help of a medieval pilgrim's guide, but the "guide" through the movieland *Kingdom of Heaven* is chiefly a guide to what's not there, to what the film has left out, added, conflated, or reconceived. Roland Barthes speaks of picture captions that function as "anchorage," something that confines the drift of the image and locates it within a particular context, framing, as it were, a picture's reference. Text and image have a particularly conflicted relationship in the DVD of *Kingdom of Heaven*, such that the film itself seems continually to strain against attempts by "The Pilgrim's Guide" to tether its characters and events to history. The effect is rather like René Magritte's celebrated series of paintings of "This is not a Pipe," especially the 1922 ("L'usage de la parole I") version where the pipe and caption exist in a common space on the same plane.[30] "The Pilgrim's Guide" rather obstreperously insists "This is not History" or "This is not really Balian of Ibelin" or "This really never happened." But like Magritte's caption it is positioned within the frame, obscuring the lower portion of the film, it competes for our attention and makes us aware of the differences between watching and reading. Viewing the filmtext's remediation of the theatrical cut makes a "willing suspension of disbelief" almost impossible; the demands placed upon a viewer turn the experience into a continuous agon between talking pictures and text. If "The Pilgrim's Guide" is a "companion," it is an attention-seeking and disruptive one, which impedes our progress through the diegesis, offering pop-up factoids that contradict or have little relevance to what we are seeing and hearing.

What W. J. T. Mitchell calls the "pictorial turn" in culture is haunted not only by the agon of poetry and painting but also by the mutual interdependence and exclusivity of sign and icon. For Mitchell the task of contemporary theory is most certainly not an iconophilic championing of the culture of the image nor is it to engage in iconophobic rants about the media age, but rather to explore how interactions of what he calls the "imagetext" challenge contemporary theory and mediate our experiences of the world.[31] The filmtext of *Kingdom of Heaven* offers an instructive case in point. Text commentaries in DVD formats are usually overwhelmingly iconophilic, providing fan information on the stars, anecdotes about the making of the film, production notes, and technical explanations of particular shots or effects. The PG, however, produces what is fundamentally an iconophobic correction of the movie's many transgressions against historical accuracy, offering the penitential spectacle of a movie laboriously confessing its own sins. One is forced to look at the film — or at least large portions of it — literally and figuratively *through* the semi-transparent, superimposed guide, and its corrections of the film help to privilege text over image and sound, thereby reasserting the inferiority of images to words that Mitchell claims has dominated Western culture since the Jews were rebuked for turning from God's commandments to worship the Golden Calf. As such it participates in the dire, iconophobic predictions about the effects of the film on audiences, made by Riley-Smith and Abou El Fadl. But as we shall see, The PG possesses its own spirit of waywardness, departing freely from the image it is supposed to elucidate and, seemingly tempted into presumption by the precedence it assumes, it detours recklessly into the trite and the trivial, leading us down its own paths of historical errantry and irrelevance. Also, the agon between image and text is not one-sided. The lusciously rich mise-en-scène of Scott's film and the internal consistency of its storyline, as well as our growing sympathy with its characters, encourage a cinephilic rejection of the PG as a needless appurtenance, or in the Derridean sense, as a dangerous supplement, which, whatever it does to history, detracts from our appreciation of the film in its intrusive remediation of the images. In this sense, perhaps the most precise pictorial analogue to the *Kingdom of Heaven*'s filmtext is Magritte's late contribution to his ongoing dialogue between words and images, "The Air and the Song" (1964). Here the picture is of a three-dimensional pipe mounted on a hand-carved three-dimensional frame. The endlessly repeated and endlessly elastic caption, "Ceci n'est pas une pipe," is here burned into the wood upon which the pipe has been mounted, and the first letter "C" contains a star, suggesting the caption is a note to the picture (or is it a flaw made by the wood-burning tool?), but the pipe itself casts a shadow and smoke rises up out of the frame from its tobacco-filled bowl. The treason of images is here countered by the treason of the text about the image and the image's irrepressible "reality effects" such as the casting of shadows and the billowing of smoke, which floats beyond the internal frame and hence beyond the sphere of influence of the caption. Likewise, in *Kingdom of Heaven* the movie exceeds the filmtext's attempts to frame it (many details go unremarked, whole scenes are left unanchored by text, and the PG ends well before the conclusion of the film). Perhaps more importantly, the guide's many omissions and silences, its digressions and irrelevances, gesture finally not simply toward the unreality of reel history but to the Lacanian real of history as a place we can only revisit.

Often the PG imitates the textual model of a footnote, providing further information or citing the sources of quotations, such as that early on which completes Godfrey's reference to Luke 24:47:

> (Godfrey) "Some say Jerusalem is the very center of the world for asking forgiveness...." (PG) "... And that repentance and remission of sins should be preached in His name to all nations, beginning at Jerusalem."

But the guide also identifies the spurious nature of apparent quotations, when in the same scene, Balian translates the Latin motto he has burned into the wooden crossbeam of his smithy for a curious Viking: "What man is a man who does not make the world a better place?" A note in the PG tells us the sentiment "has no reference, it was created by the screenwriter William Monahan." "Has no reference," means it has no authority in ancient or medieval Latinity, such that the PG's annotation refers to an embarrassing lack of authenticity, and perhaps even "notes" implicitly the screenwriter's lack of erudition. Hence the PG identifies the film's first attempt to buttress its humanitarian ethos as a fraud, and with the crossbeam of Balian's ideology declared fraudulent, we are less likely to trust the stability of the edifice this ideology is made to support in the film. Later in the same scene, as Godfrey confesses that Balian is his bastard son, there begins a series of PG blazons that distance reel from real identities. We are told, among other things, that Godfrey is fictional but based on Godfrey of Bouillon, the first ruler of the Kingdom of Jerusalem, and that Balian was the legitimate son of the crusader Barisan. But unsatisfied with having pointed out the fictionalization within the screenplay, the blazons go on to provide an anecdotal biography of the historical Godfrey of Bouillon, telling how he was reputed to have cut a Turk in half length-wise, wrestled a bear, and cut off a camel's head at a single stroke. Of course, this material seldom makes its way into conventional histories of the period because it is drawn from the romantic, rather than historical tradition. Nevertheless, the size, power, and courage detailed in these exploits seem somehow still to count within the diegesis of the film. Liam Neeson's Godfrey is a large, powerful man who tells us he once fought for two days with an arrow through his testicle and goes on to fight bravely with one in his lung when the Bishop of Jerusalem's troops stage a sneak attack. We are told that Godfrey of Bouillon refused to be crowned king in the Holy Land and "so he took the title *Advocatus Sancti Sepulchri* or Defender of the

Holy Sepulchre," which makes the real Godfrey an excellent foster father for the reel Balian, because he too denies the throne when it is offered to him and becomes the leader of Jerusalem's defenses. The uncredited writer of the PG seems to be demonstrating that the life of the real Godfrey is the inspiration for many details in the reel life of Balian, like father like son. As each of the main characters is introduced on screen, they are punctiliously distinguished from their historical counterparts and the fictive nature of major plot points is stressed. Balian, we are told, had his wife and children with him in the Holy Land; he and Sibylla did not have a romantic relationship (though the PG gossips parenthetically that she may have had an affair with his brother Baldwin). She also did not poison her own child. Nor was Guy of Lusignan nearly so bad as he is portrayed in the film, though Reynald of Chatillon was probably even worse. "Tiberias" is a composite character based largely on Raymond of Tripoli, and so forth. Often the PG directly contradicts what is being said in the dialogue of the film, such as when Sibylla tells Balian she was given to Guy at fifteen and the PG tells us Guy was her second husband whom she wed much later, or when Balian says, "I am no lord" while the PG insists, "the historical Balian was a lord." It even undermines an acoustic commonplace: "Most scabbards are made of leather, and so when cinematically a sword is withdrawn and makes a metallic sound, it is a misnomer (sic). If a scabbard had metal in it, it would dull the blade."

More intriguing though are the moments when the filmtext produces what we can only assume are intentional ironies between word and image, given the blatant nature of their juxtaposition. In the scene discussed earlier, Balian is urged by his brother the priest to leave for the Crusade, as Balian heats and pounds a sword in the forge. The PG assures us that the West had much to learn about forging metal from the Arabs:

> The Muslim method (sic) of hardening swords in the Middle Ages was the *Damescene process*. This was accomplished by thrusting a super-heated blade in the body of a slave and then into cold water. Crusaders discovered that swords made of Damascus steel were more resilient and harder than those of European manufacture, and paid the price for it.... Their version was less brutal as they found that they could accomplish the same hardening by thrusting a red-hot sword into a mass of animal skins soaking in water. It is the nitrogen, given off by the skins in the water, that produces a chemical reaction in the steel to harden it.

Very soon thereafter, Balian, having discovered the theft of the small cross and that his wife's corpse has been mutilated, plunges the red-hot sword into his brother's abdomen. The intervening period is time enough for blazons outlining justifications for crusading, including Augustine's theory of the legality of offensive war when waged against those who refuse "to make reparations for wrongs committed or *fail to return seized property*" (emphasis added), as well as the more ubiquitous justification that "God wills it!" As the priest bursts into flames, Balian dispassionately watches him cook, accompanied by the editorial note listing the spices and fruits that the Crusades introduced to the West. Such alignments are probably not accidental and they do complicate appreciably our reactions to the film. Is Balian tempering a sword in his brother's belly or the list of condiments supposed to be funny? Do the authorities of God and Augustine suggest that his punishment of his brother is just, something that God demands? Certainly this film shares with many others a deeply self-righteous anticlericism. Or are these juxtapositions arranged to highlight the differences between the crusading ideal and the human beings who embraced it?

Perhaps the most disturbing example of the PG getting off-track is its odd turn in the aftermath of the Battle of Hattin (1187) to the Muslim faith and its prophet, Mohammed. It has little or nothing specific to say about either topic before or afterward, so that this single extended reference, especially given its gratuitousness, looms large. If the film was cut to avoid offending Muslims, the censorious studio seems not to have been so vigilant with the PG. Wandering through a dusty sea of Templar corpses as carrion fowl circle above, Balian and Raymond discover the head of Reynald of Chatillon and later a whole pile of heads, including that of the kindly Hospitaller (David Thewlis). The PG explains in a series of blazons:

> Beheadings are not uncommon to the Muslim faith, as Mohammed himself engaged in beheadings. He not only engaged in caravan rides early in his career as a prophet, but also in war later. Mohammed was directly involved in the massacre of Qurayza Jews wherein he "had trenches dug, and the men were led out in batches and beheaded." Ibn Ishaq's "Life of Mohammad" is the authoritative source on The Prophet, and records the event as such: "There were 600 or 700 (beheaded) in all, though some put the figure as high as 800 or 900."

This information is not merely gratuitous but also in the context of the film extremely evocative, connecting Saladin's execution of the Knights Templar after Hattin not only backwards to no less a precedent than Mohammed himself but also forward to contemporary horrors screened on Al Jazeera and rebroadcast round the world. This is not to question the accuracy of the PG on this point, which dutifully cites its source, but rather to emphasize the way this factoid is deployed within the film. Again, no other information is given about Mohammed and there is precious little about Islam elsewhere in the PG, nor forthcoming is the corresponding information that crusaders themselves routinely engaged in such acts. Rather, the conclusion we are meant to draw is that beheadings are somehow integral to the career of Mohammed and especially characteristic of the religion he founded, a tradition of summary, religious executions, stretching from the seventh century through the time of the Crusades and down to yesterday's news footage. This episode from Mohammed's biography is a favorite of conservatives wishing to cast aspersions on Islam by agreeing with the terrorists that their actions are guided by religious precedent. Indeed, this use of medieval sources to score contemporary points against Islam is present in Pope Benedict XVI's recent quotation from the fourteenth-century *flyting* between Manuel Paleologus and a Persian scholar. The pope quotes Paleologus's characterization of Islam as a religion of the sword: "Show me just what Muhammad brought that was new, and there you will find things only evil and inhuman, such as his command to spread by the sword the faith he preached." The response of Muslims to this affront was swift and predictable to the effect that "we're not medieval, you're medieval." Iran's Ayatollah Ali Khamenei called it "the latest link in the chain of conspiracy to set off a crusade." While Salih Kapusuz, deputy leader of the government of Anatolia, said that Benedict "has a dark mentality that comes from the darkness of the Middle Ages" and called the pope's speech "an effort to revive the mentality of the Crusades."

Whether or not one concludes that the Qur'an endorses the beheading of prisoners (Islamic scholars are divided on this question, though most think it doesn't), the PG's annotation of this episode is clearly inspired not so much by the movie or the history it purports to represent as by the recent controversies surrounding televised decapitations of hostages by Muslim extremists. Its purpose is not simply to situate Saladin's executions within a tradition of sacred violence. No such justification is claimed within the film and Saladin's own biographers are very clear about his motivations: on Reynald he had sworn revenge and he refused to ransom Knights of the Temple and Hospital because they would not pledge never to take up arms again and he didn't relish the prospect of having to fight them all over again on another day. Saladin did ransom the "real" Balian, but only after extracting a promise that he would remain a noncombatant — a promise from which Saladin soon released him, when Balian asked to be allowed to remain within Jerusalem and direct its forces against the siege.[32] The PG note's verb tenses, droll litotes, odd conjunction, and circular structure speak volumes ("Beheadings *are not uncommon* to the Muslim faith, *as* Mohammed himself *engaged* in beheadings." emphasis added). The sentence bites its tail, suggesting both continuity and reverent imitation. Most crucial though is the metonymy in "the Muslim faith." The sentence *doesn't* say "some Arabs have been known to decapitate people and so did Mohammed" but rather that beheadings are common to this *faith*, *because* Mohammed committed them. Implicit here, I would argue, is an approach to the supposed alterity of the Middle East, one which defines

Islam as laboring under a lack of historical distinction between the Middle Ages and the present. Riley-Smith demands we respect the multiform differences between the present and past and fears the medievalism that sees continuities between medieval and modern wars in the Gulf, and many conservatives have been quick to take up that banner. But for many of these same voices, Muslims really are "living in the Middle Ages"— to misuse Eco's famous phrase. If medievalism is conceived as error, as a failure of Westerners to recognize real historical differences, then this form of what might be called orientalist medievalism imagines Islam to be characterized by just such an error, just such a lack of historical distinction or development. The Islamic other is then in a word medieval, he does not need to "get medieval" like Westerners. The modern West is defined by its difference from the Middle Ages, Islam by a lack of development that is conceived to be not only economic and political but moral as well. Like its calendar, Islam is some 622 years behind the West, Muslims live today in the year 1386, still very much "medieval" by Western reckonings, still bound to tradition and authority in ways modernity is thought to have left far behind.[33]

The Engineer's Guide

Throughout this essay we have been tracing the evolution of responses to Ridley Scott's *Kingdom of Heaven*. As an example of what Umberto Eco would call an "open work," subsequent versions of the film not only respond to criticism but also in a sense respond to those earlier responses. A "Director's Cut," in this case as in many others, is not simply a return to an original version so much as it is a final version (or versions) prepared in reaction to earlier cuts of the film over which the director had less control, perhaps contemplated in the shooting of the film, but typically realized only after its theatrical release. One significant revision made between the DVD of the theatrical release and the "Director's Cut" is to replace the pesky "Pilgrim's Guide" with a much less obtrusive "Engineer's Guide"—a heavily revised and considerably less controversial trivia track, which highlights film credits of the major stars, includes production notes, and discusses set construction, locations, and technological innovations like CGI, particularly in the spectacular siege of Jerusalem. This new track reproduces word for word much neutral information from the PG, *but cuts everything discussed above in this chapter* and indeed almost all of the historical corrections that serve to falsify the film's version of history. For instance, the PG annotation of the scene in the smithy in which Balian kills his brother is neutered in the EG by the introduction of the actors and the stunt men who choreographed the scene. When historical details are provided, such as in the aftermath of Hattin, they tend to support and confirm what is being depicted on screen. The EG claims that Imad ad-Din was a witness to what transpired and quotes selections from his account. There is no dissonance whatsoever between the medieval chronicle quoted in the EG and what is occurring in the film itself. The EG is also completely silent on the topic of Mohammed's beheadings and their supposed role in the Muslim faith. A close comparison of the two trivia tracks can only conclude that the later version (EG) consistently revises the earlier one (PG) by deleting not only the extraneous and the controversial but also by employing historical annotation to support rather than challenge or falsify the "reel" history.

The EG also appears to respond directly to the attacks that accompanied the film's initial release. In a clear reply to James Reston, Jr., screenwriter Monahan is quoted as saying, "When I'm doing history, I'm interested in my own take." He assures viewers that his original idea for the script was "set at the time of the Leper King" and that "I am very scrupulous about going to the primary sources," listing William of Tyre, Leon Eracles, and Imad ad-Din as having provided the raw material for the screenplay.[34] The problems of Riley-Smith and other historians who found the portrait of Saladin idealized and evidence of the film's politically correct approach to the Crusades is also addressed. These academics find their own responses "footnoted" or at least referred to within the EG, which admits the portrayal of Saladin is "iconic" and notes, "Some scholars are rethinking this and casting Saladin as a ruthless man of ambition." Ghassan Massoud, the actor whose Saladin is one of the best things about the film, also defends his performance as nuanced and compares it favorably with movies made by Arabs, in which Saladin is portrayed as being without flaws.[35] Clearly the EG has not only sanitized negative elements in the PG, but it also incorporates and responds to criticism from academics and fortune-seeking popular historians, enlisting an Arab actor to champion the depth and nuance of Ridley Scott's Saladin over the hero-worship that limits Arab versions.

Living in the Memento Mori: The Look
of the Past in Scott's Cut

Walter Benjamin insists that we live in a continual state of emergency and that it is the challenge of historiography to come to terms with this fact (p. 257). For Frantz Fanon (p. 83), states of emergency are the endlessly reiterated order of the day in colonialism and lead to a doubling or splitting of consciousness that is characterized by what he calls "Manichaean delirium."[36] Homi Bhabha reads Benjamin's states of emergency through the work of Frantz Fanon as a "state of emergence" "where collaborations of political and psychic violence within *civic* virtue, alienation within identity, drive Fanon to describe the splitting of the colonial space of consciousness and society as marked by 'Manichaean delirium'" (p. 62). Giorgio Agamben (pp. 1–31) demonstrates how common "states of exception" really are, how they do not simply suspend the regular functioning of the law but are a kind of continuing precondition of governance itself. The return to Iraq and the promise of a continuing Western "presence" there for many decades to come not only reminds us that there is likely to be no real "post" to colonialism but also of the extent to which states of emergency and exception have again become quotidian in that most recent of posts — post–9/11. The attacks of academics on *Kingdom of Heaven* were launched from/in such states, as were the defenses mounted in the editing of the film, the creation of the "The Pilgrim's Guide," and its wholesale revision in "The Engineer's Guide." In our own state of emergency the past refuses to be confined to another country and has become instead a region, an ideology, perhaps even, despite all claims to the contrary, a religion. "Manichaean delirium," I would argue, underlies *Kingdom of Heaven*'s ambivalent historical typologies as well as its deployment of repetition and specular imagery.

Representations of war are among the most hotly contested sites in any conflict and the lines between representation and participation are as often redrawn as those within a theater of war itself. This volatility is perhaps most clearly demonstrated by reference to representations staged by combatants themselves, because they (often unintentionally) point to realities not reflected in official discourses about war. One such attempt at self-representation occurred at the siege of Acre in the winter of 1190 when a stalemate was reached. Amidst what Amin Maalouf calls a "carnival atmosphere" of mutual civilities, banqueting, and ludic entertainments, mortal opponents stage what appears to be a send-up of their own conflict:

> One day, the men of the two camps, tired of fighting, decided to organize a battle between children. Two boys came out of the city to match themselves against two young infidels (i.e., Christians). In the heat of the struggle, one of the Muslim boys leapt upon his rival, threw him to the ground, and seized him by the throat. When they saw that he was threatening to kill him, the Franj approached and said: "Stop! He has become your prisoner, forsooth, and we shall buy him back from you." The boy took two dinars and let the other go [p. 207].[37]

Of the many remarkable things about this anecdote perhaps the most striking is the way the soldiers' parody of the chivalric ethos is absorbed into the real conflict. A duel was the literature of chivalry's most vaunted means of settling disputes; between opposing sides four children are sent forth to mimic a chivalric tournament, almost as if the adults were playing at without actually having to commit themselves to a winner-take-all contest. The adults attempt to produce a harmless spectacle, to carnivalize knighthood, but the children's mimesis of their elders threatens to become all too faithful. Interestingly, no attempt is made to put an end to the charade; rather than simply separating the boys, the Franks offer terms and the Muslim boy accepts a ransom for his prisoner. What began as simulation is folded into the larger conflict itself and operates to reveal the economic substructure of that conflict.

Similar elements of uncontrollable masquerade and parody are also present in the now infamous photographs taken in Abu Ghraib wherein abuse and torture shade subtly from racist, xenophobic "play" to a self-terrorizing awareness of the extent to which the West now faces demons of its own construction. Indeed, many of the deliberately and elaborately posed photos display child-like, comic book combinations of dominance and humiliation, which in their infantilism seem to many to speak underlying though unintended truths. Attempting to portray a Muslim prisoner as a bogeyman of unthinking religious intolerance, cloaked and hooded in black with wires attached to his hands, the Abu Ghraib guards erect a potent image that recalls the Ku Klux Klan, witches, and executioners, but the figure's precarious perch on a cardboard box and the electrodes attached to hands and body bespeak his lack of self-determination: The bogeyman is revealed as puppet and victim. As Melani McAlister concludes: "The photographs from Abu Ghraib were images of a new kind of racial politics, one that brought the symbolics of domestic racism — itself a product of the history of colonialism and imperialism — into the service of a new, overtly imperial American power" (p. 302).

Both these images (the twelfth-century mock tournament and the twenty-first century travesty of torture as a War against Terrorism) in their unintended ironies provide an instructive context within which to view Ridley Scott's *Kingdom of Heaven*. Scott's film is often charged with political correctness, perhaps the predictable result of a film that "tries to be fair to everybody." An example of the way in which such a strategy was doomed to backfire is the shot just before the battle for Jerusalem when the villain of the piece (Guy de Lusignan), wearing what we suppose is a fool's cap, is paraded between the two armies, bound, almost naked, and seated backwards on the rump of a braying ass. Nothing like this could have occurred, since Guy was at this time being held prisoner in Nablus. But the shot, intended to heap well-deserved scorn upon the head of a pompous and narcissistic "King of Jerusalem," should perhaps rankle the sensibilities of Christians who remember that on Palm Sunday Christ rode in unassuming triumph into Jerusalem on an ass — a triumph that quickly turned to arrest, scorn, and death: "'God bless the king of Israel.' Jesus found a donkey and mounted it, in accordance with the text of Scripture: 'Fear no more, daughter of Zion; see your king is coming, mounted on an ass's colt'" (John 12: 13–15). The shot immediately follows one in which Saladin is asked by his advisor to show mercy to the inhabitants of Jerusalem and Saladin replies: "No, I cannot." The potent mixture of merciless scorn in a film at some pains to paint Saladin as heroic and courteous is disconcerting. That Saladin should be made to orchestrate such a public *parodia sacra* is certainly at variance with the respect he shows for Christianity in his more private moments. One is tempted to surmise that the disrespect is not deliberate, only the film's failure to control its own figuralism.

Clearly the film's invention of a wayward son taking up his father's crusade reflects George Herbert Walker Bush's patrimony in American foreign policy, though the film seems both to endorse as well as to be frustrated by the very recursiveness it evokes. Imad gets his chance to stand over a fallen Balian late in the film, reminds him "you reap what you sow," and then plunges a sword into the earth next to his head, duplicating Balian's earlier gesture. And despite his extension of the same mercy shown him at the oasis, Imad's mimicry savors the irony of this gesture. Like Fanon's native, Imad has experienced the dream of being in the settler's position. But what happens when mimicry turns to self-disgust at one's reflection, as Fanon suggests it always must? Must we then reap a whirlwind?

Ridley Scott's director's cut is a much darker film than the theatrical release, chiefly because it includes a number of scenes that remain more or less detached from what Deleuze terms the "sensory-motor schema." These time-images are specular and include many of actual/virtual, limpid/opaque, and seed/ environment interchanges that we explored at some length in chapter 2. One surmises these scenes were cut from the theatrical release precisely because they interrupt the plot-driven, spectacular action scenes — for which Scott has become justly famous — with extended (and ambivalent) meditations on the spectral nature of identity. These extended intervals not only interrupt the seamless alternations of situation and response that Deleuze thinks paradigmatic in popular cinema's movement-image, they also threaten to undermine its formative proposition, that one man (or woman) can make a difference.

What gives coherence to the film's specular imagery, whereby the past reflects the present and death imagery the death-in-life of the living, is precisely the Lacanian notion that identity itself is a function of the mirror. The

Memento mori. Orlando Bloom (as Balian of Ibelin) confronts the only slightly premature death mask of Baldwin IV (Edward Norton) in Ridley Scott's *Kingdom of Heaven* (2005).

phantasmagoric mirroring in the film not only haunts its protagonists but also suggests that the identity of the contemporary world is trapped by or framed within its resemblance to the world of the Crusades — its "distant mirror." I would argue then the "New World" of the film (which critics were quick to identify with "America"), trumpeted in such reverential tones by Godfrey, is undermined in a kind of double reversal by compulsive returns to the old world (the Middle Ages) of ethnic and religious warfare. In this sense Richard the Lionheart's cameo at the end of the film represents something like an historical *Nachträgelichkeit,* the return to a trauma that Western civilization obsessively misremembers and therefore repeats. The pessimism implicit in Ridley Scott's repeated evocations of medieval death imagery finally sublates the humanitarian code of meliorism that the film ostensibly champions: Balian returns home to live out his life in peace, thereby denying or least reinterpreting his commitment to "make the world a better place," but history — in the person of Richard I — goes on without him. Both Balian and Sibylla renounce their names and birthrights in order to drop out of history; in fact, Balian makes such a denial a necessary condition of their relationship: "Cease to be a queen, and I will come to you."

In two shots not retained in the theatrical release, first Balian and later Sibylla stand before a mural in Balian's residence at Ibelin. The mural appears to be a combination of the late medieval artistic themes, "the three living and the three dead" and the *danse macabre*, both of which of course grew out of a Europe-wide artistic and poetic response to the Black Death, beginning apparently in mid-fourteenth-century France. Scott's *memento mori* images then are wholly anachronistic but derive from the association of the Crusades with death imagery in *The Seventh Seal*. Both Balian and Sibylla see their own futures mirrored in the fates of the king and queen caught during the pride of life in Death's fatal grasp — a resemblance that blurs the lines between actual/virtual and self/other. Just as in Bergman's use of the topos in *The Seventh Seal* and Besson's imitation of it in *The Messenger*, Death disturbs the characters' images of themselves, doubling as both insight and despair, and reflecting the omnipresence of death-in-life.[38] These time-images threaten to trap both Sibylla and Balian but they ultimately escape the entropic pull of resemblance through a telling mixture of medieval and modern forms of self-denial. Ridley Scott's reference to Bergman is most obvious in Balian's first conversation with the leper king, Baldwin IV, which occurs over a large chessboard, where they discuss Baldwin's political situation and the role he envisions for Balian. Scott's Baldwin wears what can only be described as a death mask, familiar from a number of recent films such as *The Advocate*, *Eyes Wide Shut*, and *The Da Vinci Code*. We first see him in an ample cloak and hood, which hides his face and head completely,[39] suggesting perhaps that he is a ghost — as indeed he would have been had he interviewed Balian after 1185! Though of course the medieval conception of lepers as the already-dead, as already having suffered in the Lacanian sense a death in the Symbolic, preceding their death in the Real, helps to establish Baldwin as a kindlier though no less potent personification of Death itself. After his "real" death, Sibylla removes his mask to reveal the rotten flesh that the expressionless mask had hidden from the world.[40] In a startling evocation of narcissism chastened by *memento mori* imagery, she later hallucinates that same twisted face in a mirror as she awaits the final siege of Jerusalem. As Sibylla looks into that mirror she chops off all her hair, creating a waifish look that deliberately evokes that of Marie Falconnetti in Dreyer's *The Passion of Joan of Arc*.

In the film's most celebrated shot (christened revealingly "the maggot shot" by the crew), the camera pulls out to a perspective far above what any medieval eye could have achieved. The shot taken from a helicopter pulls us out and far above the fray to reveal a thickening pile of corpses in the lone breach in the wall of Jerusalem's defenses. As the shot reaches its distant perspective on the carnage below, it becomes a still photograph, without movement or sound, of the utter uselessness of war from the vantage point perhaps of God himself. A "maggot shot" indeed, the picture expresses a contempt for the world one finds in many forms of late medieval art, but from a perspective that modern viewers associate with photojournalism or pictures from unmanned drones that survey from a distance "hot spots" in contemporary conflicts. To anticipate my discussion of Deleuze's provocative question in chapter 7 below, this shot asks "where is the battle?" The shot blurs all differences of time or space, right or wrong, and assumes an ethical stance from the perspective of *sub specie aeternitatis*. Like Troilus's perspective from the eighth sphere at the end of Chaucer's poem, the still image expresses a palpable contempt for the world. Looking down upon Jerusalem what is most apparent is the timelessness of the image: from this distance its aporetic carnage could be from the twelfth or the twenty-first century. The claims the image makes for sublimity thus rest less on simple distance than upon this lack of historical distinction — a "still" picture then in both senses of the word.

The enormous fireballs hurled by trebuchets that crash into the towers of the city also offer rather troubling visual citations of the images from 9/11. Yet what is most important here is not the reference itself (ubiquitous in subsequent popular cinema) but rather its collapse of the differences between these two centers of the world, twelfth-century Jerusalem and twenty-first-century New York. The pull of these time-images perhaps stems from their imitation of the specular logic implicit in the *danse macabre* and *memento mori*. In their historical *mise-en-abyme* these images reach out to interpolate the audience itself: "As I am, so shall you be!" The other in the mirror is also of course the Islamic world itself, a world conspicuously without borders, which many in the West think unwilling to capitulate to modernity and its goals of progress and liberation. Scott shows how the map of our medieval imaginary has been redrawn to include the skyline of New York City: "There be dragons."

6

Digital Divagations in a Hyperreal Camelot: Antoine Fuqua's *King Arthur*

"I am Arthur!" shouted one of the children, a bucket sitting on his head like a helmet. "No!" shouted another small boy. "You are a Woad! I am Arthur!"—
Thompson, *King Arthur*, novelization, 2004

HIC IACET ARTURUS, REX QUONDAM REXQUE FUTURUS. In the Bergsonian theory of Gilles Deleuze, *quondam* and *futurus* are virtual moments that can be actualized only in the present (1986 and 1989). Cinema screens the scandal of history, that it is thoroughly presentist like memory itself. A central tenet of post–Lacanian psychoanalysis maintains that desire constructs its objects, not the reverse. One of the West's few remaining master myths, Arthur is capable of embodying almost any desire — romantic, rationalist, or racist; nationalistic, nostalgic, or New Age; fundamentalist, fascist, or futuristic; postcolonial, postideological, or even post–Twin Towers. Indeed, it is possible to take the temperature of almost any Western age or society simply by attending to what it makes of his story. Yet whether we seek him in the tomb, like Henry II, and thereby seek to fix and control his influence or lose ourselves within the *selva oscura* of hyperspace and multimedia, Arthur's ability to survive repeated incarnations is a sure sign of his immortality. Parsing the sources of the English imagination, Peter Ackroyd says that Arthur represents "the great national fount of myth and symbol," "a legend of origin combined with a legend of revival" whose endurance stems at least in part from a seemingly limitless adaptability (Ackroyd 2002, pp. 118 and 124). The Arthur desires for origins and revivals create has little to do with the *dux bellorum*, who won the day — but not the war — against the Saxons at the notorious Battle of Badon Hill. That tiny fragment of the real only becomes significant because of the legends that accrue to it, from the earliest chronicles through the romances of the high Middle Ages and down to what Kevin Harty has dubbed *cinema Arthuriana* (Higham 2002, Finke and Shichtman 2004, and Harty 2002). These Arthurs originate and stage periodic returns from a parallel universe that the myth itself calls the Isle of Avalon, but which I denote by the more prosaic title: the medieval imaginary. This chapter is concerned primarily with the ways Antoine Fuqua's *King Arthur* (2004) and its companion videogame actualize this virtual Arthur.

For Siegfried Kracauer, pre–Nazi cinema in Germany was the harbinger of coming holocausts: "Any legend immune to rational arguments can be supposed to rest upon powerful collective desires" (2004, p. 117). Kracauer's realist aesthetic and his suspicion of both fantasy and historical cinema (for him much the same thing, 1960, pp. 77–91) represent one arm of my pincer approach to Arthurian cinémedievalism and digitization. With Kracauer I view mass entertainment as the distilled expression of collective desires, which serve not merely to reflect but also to intensify things like patriotism, nostalgia for charismatic leadership, or a belief in the historical destiny of nations. I hasten to add that this does not signal a willingness to draw facile or provocative analogies, but rather my resolve to explore the production of historical fantasy in film and other media with an abiding respect for its potential influence, as well as the popular tendencies these media reflect. The second pincer of my approach is what Baudrillard has called the "procession of simulacra" into the realm of hyperreality, where both reference and history are fatally attenuated in spasms of reproduction (1994, pp. 1–42). The apparent contradiction in Baudrillard's theory of the hyperreal is his insistence upon both the erosion of reference to any reality whatsoever as well as the postmodern obsession with technologies of its accurate representation. Many recent historical fantasies like *King Arthur* lavish money and attention on material details and egregiously verisimilar effects (such as the kilometer-long Hadrian's Wall built for the film and its CGI extensions) while treating the historical record with nothing like the same care. As Baudrillard maintains: "Concurrently with this effort toward an absolute correspondence with the real, cinema also approaches an absolute correspondence with itself ... *the cinema is fascinated by itself as a lost object as much as it (and we) are fascinated by the real as a lost referent*" (1994, p. 47, italics in original). The reflexivity of Arthurian cinémedievalism is a theme in what follows, but so too is its specular ideology whereby we establish the reality of the present by fashioning its source in the past. If our desire for origins provokes us to seek him in the tomb, our desire for renewal takes it for granted that Arthur has always been a regent of the virtual.

I want briefly to take up the question of sources and how medievalists' use of source criticism can sometimes pander to popular appetites to know what *really happened* as a basis for the analysis and evaluation of these films. At its worst, this approach rarifies the discipline of medieval studies itself, reducing the complex texture of scholarly debates and ongoing revisions to a monological "received opinion" against which standard films are then measured. In his discussion of *King Arthur*, Tom Shippey trenchantly remarks, "perhaps the least truthful part of the Fuqua film comes in the first two words of the opening credits, 'Historians agree....' On this subject, historians do not agree about anything" (Shippey 2007, p. 314; see also Lupack, p. 123). Many critics find the ubiquitous appeals in such films to new evidence or to uncovering the truth behind the legend provocative, and perhaps justly so. Shippey certainly does not fall into this trap and along with other critics of the film, such as Harty, Lupack, Jewers, and Aronstein, rightly identifies *From Scythia to Camelot* by C. Scott Littleton and Linda A. Malcot as a major source of the film's depiction of Arthur's knights as a band of Sarmatian cavalry. Yet this work is also the scholarly, albeit controversial, "source" that the film's director, screenwriter, producer, actors, and its paid historical consultant John Matthews (2004) unanimously tout in marketing the film.[1] Its screenwriter, David Franzioni (rather disingenuously as will be demonstrated below) closes his interview with Matthews thus: "I'm so tired of seeing movies about movies." He urges people not "to default to the images" but rather to "default to their experiences" (Franzioni, p. 120). As we will see, Arthur may be "just a guy," but he is a guy made from other movies in nearly every detail. Franzioni's affected, hyperspace vocabulary, urging audiences to "default to their own experiences," also hints — no doubt unwittingly — at the fact that many traits of Arthur and his Sarmatian "knights" are ready-made elements designed to ease the marketing convergence of the film and its video game where we are all invited to "play the legend."

The Seven Sarmatians

I have long been struck by the extraordinary parallels between European chivalry and the Japanese warrior code of Bushido. — Howard Reid, *Arthur: The Dragon King*

The chief source of *King Arthur*'s plot, characterization, and even its "ideology" has very little to do with Arthur, historical or legendary. It is based quite closely on Akira Kurosawa's *Seven Samurai* (1954) and the reinscription of that classic *jidai-geki* in a franchise of American westerns, beginning with Preston Sturges's *The Magnificent Seven* (1960). Of course Kurosawa's film not only inspired westerns, it was also to a great degree derived from earlier films in the genre such as those by John Ford. In recent cinémedievalism the influence of Kurosawa is ubiquitous. For instance, John McTiernan's *Thirteenth Warrior* (1999) maps the three-battle structure of *Seven Samurai* onto a euhemeristic interpretation of the monster fights in *Beowulf.* The mise-en-scène of the final battle in the rain is also an extended homage. An early sequence in *Kingdom of Heaven* set in France also self-consciously evokes Kurosawa's film in its six crusaders who add the ephebe Balian to their number. There is as well a remake of *Seven Samurai* in the works, to be produced by the Weinstein Company and starring George Clooney! What we have in Fuqua's film is yet another in a long line of medievalized westerns, banking on a genealogy that includes the masterpiece of a widely recognized auteur and its commercially successful formula. It is this genealogy, not the putative Sarmatian ancestry of Arthur's knights, that most influences what happens in the film. To recall the earlier citation of Baudrillard, the postmodern desire for origins is commonly doubled in film, calqued by cinema's nostalgia for its own past. In addition, the film's focus on ethnicity (explored thoughtfully by Shippey [2007], Caroline Jewers, and Susan Aronstein) takes on a slightly different coloring when viewed through the prism of Sergei Eisenstein's *Alexander Nevsky* (1938), which provides not only the source for an important scene but also the model for the film's erotic, Manichean nationalism. In short, the Littleton-Malcot hypothesis is a pretext in both senses of the word, one that allows Franzioni and Fuqua to cloak their Russian samurai cowboys in plausibly historical garb.

As a matter of fact, what seems to have taken place here is a, by turns, intriguing and absurd synthesis that rather nicely demonstrates how historical film and film history become entangled. Whatever one thinks of the Littleton-Malcot hypothesis of the breadth and influence of Ossetian culture, one cannot but be astonished by the ways in which *King Arthur* adapts it. Some half million contemporary Ossetians live in southern Russia and on the Eurasian steppes; the survivors of a nomadic culture whose influence is said to have been vast. The western boundary of their ancient influence was Britain, where Sarmatian cavalry perhaps fought for Lucius Artorius Castus in the second century against the Picts and Scots. It is from this Sarmatian culture that Littleton and Malcor believe many elements of the Arthurian legends derive. In an idea taken up more popularly by Harold Reid in *Arthur: The Dragon King* (pp. 223–26), Littleton has also traced the Sarmatian influence eastward from the steppes all the way to Japan, where he has found Arthur's double in the hero Yamoto-Takeru (1983, 1995). For Littleton both Arthur and Yamoto-Takeru derive from a "heroic tradition (that) has managed to span the Eurasian landmass from one end to the other" (1995, p. 259). Both are thought ultimately to descend from the Sarmatian hero Batraz, whose adventures loom large in the Ossetian Nart Sagas. In attempting to do justice to the breadth encompassed by the legendary descendents of Batraz, the filmmakers seem to have wanted their own recovery of this monomyth to be equally all-inclusive. They include large-scale elements drawn from Japan and Russia in a syncretic version of the Arthur story; yet, these elements are drawn *not* from medieval folktales but rather from the films of the Japanese director Akira Kurosawa and the Soviet director Sergei Eisenstein.

Kurosawa's influence, both direct and filtered through the screen of the westerns, is ubiquitous and sometimes profound. In the film's first action sequence, Arthur and his knights ride down to the rescue in the V-formation that was the trademark shot of the *Magnificent Seven* franchise, which the screenplay's novelization cutely dubs "the dragon formation" (Thompson 2004, p. 30). Throughout the film the knights crowd the cinemascope screen, pulled into close proximity by the use of a telephoto lens. Their horses are positively frenetic, shifting and snorting their way through every sequence. These features of the cinematography are trademarks of Kurosawa's *jidai-geki*. But rather than pile up disconnected references, let us look first of all at an extended sequence that rather pointedly confirms the pastiched nature of the film's Campbellesque monomyth. The extended tour of duty forced upon Arthur and his knights surely provokes resonances with the extended and repeated tours of American soldiers serving in Afghanistan and Iraq, who were also being hounded by determined guerrilla warfare (Aronstein, pp. 205–13). And as Tom Shippey reminds us, the "final mission" topos has been a staple of post–Vietnam filmmaking for some time (2007, pp. 316–26). Yet the egregious placing of Marius's Roman villa in the north beyond Hadrian's Wall has troubled many reviewers. The mixture of historical and film antecedents here is instructive. In their journey into southern Scotland, Arthur and his knights are attacked by the Woads (Picts), directed by Merlin. One engagement that, according to medieval battle lists, did take place above the wall was the Battle of Celidon Wood (Coed Celydon), which Geoffrey of Monmouth lists as the seventh of Arthur's battles and which Littleton and Malcor following Jackson (p. 48) place in the moorlands near the upper Clyde and Tweed valleys (2000, p. 330. n10). Unlike Nennius, Geoffrey makes the Picts and Scots Arthur's adversaries in a number of engagements and Littleton-Malcor read back from this "evidence" to postulate that all twelve of their second-century hero's battles were against the Picts and Scots, the tenth occurring in Celidon Wood. For our purposes it is more interesting to note that Geoffrey's Caledonian battle, though against the Saxons, resembles that in the film.

> Arthur pursued the Saxons relentlessly until they reached Caledon Wood.... They used the shelter of the trees to protect themselves from the Britons' weapons. As soon as Arthur saw this, he ordered the trees around that part of the wood to be cut down and their trunks placed in a circle, so that every way out was barred to the enemy [trans. Thorpe, pp. 215].

In the film, as in Geoffrey, an entrapment is orchestrated by fencing off exits from the wood, and, just as in Geoffrey, the result is not a slaughter but rather a benign gesture of allowing the trapped soldiers to escape.[2] Geoffrey claims that Merlin's mountain in Scotland was "encircled by hazels and thick thorns" (*precinctus corulis densisque frutectis*) making access difficult. This detail perhaps inspired the strategy of Merlin's ambush in the film, which entraps the knights within a labyrinth of barbed ropes that cut off their retreat. The Scottish location and the Pictish foes are certainly indebted to the Littleton-Malcor hypothesis, but most of the details are drawn not from "new evidence" but directly from that much-maligned source, Geoffrey of Monmouth. In fact, both histories — medieval and modern — are really only raw materials for a scene ultimately based on the career not of Lucius Artorius Castus but on Macbeth! The sequence restages a justly famous scene from Shakespeare's "Scottish tragedy," as reinterpreted by Kurosawa. In *Throne of Blood* (alt. title, *Spider Web Castle* 1957) the Japanese reflexes of Macbeth and Banquo dash with increasing fear and frustration back and forth through "Spider Web Forest," only to come upon dead ends appearing out of thin air. *King Arthur's* spider webs are fashioned from rope studded with Geoffrey's thorns, which the Woads shoot across the paths of the knights, weaving a web to trap their prey like so many spiders.[3] In both films the riders finally conclude that they are trapped by supernatural forces: "Evil spirits," says Kurosawa's Washiro, "Inish, devil ghosts," says Fuqua's Dagonet. At the center of the web is not the "weird sisters" but a male prophet/magician, who has killed many knights/samurai but allows this particular prey to go free, vanishing into the mist. It is not surprising that the film travels imaginatively to Scotland to introduce the eldritch Picts and their sorcerer Merlin, especially given the cinematic precedent of blue face paint provided by *Braveheart* (d. Mel Gibson 1995). What is remarkable though is its detour through the Sengoku period of civil war in Japan. The result is truly *unheimlich*, like the march of Birnam Wood to the hill of Dunsinane.

More important for the film's imaginary convergence of feudal Japan with Dark Age Britain is its uncanny structuration of identity, class, and ethnicity in terms of Kurosawa's *Seven Samurai.* Upon their release from indentured servitude in the Roman legion, the Sarmatians become in effect masterless samurai, like Kurosawa's ronin, free to do as they like but alienated by their long service from home and family. *Pace* Tom Cruise, almost every great *chambara* takes "the last samurai" as its central theme. Initially Arthur's knights treat the Woads with the same contempt that Kurosawa's samurai first display for the farmers, who "hunt" them. In the *Seven Samurai* the scene that brings class conflict to the fore and for a time allays it comes when the samurai discover a cache of weapons and armor hidden in the village that the farmers have despoiled from ambushed warriors. The seventh samurai, Kikuchiyo, himself a hybrid mixture of samurai and farmer, gives the ronin a lesson in class resentment:

> Farmers are stingy, foxy, blubbering, mean, stupid, and murderous! God damn! That's what they are! But then, who made them such beasts? You did! The samurai did it! You burn their villages, destroy their farms, steal their food, force them to labor, take their women! And kill them if they resist. So what should the farmers do? Damn ... Damn!

Like Kurosawa's ronin, the Sarmatian knights were first the scourge of the people they come to defend. When they arrive at Marius's villa they discover with disgust the reality of exploitation that their military service to Rome has supported, a colonial regime of forced labor, stolen food and women, murder and torture.

Toshiro Mifune's Kikuchiyo triangulates the farmers and the samurai much as Arthur does the Sarmatians and Picts. (I will resist the temptation to compare Kikuchiyo's ["Thirteen's"] forged ancestry to that provided for Arthur in Fuqua's film.) But his place between Pict and Sarmatian is rendered heraldically in a way analogous to that of Mifune's character, though without any of the latter's endearing foolishness. The banner of the seven samurai represents this relationship schematically with six circles at the top standing for the six samurai and the character for the farmers at the bottom joined in the middle by a triangle that stands for Kikuchiyo. The six Sarmatian knights all carry golden horse standards, though Arthur's standard is a golden dragon that sports a whip-sock dragon's tail. Like Mifune's Kikuchiyo, Arthur is also provided with a back-story that depicts him as a child victim. This element has been compared to a similar scene in Jerry Zucker's *First Knight*, which it in fact resembles, but it is also important to note that this way of establishing motivation for central characters through childhood trauma has a long history in historical films beginning with Eisenstein's Ivan (*Ivan the Terrible, Part II*) and Kurosawa's *Seven Samurai* and stretching down to more recent films such as *Braveheart, The Messenger: The Story of Joan of Arc, Tristan and*

Isolde, The Pathfinder, as well as the traumatic childhood of the "monster" in *Beowulf and Grendel*, as we have seen repeatedly in prior chapters.

The recurrent shots of grave mounds with swords plunged into them would seem to echo the "Sarmatian hypothesis" but again visually at least these images descend directly from Kurosawa. Both the screenplay and its novelization (in line with Sarmatian archeology) call for the swords to be plunged to the hilt into the earth, leaving what would appear to be a small cross as a kind of headstone. The film though embeds the swords in the tumuli only a few inches, creating a marked citation of Kurosawa's film. After the first of the deaths in both films we get scenes in a graveyard on the outskirts of a village where Arthur or Kikuchiyo sit mourning a death for which they deem themselves responsible and where wine/sake is spilled onto a tumulus. These graves become an iconic marker in both films, an image to which the films repeatedly return. As Caroline Jewers remarks, these shots "echo the *ubi sunt* topos so beloved of epic" (p. 98), but this particular instantiation of the topos is recognizably Kurosawan. In fact Fuqua's original cut — absent the happy ending — concluded in more elegiac register, like *Seven Samurai*, contrasting the grave mounds and their sword markers with the solemn survivors.

In the *Seven Samurai* all four dead heroes are killed by matchlock rifles, weapons — as we saw in chapter 2 — that Kurosawa always puts in the hands of his villains. In *King Arthur* this rather unheroic imbalance is served by arming the Saxons with armor-piercing crossbows that take the lives of Dagonet and Lancelot. Tristan, like the sword master in Kurosawa's film, goes on a scouting mission and brings back an example of this questionable technology as a trophy. Ultimately he is killed not by a crossbow but by a *seax* in a duel with Cedric. Yet, as is Kurosawa, these characteristic weapons of the enemy (crossbows and *seaxas*) are used to stigmatize their fighting styles as both figuratively and literally underhanded.[4] Likewise, Arthur's knights are associated with their horses in a proleptic nod to the etymology of chivalry (Old French *cheval*) but with a nod as well toward the reincarnation and animism of Shinto Buddhism.

The notorious Battle of Badon Hill, wherever it took place, was almost certainly not a siege but a pitched battle on an open plain. Franzioni's decision to site the battle in a fortified settlement on Hadrian's Wall allows the detailed imitation of Kurosawa to be completed. The opening of the sequence shows the Sarmatian knights abandoning the town to its fate in order to take the freedom that has been given them. The scene is based closely on Sturges's *The Magnificent Seven*, in which the gunfighters leave the town before the final battle, though slowly change their minds as they again strap on their sidearms — an act that seems to recall them to their better natures. The scene in

King Arthur is much superior, there is no talking or debate, only confusion followed by stiffening resolve as they finally submit to their horses' unwillingness to continue along this rather selfish course. When they line up alongside Arthur on the hill overlooking the battlefield, Fuqua can't resist another cinematic citation: in *Robin Hood, Prince of Thieves* Kevin Costner's Robin and his Saracen friend (Morgan Freeman) converse beneath a tree in the Sycamore Gap, known locally as "Robin Hood's Tree," one of the sites offered on marketed tours of Hadrian's Wall. The Saxon spy is commanded by Cedric to climb the tree for a better vantage point from which to view the slaughter of his own people. From an impossible distance hundreds of yards away and from within the fort, Tristan draws first blood in the battle by killing the traitor with a miraculous display of marksmanship worthy of Robin himself.

As the battle begins in earnest, it is clear that Arthur gets his art of war from Kurosawa's Kambei. One would expect that the officer of a Roman legion, whatever his name, would be reluctant to open a fortified position to the enemy. Cerdic realizes early on "he's got a plan this Roman." Indeed he has, as *Seven Samurai*'s Kambei puts it: "We'll let them in, not all of them at once. As soon as they enter, we shut the rest off and trap them. They'll be helpless [....] They must be lured in." Though employing more pyrotechnics and many more extras, Arthur's plan proceeds in exactly the same fashion. He allows the first wave through the gate and then has it closed behind them, only to open it again once they have been dispatched. Here as in Kurosawa the battle plan relies upon the coordination of different groups to attack the enemy from all directions at once. Even the now (in)famous shot of Guinevere and a group of Pictish warrior-women taking down a wounded man has its source in Kurosawa, though the more recent version also nods in the direction of Boudica, valkyries, and vampires. Where Fuqua's film does finally diverge from Kurosawa's, particularly in the PG version generally released, is in its happy ending. Like Kurosawa's samurai or Sturges's gunslingers, Fuqua's Sarmatians begin the film on the cusp of a social change that obviates their place in society. This identity crisis is momentarily bridged in all three films as the samurai/cowboys/Sarmatians heroically accept their role as protectors of the weak. However, in Kurosawa this sense of belonging is cruelly foreshortened, when, after the battle, the remaining samurai realize that only the farmers have really won anything and the three survivors leave the village just as they had entered it: alone, feared, and without a home. The Western remake of the film retains this sense of a rootless, vanishing breed in the two gunslingers but cushions the blow for audiences by allowing the Mexican ephebe to turn from the hired guns and to marry a native of the village. After an unsuccessful trial screening, Fuqua was pressured into giving the film a softer ending, which ultimately concludes not only like *The Magnificent Seven* with a marriage but also with a triumphant celebration of ethnogenesis.

Seven Samurai Meets Alexander Nevsky

Where are the Germans? There are no more Germans. —*Alexander Nevsky*

While *Seven Samurai* certainly provides a key to Arthur's hybrid identity in Fuqua's film, the conflicts both internal and external in Kurosawa's work are based on class and the economic realities that underlie them. *The Magnificent Seven* goes some way toward recasting these conflicts in terms of ethnicity, wherein *gringo* gunslingers from the north aided by their own hybrid figure — a young Mexican wannabe — intervene in a conflict between bandits and villagers south of the border. However, neither in Kurosawa nor even in his epigones is the moral nature of the conflict so clearly a matter of right versus wrong, of good versus evil, as it is in Fuqua's *King Arthur*. Earlier I invoked Siegfried Kracauer's notion that "collective desires" are manifested and indeed encouraged by historical fantasies. This is perhaps no where more evident than in *King Arthur*'s imaginary reconstruction of Dark Age ethnicity *via* the Manichean binary of Sergei Eisenstein's *Alexander Nevsky*. Arguably the greatest propaganda film ever made, Eisenstein's masterpiece pits a nation uniting under a charismatic leader against a Teutonic invasion in league with a cynical and opportunistic Catholic Church. Sound familiar? Eisenstein's Manichean fantasy certainly deserves our respect, it is a superb film made in the shadow of Nazi Germany's rise to the status of an international menace, and Eisenstein's next work, *Ivan the Terrible*, devastatingly undermines the authoritarian streak of the earlier film in its evocation of tsarist cruelty and paranoid suspicion. But *King Arthur*'s deployment of Eisenstein's *Nevsky* represents what I see as a dangerous trend in contemporary cinémedievalism, which might be dubbed Manichean nostalgia. *Pace* critics who have seen the film's ideology as reflecting current or more recent wars such as those in Vietnam or the Gulf (see Shippey 2007 and Jewers for the former, Aronstein for the latter), I see the film as profoundly nostalgic for the ethical clarities of the Second World War. Such nostalgia for Manichean clarity is also evident in the recent film versions of the postwar fiction of J. R. R. Tolkien and C. S. Lewis.

Eisenstein's film was originally entitled *Rus!*— the rallying cry of the Russian forces in his film and adopted by Sarmatian knights of *King Arthur* to express solidarity with the original Ossetian culture from which they putatively derive. The cry echoes throughout *King Arthur*, particularly from the character Bors, who typically makes the connection explicit by screaming "Artorius!" and then "Rus!" After the marriage of Arthur and Guinevere has united the Sarmatians with the native peoples of Britain, Bors again bellows "Artorius!" and then sheepishly omits the "Rus!" as no longer appropriate. His silence signals a recognition of the difference this marriage makes, the imaginary unification of Britain under a single leader. Against this in both films are posed the mute synecdoches of a proto-Nazi salute: open, extended hands adorn the helmets of the Teutonic hordes in *Nevsky* and the Roman Marius receives a Nazi salute from a soldier whose body remains outside the frame. The twentieth century is proleptically signified as that which gave body and a voice to these truncated gestures of unquestioned obedience.

The extended sequence in the colonial villa of the aristocrat Marius is a devastating depiction of a Roman Catholic monster. The episode, I would argue, is a euhemerizing interpretation of the "saint" of Mount St. Michel in the alliterative *Morte Arthure* and Malory's fifth book, inspired by the equally barbarous slaughter of the innocents in *Nevsky*. As we saw in chapter 1, euhemerism is a common trope in postmodern movie medievalism, which offers rational explanations for medieval myths. The monster Grendel in *Beowulf and Grendel* as it turns out is the unfortunate result of a congenital birth defect. The *fyr-wyrm* of *The Thirteenth Warrior* is naturalized as merely the serpentine undulation of mounted cavalry, who bear flaming spears through the dark mist. Luc Besson's *The Messenger* explains Joan's visions as dissociative psychosis, provoked by childhood trauma. And Fuqua's Marius is no giant cannibal, merely a fat, petty despot who thinks himself a "saint" and who starves the native populace to death in order to enrich himself. Like the monster of St. Michel, Marius signifies the inhumanity of Rome's boundless acquisitiveness. His colonial villa has, like the Malorian Lucius, "an egle displayed on loffte" (Malory, pp. 126). But like the giant of St. Michel the dark secret of his perversity can be discovered by following one's nose "to the source of the reek" of rotting flesh (*Alliterative Morte Arthur*, ed. Benson and Foster, p.163, line 1041). If the giant is a grotesque parody of the Catholic Eucharist, Marius parodies the devotion of anchorites by entombing the disobedient in an anchorhold and slowly starving them to death, while his monks enchant masses for their souls. In *Alexander Nevsky* the Church is complicit in the Teutonic invasion, the cathedral at Pskov serves as a gibbet, and withered old men are chained to its walls. A bishop blesses the tortures and intones masses as babies are dropped into the flames in a perversion of the die-to-live paradox of Christianity. Compare the *Nevsky* priest — "Die in order that you may be saved" — with *King Arthur's* monk — "It was God's wish that these sinners be sacrificed, only then can their souls be saved." In the Arthurian tradition the Mount St. Michel episode is handled with increasing levity, the monstrous false saint, like the avaricious Lucius, must be defeated in Arthur's quest to liberate Rome from tyranny. In *Alexander Nevsky* there is no faltering of epic "high seriousness," Eisenstein's Church is the left arm of colonial enterprise that seeks to cower and enslave the people. Fuqua's Arthur, like that of medieval romance, is a Christian, but his faith is itself an illusion, a dream: the young Roman Alecto tells him, "the Rome you speak of doesn't exist, except in your dreams." The historical figures in the film, Pelagius and Germanus, were both dead for some decades before the time in which the film is set. They are revived as Manichean figures battling for the soul of Christianity, which, as in most contemporary cinémedievalism (see, for instance *Name of the Rose, The Messenger*, or *The Da Vinci Code*), is controlled by a dark power structure that renders humanitarian, libertarian, or socialist reforms heretical. Thus Bishop Germanus, famed in Bede's *Ecclesiastical History* as the leader of the "Alleluia Victory" against the Celts, perhaps simply by virtue of his name, becomes a silent partner in the "ethnic cleansing" of the Saxons. His masterful strategy in war is likewise reduced to the cowardly tactics of employing a *kagemusha* double like the morally corrupt Singen in Kurosawa's film (*Kagemusha* 1980). The complicity of the Roman Catholic Church in the final solution of Nazis thus gains an imagined analogue in Dark Age Britain, inspired by a Stalinist reading of thirteenth-century Russian history.[5]

As Eisenstein was quick to point out, the more human, less mythical side of his hero Alexander was calqued by two figures, Vasili and Gavrilo, rival suitors for the patriotic Olga. *King Arthur*, like the earlier *First Knight*, writes adultery out of the love triangle but it also, like *Nevsky*, makes the woman a prize to be won by the warrior most committed in defense of the homeland. The eroticization of nationalism is an important theme in *Nevsky*, and Fuqua's film assiduously follows suit. Lancelot loses the contest of smoldering glances to Arthur simply because the latter is the more selfless defender of Britain. The love-triangle is resolved in different ways in the two films, but crucial to each is the introduction of the Bolshevik idea of the woman warrior. Like *Nevsky*'s Vasalisy and Besson's Joan of Arc, Guinevere goes to war less as a gender warrior than as an embodiment of nationalism itself. Rather disappointingly for many, including Caroline Jewers and myself (though perhaps for different reasons), the Bacchic exploits of Ms. Knightley's Guinevere are soon complete. She discards her leather-thong bikini and paint-on tattoos for a white wedding gown. Having played her part as the woman warrior Vasalisy, she humbly assumes the role of the more docile Olga, a prize that goes to her nation's staunchest defender.

The "Battle on the Ice" of Lake Chudskoe is justly regarded as one of Eisenstein's most accomplished set pieces and *King Arthur*'s homage is a more than adept stylization. Like the "Odessa Steps" sequence in *Battleship Potemkin*, the ice battle has become a cinematic tour de force. *King Arthur* here rises to the challenge by producing some remarkable shots, like the camera tracking the cracking ice or the *memento mori* shot of the Saxon Cynric who sees the face of a drowned comrade beneath the ice. The sequence was shot in a green valley in County Kildare, Ireland, seeded with gravel and fake snow, employing dozens of cameras. The snowcapped mountains and grey sky were added later by computer graphics imaging (CGI) and the footage intercut with shots filmed in studio water tanks. While the result achieved never quite lives up to Eisenstein, who was working with a much smaller toolbox, it too is a splendid set piece. We will take up below the virtual nature of cinémedievalism and how its production of immediacy and realism relies upon the ever more complicated pastiche of multiple simulations. Here though I want rather to focus on the elemental nature of the battle itself as an example of what Frantz Fanon (1991) dubbed "Manichaean delirium" to denote the paroxysms of binary thinking that are a stubborn inheritance of colonialism. Eisenstein's sequence is rationalized in the physical world: The Teutonic army is larger; the knights and their horses encased in heavy steel, designed to evoke the armor of German panzer divisions. Alexander, spurred by a lewd joke about an unfortunate vixen wedged between two trees, employs the landscape itself as a pincer to bunch the Teutonic cavalry charge and turn their size and weight into a disadvantage. Eisenstein repeatedly emphasizes the machine-like impersonality and ponderousness of the German forces. Their bulk becomes ethically freighted, nowhere more clearly than in the final scenes of the film when their leaders are brought in like beasts of burden weighed down by huge plough-horse collars. There is nothing of this in *King Arthur*, at least not apparently. Arthur, his mounted Sarmatian knights, and a long caravan of serfs and wagons travel along the ice, eliciting little more than a few ominous creaking sounds. Their combined weight would be many times that of the small force of foot soldiers led by Cynric, which finally catches up to them on the frozen river. Since neither of the opposing leaders thinks to hug the shoreline, the two armies face off and prepare for battle on (relatively) thin ice. The first clue that we have entered an imaginary world of moral physics comes when Cynric's archer fires an arrow that skids to a stop a hundred feet or so before reaching its target. Tristan and Gawain respond in kind, the former shooting three arrows at once, all four of which find their marks in Saxon chests with such force that they are knocked over backwards. There is no wind in the scene; the success of the Sarmatians clearly points to an abundant superiority, but of what kind exactly? As the Saxons advance, Arthur instructs his archers to "make them cluster," employing mutatis mutandis the pincer tactics of Alexander. When it refuses to break, Dagonet runs into the breach and chops a hole in the ice, which does not fracture radially but rather beats a direct path for the Saxons and explodes into large fragments. There are accomplished shots of Saxons sliding down vertical planes of ice into the cold water that faithfully reproduce those of Eisenstein. The cracking ice takes some time to turn back in the other direction and threaten the Sarmatians, but none fall through the ice except for Dagonet, who is already dead before he hits the water. The ice weighs in balance the fates of the two sides and evil is plunged down. Only when most of the Saxons have already fallen into the water does the balance shift and the miraculous crack turn in the opposite direction. This strange physical world is only explicable in Manichean terms, the Sarmatians' arrows fly farther and their feet tread softer than the Saxons: the spirit riseth up and the flesh presseth down.

Like Eisenstein, the novels of Tolkien and Lewis are deeply imbued with Manichaeism — a worldview that is not only excusable but to some degree just.[6] What rankles is the avid renaissance of their Manichaeism in contemporary times, intensified to the point of delirium, in recent films such as *King Arthur*, the *Lord of the Rings* trilogy, and the first installment of *Narnia*. Indeed

Clive Owen as Arthur (front and center) leads his band of Sarmatian cavalry out on to the ice in Antoine Fuqua's *King Arthur* (2004).

the latter two films seem to adopt Boethian view of the ultimate nonexistence of evil. Once its leader has been defeated whole armies quite literally blow away like dust in the wind. This is more than a simple CGI convention, it is the immaterial correlative of an ideology that clearly determined the world-view of George Bush upon his invasion of Iraq. The dark lord was eventually found, tried, and executed, yet the "evil" stubbornly refuses to evaporate.[7]

Romancing Genetics

The peoples of Germany have never been tainted by intermarriage with other peoples, and stand out as a nation peculiar, pure and unique of its kind.— Tacitus, *Germania*

Are these ... "toads" apt to strike again?— Thompson, p. 48

There's a much better chance that the Saxon leader Cerdic actually was the historical Arthur than that he and his son Cynric were killed at the Battle of Mt. Badon. Cerdic went on to found the West Saxon dynasty, which his son continued. He is certainly the ancestor of the salt-of-the-earth Cedric the Saxon in Walter Scott's *Ivanhoe*. The film's Cerdic despotically enforces genetic purity among his soldiers: The abortive *witena gemot* on the rights of victors to the spoils of war ends abruptly when he executes a soldier attempting to rape a native — and then shocks the grateful damsel in distress by ordering her death as well. "Don't touch their women. We don't mix with these people. What kind of offspring do you think that would yield? Weak people, half people. I will not have our Saxon blood watered down by mixing with them." Cerdic's antimiscegenation policy in many ways takes its clue from the now discredited Anglo-Saxonism or Aryanism of the nineteenth and earlier twentieth centuries, which judged the Isles overwhelmingly Germanic — the native inhabitants having been geographically marginalized, exterminated, or bred nearly out of existence. A number of recent books trace the rise and obsolescence of what Hugh A. MacDougall calls "racial myth in English history," which conceived Germanic peoples as marked by their unmixed heredity and the English as the especially favored descendants of these tribes, pioneers of personal liberty and political freedoms (MacDougall; see also Frantzen, Geary, and Higham). Now the pendulum has swung in the opposite direction and connections are routinely drawn between Anglo-Saxonism and Victorian imperialism. The rise of historical linguistics in the nineteenth century eventually mooted underlying assumptions about connections between race and language. And the advent of Nazi Germany demonstrated the horrors that grow not simply from racism itself but from attempts to connect race and nationality.

From the perspective of contemporary advances in genetic mapping, such as the celebrated lab at Oxford headed by Brian Sykes, Cerdic's quest for Saxon purity has been dealt a mortal blow. Modern geneticists have diminished significantly nineteenth- and early twentieth-century estimations of the Germanic inheritance of modern Britain. Sykes puts the total genetic inheritance of Germanic peoples in the British Isles at no more than 30 percent and attributes the lion's share of that to the later Viking/Norman incursions. For our purposes what most fascinates in Sykes's approach are his delightfully wistful meditations on how gender differences are expressed in the gene pool of Britain. He affirms a clear, personal preference for mitochondrial DNA, which records the female line and a marked contempt for the weak and unstable Y-chromosome.

> ... the brightest and strongest of these threads (is the) one through which we are joined to our ancestral mother. An infinite umbilical cord which courses smoothly from mother to mother back to the mist of our ancestry. The other, which only men possess, thrusts its way from generation to generation. Erratic, illogical and passionate, it lives a life free from responsibility. But it enslaves its host and drives him to violence, murder and conquest. Follow this thread into the past at your peril. Sooner or later you will spend a generation or two in the testis of a warlord [....] The first conclusion, blindingly obvious now I can see it, is that we have in front of us two completely different histories. The maternal and the paternal origins of the Isles are different [....] On our (i.e., British) maternal side, almost all of us are Celts [Sykes 2006, pp. 279–81].

In Eisenstein's *Alexander Nevsky* the Teutonic warlord orders a holocaust: "Wipe them off the face of the earth." Cerdic in *King Arthur* is equally unequivocal: "Burn it all. Never leave behind you a man, woman or child that can ever bear a sword."[8] Indeed, like the German commander in *Alexander Nevsky*, Cerdic is a Nazi calque. The novelization of the screenplay has him exclaim, "We must cleanse the earth!" (Thompson, p. 97). Later, he recalls the clansmen of Griffith's *Birth of a Nation* when he rears a burning cross in front of Hadrian's Wall: "The massive flame cracked and roared. No one had encountered such a thing before, but they all knew what it meant. The Saxons were promising total defeat, absolute annihilation" (p. 258). Not surprisingly this needlessly provocative image was left out of the film. On the other hand, Fuqua's Guinevere represents the Celtic bedrock, a daughter of one of Sykes's seven daughters of Eve, probably Jasmine, whose descendants appear to have migrated after the Great Ice Age over the course of many generations from the Near East through Portugal and Spain to settle eventually in "Cornwall, Wales and the west of Scotland" (Sykes 2001, p. 209). It would be impossible to prove that modern genetics and not the neo-Celtic resurgence in popular culture and films such as *Braveheart* is at the base of the film's celebration of a pan-Celtic ethnogenesis at the end of the film.[9] Sykes does, however, claim that the evidence of the British gene pool moots older theories about the Picts dying out and suggests that genetically at least Picts and Celts are nearly indistinguishable. Also lumped into a single group by their lack of genetic differences are not only Angles, Saxons, and Jutes but Danes and Normans as well. In Sykes's analysis of the gene pool of the Isles the great divide is that between Germanic and Celtic, and there is no doubt which is the deeper end of that pool.

Guinevere early on tells Arthur "I belong to this land" and then goes on to equate Arthur's father having chosen a native Briton as his wife with an affection for Britain itself in an erotically charged piece of dialogue. The ethnic components of Arthur's identity are parsed, she detests his Roman side and appeals both sexually and politically to his Celtic side. Arthur's hybridity limes the structure of what Jeffrey Jerome Cohen has dubbed "the postcolonial Middle Ages" quite distinctly. Guinevere chips away at his collaboration

Keira Knightley (as Guinevere) leads her Woad women warriors into battle against the Saxons in Antoine Fuqua's *King Arthur* (2004).

with the Roman oppressors of a people he belatedly will accept as his own. In yet another example of rationalist euhemerism in the film, Arthur pulls Excalibur from the ground in a failed attempt to save the life of his Celtic mother. As Merlin tells him: "It was love of your mother, Arthur, not hatred of me that freed that sword." The pulling of the sword from the earth, then, signifies that Arthur's legitimacy to rule comes not from Rome but from his "feminine," Celtic side. Personal liberties and political freedoms are shown to descend not from ancient "democracies" or the "English Constitution" so touted by traditional classicism or Anglo-Saxonism, but rather from the oppressed, blue-faced but red-blooded Celtic fringe of *Braveheart.* The reincarnation central to the Arthurian myth of a once and future king is also given a politically correct twist. Boudica-like, Guinevere is entombed by the Romans but revived by Arthur to lead her people in their time of need against a new enemy, the Saxons![10]

Playing (with) the Legend

> *It almost felt to the two friends as if they were playing some sort of brutal game.* — Thompson, p. 38

One thing that perhaps helps to account for our frustration with the fantasy history of cinémedievalism is the promise that the medium once held for many in its capacity to deliver faithful representations of reality. Discussing Andre Bazin's comment on the advance of cinema technologies that "every new development must, paradoxically, take it nearer and nearer to its origins," Robert Burgoyne remarks that this has in fact come true, though in a very different sense than anticipated.

> Although Bazin probably meant that cinema would eventually arrive at a perfect replication of the real, computer generated imagery in fact pushes the cinema's origins back beyond the nineteenth- and twentieth-century dream of the mechanical or electronic reproduction of reality, all the way to premodernity, to medieval or mythic times when the line between fantasy, fact and speculation was not yet clearly drawn [p. 234].

We are now only at the outset of a technology that can represent history and legend almost exclusively by computer-generated animation. Lev Manovich suggests that the digital revolution has the consequence that "cinema can no longer be distinguished from animation. It is no longer an indexical media technology but, rather, a sub-genre of painting" (p. 175). On the one hand, the proliferation of Arthurian materials across a dizzying array of media perhaps resembles nothing so much as Borges's garden of forking paths, alternate and incommensurable realities that can be compassed only by a hypertextual model of transmedia storytelling. On the other hand, as Baudrillard knew, the procession of simulacra is an ideological force capable of implanting its rootless images as false historical memories, a phenomenon increasingly common in a world of cinema, experiential museums, and digitality, which has been dubbed "prosthetic memory" by Alison Landsberg (1995).

These are issues too large to unpack in any further detail here; instead, I want to focus briefly in the conclusion of this chapter on how the reality effects of film serve to anchor further excursions into the virtual space of video games through the cinematic device par excellence, montage. My argument is that virtual representations are often posed as hidden or spiritual realities beneath, behind, or beside the world as we have been led to know it. This spiritual reality is animated, like the classical moving picture itself, by rendering continuity through an erasure of the boundaries between discrete images. Follow if you dare the imaginary archaeologist Lara Croft of *Tomb Raider: Legend* beneath the tourist shops of Glastonbury to discover Arthur's tomb in the Avalon hidden beneath. Recover with her from the four corners of the earth pieces of the sword Excalibur, which only the Ghalali Key (sic) can reassemble. Return the reforged sword to the stone, and use it as the lever of a time machine. Gerald of Wales claimed that both Glastonbury and Avalon were names for the same place in different languages, denoting a city of glass and an isle of apples. Lara watches through a glass darkly as her mother, in a parallel universe, again makes the fatal mistake of pulling the sword from the stone, urged on by a doltish Eve-figure Amanda, ensuring that the past is repeated. In the made-for-TV miniseries *Mists of Avalon*, Morgaine learns to part the mists of Glastonbury to gain access to the hidden world of Avalon, which also seems to exist in a parallel space-time continuum. These games and films actualize virtual spaces that one could argue are present in the legend from the outset, the spaces of an imaginary archaeology typically gendered feminine, which invite descendants to participate in their recovery while exposing them to the dangers of compulsive repetitions.

Gilles Deleuze's cinematic philosophy of the time-image exfoliates from the notion that the virtual and actual, the transparent and opaque can achieve a point of indiscernibility, a crystalline image of the multifaceted nature of time itself. Deleuze valorizes the powers of the false because they deterritorialize the possibilities of our future perceptions. Ideally, video games made to accompany digital cinema would be crystalline images of the worlds they supplement, allowing players to deterritorialize films, to actualize what is only virtual in them, to render the opaque transparent. Recent franchises like *The*

Matrix, *Stars Wars*, or *Harry Potter* spread their stories across a series of media, encouraging the audience to participate in what Henry Jenkins (2006) calls "transmedia storytelling." Certainly the economic motivations of such a marketing strategy are paramount, creating multiple points of access to a franchise and encouraging brand loyalty by the dispersal of information across old and new media. Saturation marketing invites audience participation as nominal co-creators of a franchise through a "fan culture" of merchandising, Internet chat, fan fiction, and even fan cinema. *King Arthur* in many ways represents a much less successful attempt to capitalize on this "culture of convergence." Yet its strategies of convergence do represent a trend with which students of movie medievalism will increasingly be forced to reckon.

The syncretic monomyth of *King Arthur*, which mixes different national film traditions according to a recipe unwittingly provided by the Littleton-Malcor hypothesis, is one element of its participation in the culture of convergence. Another is the nearly seamless character of its iterations across a number of media platforms. Publicity for the film included its ghost-like presence in a number of documentaries made around the time of its release, such as Francis Pryor's *King Arthur's Britain* (2004), which uses lap dissolves to embed numerous shots from the film into a survey of Arthurian sites. The video game itself begins with an extended "cut scene," which reproduces the opening of the film up to the point when the *kagemusha* "bishop" looks out the window at the invading Picts and three bolts smack the carriage next to his head. Here a match cut takes us to this same shot in virtual reality, easing our integration from film to game world. In fact, the cut scenes, in their low-density resolution, closely resemble the pixilation of the game's virtual world. Interestingly the transition between film and game takes place at a window, the metaphor par excellence for hyperspace: part screen, mirror, and window. As Stanley Cavell remarks: "The screen is a barrier. What does the silver screen screen? It screens me from the world it holds — that is screens its existence from me" (p. 24). Like the mists of Avalon and the glass of Glastonbury in the examples discussed above, the window in the film/game is the threshold that marks an ontological cut, a window within a window whose *mise en abyme* is charged with a titillating bit of scopophobia (on windows and virtuality, see Friedberg 2006).

Unfortunately, things through the looking glass are pretty much the same. The goal of the game, interspersed with cut scenes, is to reproduce precisely what happens in the film. Failure to do so results in death and an invitation to restart the challenge. The game maps the film as a quest along a circular path through the Midlands and the north of Britain, punctuated by six rabbit holes into virtual space, proceeding roughly due north and returning on a parallel road south. Killing sufficient numbers of the enemy endows one with a shining aura that, as in the Homeric *aristeia*, invests the warrior with superhuman powers. Passing through the various levels one earns things, such as increasing strength or experience, until, fully charged with all available powers, one meets Cerdic in a final showdown at Mt. Badon. To reach this duel one has to have killed something very close to the 960 enemies Arthur himself is credited with in the early histories. The "synergy" between film and game begins in fact to look like part of an original strategy rather than something added post hoc. One would expect a Roman legion to fight with spears and *gladii* and to dress in the same uniform. However, each of Arthur's Sarmatian knights is distinguished by his weaponry, dress, and movements. For instance, Tristan wears what appears to be a Sarmatian pointed cap and sports a Saracen sword and recurved bow. Gawain's weapon of choice is a giserne, Lancelot is the knight of two swords, and Bors wields a ninja-like configuration of brass knuckles and forearm blades. All this paraphernalia can be a bit distracting in the film, but, along with the individuated fighting styles of different characters, the details seem to stem from a planned convergence with the world of the video game, where such means of characterization are a staple of game programming. Thus in both film and game Arthur's "signature moves" include a slashing pirouette and a kill-shot performed with the sword held overhand below shoulder level; Lancelot turns his two swords into a pair of scissors to cut off the heads of his victims; and Tristan has a rapid-fire feature allowing him to loose three arrows in machine gun-like succession. Conversely (and absurdly) the ice battle sequence recalls a carnival arcade game in which sheets of ice stand on end and one must shoot through the gaps to kill the Saxons on the other side. Albeit rarely, one does get to walk through doors the film doesn't open, such as the battle fought within the walls of Marius's palace. The game and the film seem part of an overall design in which both convergence and divergence are designed to compose a variegated world.

Finally, from my discussion of Fuqua's *King Arthur*, it is possible to draw at least three more generally applicable lessons for the study of contemporary cinémedievalism. First, while medievalists will always be tempted to compare these films to medieval sources or academic scholarship, cinema too has a history through which it interprets and reconstructs the past. This particular film's convergence of speculative scholarship with auteur cinema is remarkable, but the phenomenon of such mixtures is not. Second, we must be attuned not simply to the risible rhetoric of "new discoveries" but also to the popular science that underwrites this endless production of a "more authentic" past. Last and perhaps most importantly, we must not reerect the wall that used to separate film and written documents between film and newer media. The works that increasingly engage students of cinémedievalism are perhaps best described by Jenkins's term "world-making," which includes not only their imaginary ontology but also their desire to produce a sustainable and multivalent media franchise, coherent in itself but opened to future development. Increasingly these franchises, and not simply the films in isolation, will become objects of study. All three lessons fit neatly under a single rubric: convergence. But of course convergence has been the defining if not enabling trait of medievalism as well as Arthurianism right along, at least since the moment Caxton decided to merge Malory's tales into a printed book and thereby initiate the single most successful franchise in storytelling history.

7

Postmedieval Paranoia: The New Middle Ages of *Night Watch* and *The Da Vinci Code*

We are all sufferers from history, but the paranoid is a double sufferer, since he is afflicted not only by the real world, with the rest of us, but by his fantasies as well. — Richard Hofstadter, *The Paranoid Style in American Politics*

We are in a conflict between good and evil, and America will call evil by its name. — George W. Bush, West Point Commencement Address, 2002

What would he do if he ever made a mistake? If he killed someone who wasn't an enemy of the human race, but just an ordinary person? — Sergei Lukya-nenko, *The Night Watch*

To the long list of terms proposed to describe what happens after post-modernism (postideological, posthuman, etc.), I would like to offer the fol-lowing addition: "the postmedieval." Some of what I intend the term to embrace will be explored in this final chapter as a kind of parting (or Parthian) shot, though I hope to trace further resonances of the concept in more detail in the coming years. Let us begin with Burgoyne's notion, discussed in the previous chapter, of technologies of the virtual that blur the distinction between fantasy and reality to a degree thought to be characteristic of "medieval or mythic times." In the postmodern films analyzed in chapter 1, such as Terry Gilliam's *Brazil* or *The Fisher King*, the medieval is the space of paranoid fantasy papered over by an information age, which interpellates its subjects with the white noise of postmodernity. Here the medieval imaginary exists as a phantasmagoric reaction to the random violence and numbing impersonality of the contemporary urban landscape. Postmedievalism, on the other hand, positions the Enlightenment and its aftermath as the aberration, the hiatus, or mass delusion from which we are only now beginning to awaken. We wake, of course, into the new Middle Ages: a time of interhemispheric religious wars, sectarian violence, and apocalyptic fervor, in which Jerusalem is once again the center of the world. But being postmedieval we also wake to realities the "Dark Ages" had concealed even from modernity itself, the transcendental reality of a Manichean universe. What would it mean to be "postmedieval"? Least obtrusively, it would mean the acceptance of the metanarrative, which positions the Middle Ages as the period from which most modern institutions and beliefs derive, combined with an elegiac nostalgia for these times as a site of loss or repression. The postmedieval world is only superficially different from the Middle Ages, beneath the apparent change lies a dark continuity, masked by narratives of historical progress or rupture. This postmedieval world is then positioned as the fateful stage of a delayed medieval apocalypse, a return of the repressed, the macrocosmic homology with Freud's *Nachträglichkeit*, or "delayed action." In short, the postmedieval is a paranoid/schizoid formation. This formation is readily apparent in the name-calling slurs emerging not only from all political positions in a post–9/11 world, each of which seeks to identify their enemy as "medieval," but also, as Bruce Holsinger demonstrates, in the "neomedievalism" of academic and "think-tank" movements to characterize globalization as a return to the feudal and ecclesiastical political structures of the Middle Ages.[1]

The Night Watch

One thoroughgoing example of postmedievalism is Timur Bekmambekov's *The Night Watch* (2004), a rich, kitschy pastiche of *The Matrix* and the *Lord of the Rings*. The opening voice-over narration provides an introduction to the apocalyptic legacy of the Middle Ages, its repression of Manichean realities, and their reemergence in a final, postmedieval conflict.

> As long as humanity has existed there have been Others among us. They're human, yet they have abilities beyond those of ordinary men. Witches, sorcerers, shape-shifters — the Others are as varied as the stars in the sky. The Others are soldiers in the eternal war: the struggle between Dark and Light. Light Others protected mankind from the Dark Others who plagued and tortured humans. Legend tells of the day when the two armies met on a bridge. Gesser, Lord of the Light, and Zavulon, General of the Darkness, faced each other. And neither one would give way. And so began a great battle, bloody and merciless. Zavulon gloried in the slaughter, but Lord Gesser wept. As the screams of the dying reached heaven, Gesser realized the armies were equally matched ... and he knew that unless the fighting was stopped, every last soul would perish. So he stopped the

battle. Thus the forces of Light and Darkness forged the Truce. Gesser spoke for the Light and Zavulon spoke for the Darkness. And these things were agreed: No one could be forced to good or evil without choosing freely. The soldiers of Light would be called Nightwatch, making sure Dark Others obeyed the Truce. And the soldiers of Darkness would be called Daywatch, to do the same. And so the balance would kept for centuries to come. But one day an Other would come, more powerful than any before him. Like all Others he would have to choose between Light and Dark. And his choice would change the balance forever.

I have quoted this opening voice-over narration in its entirety to emphasize not only its by-the-book Manichaeism but also its placement of a fundamental medieval aporia as the core reality of the contemporary world. In Lacanian terms the Middle Ages creates this Real by repressing it, the "Truce" forms the symbolic order, the armies of Light and Dark, its Big Other(s), as the invisible ground upon which all subjectivization occurs. As if to demonstrate how the field of battle changes with this medieval truce, we move from the wide shot on the bridge to a tight shot on the face of a single, frightened mortal. The lords of the Light and the Dark, Gesser and Zavulon (respectively), take their war from the bridge to the mind of a man. They whisper their cases on either side of the man's head, speaking for the Light and the Dark but also blighting the subject of their warring interpellations, who ages in an instant.[2]

The field of battle in Prudentian fashion has been fully internalized. Throughout the film the Others view human beings through "the twilight" or "gloom" from a kind of MRI perspective, which renders their central nervous systems visible. These shots perhaps confirm J. Alfred Prufrock's fear of "a magic lantern" throwing "the nerves in patterns on a screen," the ultimate modern paranoia in which no inside is safe from insight.

For Žižek, "The original question of desire is not directly 'What do I want?' but 'What do *others* want from me?' 'What do they see in me?' 'What am I to others?' A small child is embedded in a complex network of relations, he serves as a kind of catalyst or battlefield for the desires of those around him" (1997, p. 9). The narrative of *Night Watch* ultimately resolves to just such a battle for the soul of a child whose choice will break the thousand-year stalemate between the Light and Dark Others. The opening sequence then stages the internalization of Freud's fundamental fantasy unto the ground of the unconscious, where as Žižek reminds us "fantasy tells me what I am for my others" (1997, 9).[3] But that internalization is also the moment of a repression: "fantasy, at its most elementary, becomes inaccessible to the subject. It is this inaccessibility that makes the subject 'empty,' as Lacan puts it." The apparent time-lapse photography, which tracks the rapid aging of the central figure between Light and Dark, records this blighting of the subject, perhaps understood ambiguously as both the rapid wasting of a life as well as a natural lifespan spent as the ground of a warring Real that quite literally "interpellates" the subject.

Viewers of this framing fantasy might well ask with Gilles Deleuze: "Where is the battle?"

> If the battle is not an example of an event among others, but rather the Event in its essence, it is no doubt because it is actualized in diverse manners at once, and because each participant may grasp it at a different level of actualization within its variable present. [...] But it is above all because the battle *hovers over* its own field, being neutral in relation to all of its temporal actualizations, neutral and impassive in relation to the victor and the vanquished, the coward and the brave; because of this, it is all the more terrible. Never present but always yet to come and already passed, the battle is graspable only by the will of anonymity which it itself inspires. This will, which we must call will "of indifference," is present in the mortally wounded soldier who is no longer brave or cowardly, no longer victor or vanquished, but rather so much beyond, at the place where the Event is present, participating therefore in its terrible impassibility. "Where" is the battle? [Deleuze 1990, p. 100].

In the film, the freezing of the Manichean war on the bridge essentializes the event and thereby renders its neutrality with respect to its "temporal actualizations" across the thousand years of subsequent history. Its "freeze frame" embraces not only the Cold War proper but also, as it were, "hovers over" the whole of the millennium in its aporetic neutrality. The Rembrandt painting from which the film borrows its title has been in recent years the subject of numerous actualizations in Denmark to mark the artist's 500th birthday, including role-playing masques and a patio sculpture that allows visitors, in effect, to enter the painting within a three-dimensional space. The film's reification of the battle functions in analogous ways. As Žižek asks regarding *The Matrix*: "What if the virtual character of the symbolic order *as such* is the very condition of historicity?" (2001, p. 213). The lone peasant, himself a calque for human subjectivity under the pale of this "event," shudders in the thrall of "its terrible impassibility." For Deleuze this indifference is finally embodied or grasped only at the point of death — a realization beyond any single actualization. The trajectory in Deleuze's description of the battle moves from the indifferent battle to the single, indifferent soldier — exactly the same traversal of fantasy that the opening sequence of *Night Watch* undertakes. But it is as if being reinscribed within the human mind, the battle, with its opposing sides, now takes the psyche itself rather than the material world for its field of battle. Malcolm Bowie says: "psychical time is different from 'natural' time [...] because the present can change the past" (p. 181). As we have seen throughout this book such is the central wager of medievalism itself. Here the wager is ultimately tied to the battle in the soul of a young boy,

The battle of Dark and Light Others in Timor Bekmambetov's *Night Watch* (2004).

whose choice will finally tip the balance and bring the "Middle Ages" — conceived as the sublimation of a real Manichean conflict — at long last to an end.

In Deleuze's impassive impasse, the battle bears striking affinities to Žižek's valorization of the Real as that which both precedes the Symbolic but also comprises its remainder, its excess. As Tony Meyers explains, the Real is "the arena of dialectic, where opposing terms can coincide" (p. 27). The truce between Light and Dark Others in the film creates then the Lacanian Order of the Real, not only invisible for the most part to human beings but also containing the violent and beneficent forces that erupt into human lives, though the forces elude their comprehension. The battle and the truce repeat quite rigorously Žižek's insistence that the Law conceals its obscene supplement, the inhuman, uncivilized violence through which the rule of Law is instituted. And as Georgio Agamben's work would lead us to expect, this Law itself seems defined by complicated "states of exception," in which the torture and murder of human beings is sanctioned within complicated systems designed to maintain a balance of power. The Others are themselves Žižekian calques, each is possessed by a little other — that monstrous element that not only estranges them from their human selves but also serves as the core of their special powers as magicians, shape-shifters, vampires, and so forth. And each is subject as well to a Big Other (Gesser or Zavulon), who compels them to honor or break the truce with a Kafkaesque capriciousness. In this imaginary world all of humanity become potential *homines sacri* and the Law, as Žižek claims for Judaic law, "is strictly correlative to the emergence of the neighbor as an inhuman Thing" designed to "shield us from the monstrosity next door" (2006, p. 44). In the world of the Night Watch the vampire lives next door and one can borrow a cup of blood if the cupboard is bare.

The apocalyptic thaw in this virtual freeze self-consciously tracks stages in the development of the movement-image from the persistence of vision through virtual simulations, as though technology itself in its increasing capacity to mimic reality represents a Pygmalion gambit, capable of freeing the geniis from their bottles. In an early scene, Gesser doodles in the margins of an old book entitled *Legends of Byzantium*, which contains the story of a cursed virgin. But as the virgin's powers to blight all she touches take hold, the magician's marginal stills illuminate his voice-over as a low-tech moving picture. The images in the margins not only animate her story — everything she touches dies — but seem to awaken, to animate progressively this evil force itself. Later, in a tour de force of this apocalyptic continuity, the virgin serves as the site of a vortex that sucks a screw from a plane 30,000 feet overhead so that it falls through an airshaft and into her cup of tea. Meanwhile the millennial boy over whose soul the battle will be rejoined is a latchkey kid watching *Buffy the Vampire Slayer* on TV while a "real" vampire prowls the hallways of his apartment building. Zavulon, the Lord of the Dark, bides his time playing video games, but the game he plays is actually a simulation of virtual futures, a virtual battle in which he practices for his final duel with Anton for the life and the soul of this apocalyptic child. Having honed his moves in virtual reality, Zavulon is able to duplicate them in reality, thereby saving the boy from his father Anton, who had determined to sacrifice his own child in order to save the world. Here the Christological allegory receives an Oedipal twist. In being willing to kill his own son for a higher cause, Anton has lost him to the Dark Side and now the plague of absolute justice can fall upon humankind unencumbered by any hope of grace. The Law, which the Truce had represented, will, not, in the terms of Flannery O'Connor's "Misfit," be thrown out of balance by a sacrifice that profoundly alters time itself.

What happens instead is Freud's *Nachträglichkeit* ("deferred action") projected from the realm of individual psycho-dynamics and back unto the historical field itself. As the frozen medieval battle is rejoined on a twenty-first century Moscow rooftop, Deleuze's question "Where is the battle?" receives a presentist response, but one that neatly balances relativism and determinism. As Žižek puts it in *The Fragile Absolute*:

When we say that the present redeems the past itself, that the past itself contained signs which pointed towards the present, we are not making a historicist-relativist statement about how there is no "objective" history; how we always interpret the past from our present horizon of understanding; how, in defining past epochs, we always — consciously or not — imply our own point of view. What we are claiming is something more radical: what the proper *historical* stance (as opposed to historicism) "relativizes" is not the past (always distorted by our present point of view) but, paradoxically, *the present itself* — our present can be conceived only as the outcome (not of what actually happened in the past, but also) of the crushed potentials for the future that were contained in the past.... It is also that we, the "actual" present historical agents, have to conceive of *ourselves* as the materialization of the ghosts of past generations, as the stage in which these past generations retroactively resolve their deadlocks [2000, pp. 90–91 (emphasis in the original)].

There is a common elegiac strain in movie medievalism for the "crushed potentials" of the past (see, for instance, my discussion of *The Name of the Rose* in chapter 1), but the "stance" of *Night Watch* is in some ways more of a historical metapsychology than even Žižek attempts. The Middle Ages are posed as the site of an aporetic battle, which itself seems to allegorize the medieval suppression of Manichaeism in its many forms. The film introjects that conflict, much as Augustine and Prudentius did, into the soul of human beings. Finally in the "actual" present, an age of paranoia and Manichean delirium, this virtual conflict is once again externalized or projected onto the neopagan screen of popular culture. Of course, Freud himself came to much the same Manichean conclusion in *Beyond the Pleasure Principle*, in which he postulated the "death instinct" as the equal or even superior *other* of the pleasure-seeking Eros. Freud's embittered reaction to the rise of Nazism and his own personal tragedies in *Civilization and Its Discontents* also led him to diagnose the externalization of the death instinct and its final triumph under the growing shadows of World War II.

This later Freud is somewhat of an embarrassment to Lacanians, who see him as having repressed in these later writings his early insights and as having failed to remain with Nietzsche "beyond good and evil." The solution that *Night Watch* poses to the problem of Manichaeism is, however, both beyond history and beyond good and evil. It accepts as a fundamental reality the Reaganesque construction of postwar history as a stalemate between good and evil and accepts as well the seemingly antagonistic neo-Marxist notions of false consciousness and the administered self. Its human beings exist in a world of illusion whose eruptions are determined by unseen forces of dark and light; it is only the Others who have free choice and that choice is limited to which of the two sides they choose to join. Like Frodo Baggins, Luke Skywalker, and Neo, the boy of *Night Watch* has a choice to make that will tip the balance between good and evil, but, unlike them, he makes this choice in the presence of the audience where the delirium that Manichaeism produces in the good, Light Others is much in evidence. As another sacrifice of Isaac is interrupted, the boy can only turn and follow his liberator, Zavulon the Lord of the Dark Ones, who, like the West during the Cold War and in its increasingly delirious aftermath, are dedicated to the preservation of their own freedoms at whatever price.

The Da Vinci Code

Ron Howard's *The Da Vinci Code* (2007) and *Night Watch* may at first appear odd bedfellows indeed. Superficially they bear little resemblance; yet, both films appeal to the particular brand of Manichean delirium that I have dubbed postmedieval. The film's conspiracy theorist *cum* grail scholar, Sir Leigh Teabing, describes the repressed Manichean inheritance in what are by now familiar terms.

> We are in the middle of a war. One that has gone on forever. On the one side stands the Priory. On the other is an ancient group of despots with members hidden in high-ranking positions throughout the Church. This Council of Shadows tries to destroy the Grail documents as devoutly as the Priory fights to protect them.

Just as in *Night Watch*, the conflict between the light Priory of Sion and the dark power structure of Opus Dei is posed as the fundamental Real beneath the apparent chaos of history, a stalemate whose recognition is *parousia* or *gnosis* and whose resolution promises to alter fundamentally the balance of knowledge and belief.

Intriguingly, *The Da Vinci Code* is its creative team's second bite at the apple of conspiracy. Director Ron Howard, producer Brian Grazer, and screenwriter Akiva Goldsman also collaborated on the 2005 Academy Award–winning film *A Beautiful Mind*. Both films employ the same special-effects techniques of highlighting and shifting letters to mimic the process of a mind solving hidden anagrams. The earlier film chronicles the life of the Nobel Prize–winning mathematician John Nash from his early brilliance through his descent into paranoid schizophrenia. Nash's mind becomes the screen upon which the search for mathematical proofs explaining the complex interactions of groups slowly becomes corrupted by delusions of grandeur and persecution, which provoke him to search for secret codes concealed within newspapers and magazines. Nash's psychosis seems not simply imbued with Cold War paranoia, but instead is presented as its inevitable by-product. Yet if Howard and his team were quick to dissect the will to power in McCarthyism, they strangely appear to have fallen head-over-heals for its new-age counterpart, the even less credible fabrication of a millennium-long war of conspiracies in Dan Brown's novel. I don't intend to engage here in refutations of Brown's conspiracy theory nor in refutations of the many attempts to demonize him or the novel; however, what does fascinate is the championing of paranoia in both the novel and the film as the keystone of a new, decidedly postmedieval spirituality.

What is the relationship between religious belief and the belief in grand conspiracy metanarratives? The apparent difference is that cynicism poses no bar to belief in overarching conspiracies; indeed, cynicism serves contradictorily as the very ground of such beliefs. Žižek follows Peter Sloterdijk in terming this style of thought "kynicism:" "a form of sarcastic or ironic response to authority, one which ridicules the hypocrisy of ruling institutions" (Myers, p. 65). Such kynicism is everywhere apparent in both the novel and the film versions of *The Da Vinci Code*, and it loops back into the revelation of a Manichean struggle in a way common to much conspiracy discourse. Begin with the generally accepted notion that there are wheels within wheels, that power masks its deployment and motives behind political propaganda, and you are half way to the willing suspension of disbelief that comprises the epistemology of a conspiracy theorist. How though do we travel the remaining leg of the journey to end up kneeling before the glass pyramid in front of the Louvre, secure in the belief that the tomb of Mary Magdalene lies hidden hundreds of feet below? Žižek's answer to the problem of religious faith in the contemporary world is Pascal. We wager that God exists because to bet on the contrary holds no prospect of benefit if we are correct and significant penalties if we are wrong. Belief for Pascal is not simply expressed or affirmed in ritual but rather produced by it, if you would believe you must first kneel and pray. "Pray and you will believe" becomes for Žižek the model for ideological apparatuses in a supposedly "post-ideological" world (see Žižek 1989, pp. 33–35).

The curious fusion of cynicism and belief in the ideology of conspiracy pays similar dividends even for its least committed adherents. Its wager is, like Pascal's, on the existence of God: The rewards of belief are potentially much greater than disbelief, just as buying a lottery ticket involves a minuscule chance of success, though an equally small investment for the possibility of an enormous gain. More to the point, imagining that one has the winning ticket or the key to history itself involves a thrill, however fleeting. Though for true believers — unlike casual buyers of lottery tickets, paperbacks, or movie tickets — falsification is well nigh impossible: "just because you're paranoid doesn't mean they're not out to get you." Sir Leigh Teabing's response in the film to the news that the Priory of Sion documents had proven a forgery nicely exemplifies this defense mechanism: "Yes, and that's just what they want you to think." Of course, deciding what it is "they" want us to think and determining to think otherwise is also the hallmark of the post-modern "hermeneutics of suspicion" and drives a good deal of academic discourse in what were formerly known as the humanities. Be that as it may, I want to return to the second of Pascal's formulations, "Pray to believe." How can *The Da Vinci Code* be at once (as Dan Brown at various intervals has claimed): (a) just a novel or movie; (b) the revelation of an enduring, real conspiracy to distort the meaning of Christ's life and repress the sacred feminine; as well as, (c) the recovery of a pre–Christian balance between masculine and feminine that was lost in the eclipse of paganism? The answer perhaps is that one has to *play* in order to believe. Both the film and the novel attempt to suture the audience into the machinery of the mystery-thriller genre whose successful resolution depends on its cryptex-like alignment of esoterica. To follow the suspenseful plot of the murder mystery is also to acquiesce to some extent in its concatenation of conspiracy history. Dan Brown, like the popular nonfiction authors of *Holy Blood, Holy Grail* and *The Templar Revelation*[4] from whom he draws many of his theories, is not merely a cynical opportunist but rather his own ideal reader, someone who plays at belief and ends up believing, if not in every detail then in the possibility that beyond faith in conspiracies lies faith itself.

Umberto Eco's *Foucault's Pendulum*, like all great parodies, continues to sting even books written decades later. Certainly it takes the measure of the likes of Dan Brown and his recent epigones proleptically. As meisters of esoterica none are fit to hold Eco's cloak. Everyone who has delighted in *The Da Vinci Code* should be sentenced to slogging through *Foucault's Pendulum*. Eco's own categories of medievalism in his essay "The Return of the Middle Ages" anatomizes the genre mercilessly:

> The Middle Ages of the so-called *tradition*, or of occult philosophy..., an eternal and rather eclectic ramshackle structure, swarming with Knights Templars, Rosicrucians, alchemists, Masonic initiates, neo-Kabbalists, drunk on reactionary potions sipped from the Grail, ready to hail every neo-Fascist Will to Power.... Antiscientific by definition, these Middle Ages keep going under the banner of the mystical wedding of the micro- with the macrocosm, and as a result they convince their adepts that everything is the same as everything else and that the whole world is born to convey, in any of its aspects and events the same Message. Fortunately the message got lost, which makes its Quest fascinating for the happy few who stand proof-tight, philology-resistant, bravely ignorant of the Popperian call for the good habit of falsification. [1998, p. 71].

Still it is surprising to find Eco fifteen years later pursuing wholeheartedly (if a bit whimsically) the genre he had so roundly trounced. Perhaps less surprising though, if we understand the homologies between conspiracy theory and medievalism in whatever form, as a crucial component of the project that seeks to establish continuities between the Middle Ages and the modern world. In *Foucault's Pendulum*, Templar conspiracies are at first equated with a lunatic fringe: "For (the lunatic), everything proves everything else ... whatever he comes across confirms his lunacy. You can tell him by the liberties he takes with common sense, by his flashes of inspiration, and by the fact that sooner or later he will bring up the Templars" (pp. 57–58). But with the aid of a supercomputer, the trio of bored editors begins to weave a conspiracy of conspiracies, a web of arcane knowledge, a hoax in which they themselves are slowly compelled to believe. Others believe it too and a malign conspiracy called the Diabolicals, seemingly conjured into existence by the game itself, begins ruthlessly hunting for the secret. Eco's pilgrimage through hermetic knowledge ends where it began: with a paranoid man hiding in a museum awaiting the fatal encounter that his own conspiracy theories have called into being. When Belbo is hung from the wire of the pendulum, his head functions as the still point that demonstrates the turning of the world. Eco's merciless satire sends up the trio of authors (Michael Baigent, Richard Leigh, and Henry Lincoln) who composed *Holy Blood, Holy Grail* and Dan Brown's *The Da Vinci Code* is filled with punning references to their names and the sites of their "discoveries." As the world revolves round Belbo's head, he at last gains access to the great secret. Roughly stated the secret is this: everything *is* connected, because human beings make meaning by drawing connections. And those who attain this secret knowledge are forever haunted by the embodiments of their labors, those who refuse to accept that their profound sense of alienation is simply a function of the gap between signifier and signified.

The Time Image as a Technique of the Imaginary

Alfred Hitchcock always insisted that the object of desire in the mystery-thriller is essentially a null set, what he called a McGuffin, around which the plot circulates but which itself has no real importance or significance, like the radioactive dust in *Notorious* (1946) or the microfilm in *North by Northwest* (1959). Of course, the ubiquity of the grail in popular fiction and film threatens to make it the supreme McGuffin (McGrail?), but Brown's plot rather ingeniously collapses the thriller's objects of desire, the feminine and the precious prize. Film noir often partially collapses objects and women in a similar way, although the resolution of the mystery typically reveals the falsity of both the object and the woman. The quest of the noir detective/ knight (note that Robert Langdon is dubbed both in the film) is to remain essentially unmoved by this dual assault of cupidities. The paradigmatic film in this regard is John Huston's *The Maltese Falcon* (1941), in which both idols, the woman and the figurine, are finally exposed as false, "the stuff that dreams are made of." Brown's mystery-thriller opens to predictable noir dangers, with Langdon the harassed victim of a cop trying to pin a murder on him and subject as well to the attentions of a seemingly unbalanced femme fatale, who involves him in the patently ridiculous search for the grail. Yet in transforming the grail into an imaginary genealogy, Brown appeals more directly to the idealized chivalric quests of which the knights of hard-boiled fiction, such as Sam Spade or Philip Marlowe, could only dream.

Hitchcock also insisted upon a clear distinction between cinema and "pictures of people talking." The challenge for anyone trying to film Dan Brown's novel was how not simply to give way to a storyline that consists almost exclusively of people talking, or worse, people thinking. Ron Howard's solution to these problems is less than ideal, although it does provide an interesting example of recent attempts to wed what Deleuze calls the sensory-motor schema of the movement-image with the crystalline faceting of time he valorized in the time-images of modern cinema. The film pits the dark, noir universe of secrets, conspiracies and murder mysteries against the multifaceted illumination of the time-image, which offers both psychological and historical *gnosis*. In the remainder of this chapter, I trace the film's images of time through the conflation of personal and cultural pasts, what Umberto Eco calls the "mystical wedding of the micro- with the macrocosm."

Throughout this book we have looked at numerous examples of imagined back stories of childhood trauma that movie medievalism invents in order to calque the troubled relationship of modernity to the Middle Ages. Just as the child fathers the adult, so too does the Middle Ages father a modern world prone to the unresolved conflicts of its traumatic childhood. *The Da Vinci Code* has a trio of these victims: Silas, the Opus Dei albino assassin traces a familiar trajectory from abject to divinely sanctioned warrior of God, while Robert Langdon and Sophie Neveu together seek more socially acceptable forms of liberation from their traumatic pasts in the deciphering of codes that yield both psychic and historical insights. All three though are "sufferers from history," in Richard Hofstadter's terms, because, in the mode I have termed postmedieval paranoia the darkness of their own pasts is bound up with the secrets the Dark Ages repressed. In chapter 1 we looked at how the cinema apparatus permits the construction of temporally multivalent images, collapsing the distinction between historical epochs into an imaginary co-presence. For example, in Cecil B. DeMille's *Joan the Woman* (1916) the saint haunts the battlefield and spurs the reincarnation of her lover, Eric Trent, to a self-sacrificing expiation of his crimes against her and his own country — an expiation that atones in the trenches of World War I for the English occupation of France in the fifteenth century. For Žižek, contemporary subjects serve as "the materialization of the ghosts of past generations, as the stage in which these past generations retroactively resolve their deadlocks" (2000, p. 91). In the postmedieval world of *The Da Vinci Code* this retroactivity is everywhere apparent at both the psychic and the metapsychological levels, through an extensive series of flashbacks that construct the film itself as a complex, if very conventional, time-image. Indeed, the remembering, repeating, and working through of childhood traumas calques the solution of modern codes as well as the discovery of secrets the medieval church is supposed to have repressed.

The Da Vinci Code is probably the most complete example of the two theoretical foci outlined in my opening chapters, a veritably mystical wedding of the techniques of the imaginary to the crystalline time-image. The film's flashbacks are presented in two-toned, predominantly silver images in which symbolic objects (such as roses or Templar crosses) are brightly colored red in post-production. These flashbacks avoid Hitchcock's warnings against "pictures of people talking" but also weave, in concert with the frenetic cutting between the various present-day players in the hunt for the grail, a dense conglomeration of time and space. It is worthwhile to survey these flashbacks before attempting to demonstrate how they function in the film's wedding of the micro- to the macrocosm.

1. The sight of Saunière's corpse on the floor of the Louvre provokes a memory in flashback of Sophie as a child running through a field of roses colored red.

2. Brief flashback (5 seconds) of a modern Priory ceremony (I), described hypothetically by Langdon but remembered by Sophie.

3. Silas's childhood, his murder of an abusive father, and his imprisonment. Aringarosa rescues him from prison (lap-dissolve on Aringarosa as Christ) and then is in turn rescued by Silas from Church robbers.

4. Sophie as child on treasure hunt, connected by the scene in the Bois de Boulogne to the next flashback narrated by Langdon.

5. Langdon in voice-over narrates to Sophie a flashback of First Crusade in the late eleventh century as a clandestine hunt for a secret treasure by the "Priory of Sion and their military arm, The Knights Templar." His own image is present in an apparent double-exposure within the frame of the historical events he chronicles.

6. After a brief return to the present, Langdon then goes on to narrate the early fourteenth-century persecution of the Templars by the Church, as well as the Church's search for their treasure whose disappearance is symbolized by a single rose in an empty crypt.

7. Flashback in the armored truck of Langdon's childhood trauma, the fall into the well, though the meaning of the image is not yet apparent.

8. Flashback to Saunière giving a cryptex as a gift to Sophie, preceded by shots of "Da Vinci's design" of cryptex, its inner workings and its fail-safe mechanism.

9. Rubbing Langdon's temples to relieve his claustrophobia, Sophie flashes back to the accident that killed her family — although again the significance of the image to Sophie herself is not yet apparent.

10. Lecture at Chateau Villette (flashbacks 10–16 occur in this setting, itself cluttered with technologies of reproduction): Teabing narrates this flashback and remains a shadow in its foreground as he tells of the "lifelong pagan" but "pragmatist" Constantine, pagan culture's balance of the masculine with the "sacred feminine," the Christian versus pagan wars in Rome, and the resulting Council of Nicaea, said to be responsible for the deification of Christ and the repression of the "Gnostic Gospels," which suggest otherwise.

11. Momentary flashback to the dead body of Saunière as Sophie asks "Who is God, who is man? How many have been murdered over this question?"

12. Ancient Jerusalem, the pregnant womb of Mary Magdalene and her legendary flight from the Holy Land to France, followed by the birth of her daughter, Sarah.

13. Sophie's skeptical question ("People found God through sex?") provokes a second flashback to the modern Priory ceremony (II) with its robed and masked figures, containing only the scarcest hint at the extreme of the frame of what is going on within the ritual circle.

14. Shots of the Inquisition, which "soon publishes" *The Melleus Maleficarum*, "the most blood-soaked book in human history."

15. Shot of a modern copy of this book in Teabing's study spurs another flashback to the Inquisition's torture and execution of "free-thinking women."

16. Sophie as a child dancing to "riddle songs" and working puzzles alongside split screen of her in the present.

17. From Teabing's plane the brief flashback of Mary Magdalene being interred in a sarcophagus decorated with her effigy, followed by shots of her knights, the Priory of Sion, worshipping at her tomb, that is, the Holy Grail.

18. Flashback of only a few minutes of diegetic time showing how Langdon, Sophie, and their prisoner Silas managed to exit the plane within the hanger seconds before the police arrive to search it.

19. Outside Temple Church, London, a flashback to seven-year-old Langdon falling into a well, narrated by Teabing for Sophie. Though apparently cured of his claustrophobia, Langdon is still admonished by Teabing: "You above all people shouldn't be one to dismiss the influence of the past," collapsing personal and cultural pasts as the film itself does throughout.

20. Outside Westminster Abbey the sense of being in history is confirmed as what appears a double exposure gives us a London of the twenty-first- and the seventeenth-century funeral of Sir Isaac Newton. Skyline of famous buildings along the Thames morphs from the present, featuring the London Eye (or Millennium Wheel) to the largely identical seventeenth-century cityscape, as Langdon and Sophie enter Westminster.

21. As Langdon tries to open the cryptex, a vision of Newton's tomb appears and then the universe it represents, the planets and stars swirling around him, as Langdon tries to identify "the orb that ought be on his tomb." The image evaporates as Langdon apparently fails to solve the password riddle.

22. Apparent audio and visual hallucination in Rosslyn Chapel where Sophie regresses to a chapter early in her life. Past and present occupy the same space and time: Sophie sees herself in her past as a young girl in a red coat as well as Langdon in the present, both in the chapel.

23. Rosslyn Chapel: a flashback to the effigy of Mary Magdalene once entombed at this site, her absence in the present marked by a single red rose.

24. Set in the basement archives of Rosslyn Chapel, a flashback to Sophie doing research as a child in Saunière's study, attempting to discover how her parents died. She is caught and chastised by her "grandfather" Saunière. She runs through the field of roses we saw in the first flashback.

25. In the final flashback, Sophie as a teenager returns unexpectedly from boarding school and witnesses the secret ceremony of the Priory (III) in her grandfather's home, which she is now able to understand was not a demonic rite but rather a sexual sacrament.

Certainly one could quibble with my enumeration here but it was earnestly set down and perhaps not surprisingly yields the magical squaring of the pentacle most familiar from the numerology of *Sir Gawain and the Green Knight*. There are thirteen flashbacks from the traumatic childhoods of Sophie, Langdon, and Silas (1, 2, 3, 4, 7, 8, 9, 13, 16, 19, 22, 24, and 25), ten historical flashbacks (5, 6, 10, 12, 14, 15, 17, 20 21, and 23), while two (11 and 18) concern the present world of the film. For Deleuze the simplest explanation of the time-image is the Bergonian insistence that time is not in us but rather that we are in time. Sir Leigh Teabing in his Lear jet exuberantly gives voice to the poetics of the film as a whole: "We're in history now." The temporal lisibility of the film's mise-en-scène not only renders personal and distant historical pasts as crystalline, virtual realities within the present, but it also situates the present as the site of the past's actualization, an apocalypse that reveals once and for all what will have been.

These two-toned images of pastimes are themselves deliberately puzzling and often misleading, the truth particularly of repeated flashbacks emerges slowly across the film's diegesis and is finally clear only after images of the past have been shuffled like the letters in an anagram to provide the final solution. This solution is paranoid not simply in Eco's sense that all of history hides the same secret message but in the more clinical sense in which the message, the gnosis is the "new gospel" of Sophie Neveu herself. Sophie's final insight — that her "secret identity" is the solution not only to her own personal alienation but also to that of all women — perfectly unites delusions of persecution and grandeur, the micro- with the macrocosm, even as it heralds a return to the ancient balance between yin and yang, male and female. In Freud's most famous case history, "The Wolf Man," the "primal scene" and its expression through *nachträglich* fantasies and compulsions is closely tied to sexual position — the *a tergo* intercourse of his parents witnessed by the "Wolf Man" as a child (1989, pp. 400–28). The gradual unveiling of Sophie's primal scene proceeds not through dream analysis but rather through a series of flashbacks that represent fragmentary or blocked memories. The second flashback (#2 above), in its sightlines through two windows, mimes the montage of cinema apparatus itself and also emphasizes the partial and obstructed nature of what both we and Sophie are able to "see" in her mind's eye, thereby duplicating the subjective nature of memory within the mechanisms of repression. The ceremony, only briefly and partially witnessed, seems occult, not least by its imitation of similar shots in Stanley Kubrick's vastly superior *Eyes Wide Shut* (1999). But later through the assemblage of subsequent flashbacks, this moment is seen from a closer and higher angle (as though her memory itself had grown taller!). The reconstruction and final recognition of this memory is delayed within the film itself for almost two hours. Indeed, the "truth" about what Sophie saw is not clear until the final flashback (#25) near the end of the film. The first flashback (#1) is provoked by the adult Sophie viewing her grandfather's corpse on the parquet floor of the Louvre, posed like Da Vinci's Vitruvian Man, the circle around his extremities and the pentacle emblazoned across his chest inscribed with his own blood. The "sign of Venus" on Saunière's chest thus duplicates the "woman on top" position that Sophie witnessed in her youth and which estranged her from Saunière. The Paris detective Bezu Fache assumes that the pentacle signifies demon worship and, as a member of the conservative order of Opus Dei, is disgusted. Even though Langdon is there to set him straight, insisting that the pentacle for Saunière would certainly have meant fertility, Venus and the sacred feminine, Fache remains unconvinced. Sophie's own flashbacks to her past intimate much the same thing, the scandal of his corpse jibes with her early impressions of her grandfather as a crazed, perverse occultist.

When Langdon and Teabing unfold for her in Chateau Villette the mysteries of the sacred feminine and the Manichean conspiracies of history, Sophie remains incredulous: "So people found God through sex?" Yet the idea provokes a second, longer flashback (#13) of the Priory ceremony, which includes a woman's bare arms flailing at the edge of the frame. Given the context, however, it is not at all clear whether this figure is miming the throws of sexual ecstasy or the kind of physical torture that Langdon and Teabing are reporting the Inquisition meted out to the "free thinking woman" accused of witchcraft. This dangerously ambiguous, even Bataillean, vision of transcendence through excess is finally brought fully into focus and under control in the last flashback (#25), in which her grandfather is revealed at the center of a circle of worshippers, flat on his back (as he would be in the Louvre) with a woman on top of him enjoying to the hilt her role as the goddess. Sophie only gradually pieces this memory together, as the film itself slowly debunks the "dark con," which tragically split sexual and religious ecstasy.

Yet while the film greatly elaborates the brief mention of such a scene in Brown's novel, it is strangely much more reserved in its depiction of Sophie herself as a sexual human being. Not only is the growing romantic attraction of the novel almost completely lacking between Tom Hank's Langdon and Audrey Tautou's Sophie, but there is never any intimation that more is to come. Brown ends the novel proper on a tritely romantic note with a promised rendezvous in a luxury suite in Florence:

> Sophie leaned forward and kissed him again, now on the lips. Their bodies came together, softly at first, and then completely. When she pulled away, her eyes were full of promise. "Right," Langdon managed. "It's a date."

Far be it from me to lament the absence of so conventional an ending, yet Langdon's final brotherly kiss on Sophie's forehead in the film does give one pause. In fact the film gives us every reason to think of Sophie herself as a virgin. In playing Brown's legend the makers of *The Da Vinci Code* have come to believe, so much so in fact that their respect for this descendent of Jesus will not permit any luxury hotel suites in her foreseeable future. With the *hieros gamos* not simply deferred but excluded as a possibility, the film's whole thrust seems to founder on the rocks of its shallow neo-paganism. Paradoxically, the new-age religiosity returns to the very absurdity it refused to accept: the chastity of its progenitors. Of course this paradox is precisely Lacan's provocative thesis that "Woman does not exist" and the resultant impossibility of the "sexual relationship." Woman cannot be the sublime object, the Thing, which as Žižek puts it "could fill out the lack in man, the ideal partner with whom the sexual relationship would finally be possible" (1991, p. 80), for the simple reason that "the sublime quality of an object is not intrinsic, but rather an effect of its position in the fantasy space" (1991, p. 84). Perhaps this is why, having established Sophie as a sublime object, the filmmakers cannot bring themselves to threaten that place with the taint of sexuality; instead, they simply rear a new idol to the Virgin in the space cleared by Dan Brown's iconoclasm.

The film's imaginary genealogy also rewards comparison with the use of genetics in *King Arthur*. Here though the desideratum is not simply the connection of race to nationality, but rather the attempt to euhemerize the "actual" immortality of Christ in the survival of his DNA down to modern times. The tomb of Mary Magdalene at the end of the film opens the possibility of a DNA analysis that would connect Sophie to a select line of true "Christians," stretching back to Mary and her daughter Sarah — the first *real* Christian. This line is imagined as passing through the Merovingian kings down into the contemporary world, where the ultimate Calvinist blood-lottery would surely be held in order to determine the truly elect inheritors of the line of Christ. Belief is no longer necessary once knowledge of Christ's real presence through history is finally established. And Pascal's wager would no longer be necessary, a cotton swab could soon determine whether or not one is in fact a Christian. Such would truly be the "hysterical Christianity" of which Žižek speaks, a religion in which the most revealing of codes is the genetic one, the real soul of human beings.[5] Žižek defines Lacan's *objet petit a* as "the hidden treasure, that which is 'in us more than ourselves,' that illusive, unattainable X that confers upon all our deeds an aura of magic, although it cannot be pinned down to any of our positive qualities" (1991, p. 77). Of course the "hidden treasure" of the hunt for the grail turns out to be Sophie herself, though precisely that something which is in her more than herself, her genetic inheritance, whose discovery retroactively bestows on her gentle qualities (with the drug addict and with Langdon's fear of closed spaces) the aura of the supernatural. Sophie's only faith — "in people and that they can sometimes be kind" — then becomes a full-fledged if unintended pun, her own kindness serves to prove her descent, a clear instance that what is bred in the bone will out in the flesh.

The historical flashbacks, as I mentioned above, are linked to the personal ones in their use of two-toned shots and objects colorized red, and they also construct multivalent time images characterized by virtual/actual interchanges whose significance is altered in successive flashbacks. In the first of

In Ron Howard's *The Da Vinci Code* (2006), Audrey Tatou as Agent Sophie Neveu is juxtaposed with Da Vinci's Mary Magdalene at the Last Supper; their bodies form the V-shape or chalice, which signifies the "sacred feminine."

these (#5), Langdon rather incredulously narrates the "myth" that the First Crusade was in fact "orchestrated by a secret brotherhood, the Priory of Sion and their military arm, the Knights Templar" in order to locate "an artifact lost since the time of Christ, an artifact, it was said, the Church would kill to possess." The scene immediately prior to this one shows Silas bashing a hole in the floor of Saint-Sulpice and unearthing not the keystone but instead a stone-cold dead-end referencing Job 13: 11: "Thus far shalt thou come, but no farther." As Langdon's narrates in voice-over, the twelfth-century Templars also smash through a wall and find hidden there a confusing hoard of possible grails — cups and reliquaries, reminiscent of the scene from *Indiana Jones and the Last Crusade* — though they are subsequently shown kneeling before a sarcophagus, which, only much later in the film, is identified as that of Mary Magdalene. Langdon's skepticism is palpable throughout his narration of this Templar "myth." He is himself superimposed within the frame of a round table, decorated with the templar fleur-de-lis, on which the "keepers" of the grail lay their swords in a ritual expressing their promise to protect the "secret." Of course, Langdon's appearance within this scene ostensibly casts doubt upon its authenticity but in fact proleptically enlists Langdon himself as one of the keepers of the grail. The notion that the present perversely reconstructs the past is slowly, almost imperceptively overtaken by the idea that the past determines the destinies of the present, as Langdon is made the unwilling embodiment of the very "myth" of Templar guardianship that he relates.

The next flashback (#6), again with Langdon as a skeptical presence in the foreground, includes scenes from the trial of the Templars and the Church's fruitless search for the grail. As the published screenplay directs: "Soldiers burst into the ancient, buried chamber, now empty save for the outline of a sarcophagus in the dirt floor" (Goldsman, p. 86). This of course denotes the ancient remains of the Temple of Solomon, where the Templars reportedly unearthed the Holy Grail, yet the filmed version includes the further detail of the single red rose that occupies the place of the missing sarcophagus. This rose becomes the repeated symbol of Mary Magdalene, the trace in the film that marks both her absence and her continuing existence. Later, in flashback #17 we see her being interred in what is retrospectively identified (flashback #23) as the fifteenth-century Rosslyn Chapel, where Langdon and Sophie seek her out, only to discover once again her trace in the form of outlines in the dust and the single rose but also the grail documents that

Robert Langdon (Tom Hanks) pays his respects at the tomb of Mary Magdalene in Ron Howard's *The Da Vinci Code* (2006).

connect the long genealogical line between the rose Mary Magdalene and Sophie Neveu.

In what must be admitted is a clever if belabored bit of wordplay the sarcophagus of Mary is finally "found" by Langdon beneath the ancient "rose line" and the modern pyramids of the Louvre. This last shot of the film rather tidily unites the modern grail knight's personal quest for belief with the personal and historical flashbacks that have punctuated his quest. Like St. George in Book I of Spenser's *Faerie Queen*, Langdon's quest for the sacred feminine is baptized by a fall into a well, which both inspires and also impedes his search for that which is secret and profound. His prayer, hundreds of feet above the buried crypt of Mary Magdalene, brings him in belief to a secret but literal existence revealed by knowledge. Throughout the film, the sarcophagus is filmed in black and white, its absence signaled by the red rose. Here, the sarcophagus is actual (in living color) not virtual, and it is the rose alongside her golden tomb that has lost its hue, as the signifier loses its beauty in the presence of its signified. This (non)flashback is the fulfillment of all the previous flashbacks and brings the virtual past and the actual present together in what is meant to seem a sublime, synchronous unity. Langdon's veneration of Magdalene, the holy grail of the postmodern passion for the real, significantly shows him committing the gross error for which Mary herself was perhaps falsely accused: He seeks her in the tomb.

Chapter Notes

Chapter 1

1. See Harty (1999b) and Freud's *Beyond the Pleasure Principle* (ed. Gay, 1989, pp. 594–625): "I eventually realized that it was a game and that the only use he made of any of his toys was to play "gone" (*fort*) with them [....] The child had a wooden reel with a string tied round it [....] What he did was to hold the reel by the string and very skillfully throw it over the edge of the curtained cot, so that it disappeared into it, at the same time uttering his expressive 'o-o-o-o.' He then pulled the reel out of the curtained cot again by the string and hailed its reappearance with a joyful '*da*' ('there'). This, then, was the complete game — disappearance and return. As a rule one only witnessed the first act, which was repeated untiringly as a game itself, though there was no doubt that the greater pleasure was attached to the second act" (599).

2. See for instance: Keathley (2006); Rosenstone (1995a, 1995b, 2006); Toplin (2002); Landy (2001); Wyke (1997). Popular treatments of cinema history include: Sanello (2003); Carnes (1995) and MacDonald Fraser (1988). Two recent books on movie medievalism based on the reel/real distinction are Harty (1999) and Aberth (2003).

3. See Carolyn Dinshaw's provocative exploration of this exemplary phrase (1997, 116–63) and the somewhat different version of the essay (1999, 183–206). Dinshaw emphasizes the term's abjection of blacks and homosexuality and how the film itself fails to "get medieval" or fails to queer the white male heterosexual stereotype. I would rather emphasize how the "medieval" is both beyond representation and still a part of the Real in which moderns can participate.

4. Kevin J. Harty (1999, 188) is surely correct in noting that "what is being skewered here is not so much the legend of Arthur as previous cinematic treatments of that legend."

5. Such effects were almost a kind of signature of the French New Wave; see for instance the opening of Jean-Luc Godard's *Breathless* (1959).

6. See also the opening scene of Raymond Khoury's novel *The Last Templar* (2006) in which four Templar knights interrupt a gala opening at the Metropolitan Museum of Art. The appreciative crowd applauds, delighted with the publicity stunt, until the Templars begin killing the assembled rich of New York.

7. The no-exit ending was so frightening for the studio that, at first, it released a conventional happy ending in which the hero's soaring imagination and reality are made to coincide. Sam and Jill head for the hills where they live out their lives in pastoral bliss. Thus the history of the film's release replays its own Matrix-like presentation of transcendence as false consciousness: the film's real horror is hidden beneath the studio's imaginary projection, in which the couple flies off beyond the towering reach of the modern world. The studio's initial release thus "plugs in" its audience, offering up an escape from the Symbolic into the Imaginary that both demonstrates and masks its complicity in the same kind of ideological false consciousness the film itself so relentlessly lampoons. For the theatrical history of the film see especially Jack Matthews, *The Battle of Brazil* (1987) and his contribution to the *Criterion Collection* edition (1999) of the DVD, "The Battle of *Brazil*: A Video History."

8. Though it should also perhaps be noted that Perry, dressed in rag-tag knightly get-up does "get medieval on the ass" of a young

vigilante who attacks homeless people. He first incapacitates the knife-wielding assailant and then leaves him tied up in the junkyard, bent over with his pants pulled down, as an open invitation to the barbarian hoards who nightly scavenge the dump in search of treasure.

9. This reading of the pre–Civil War South is still quite apparent in the opening of *Gone with the Wind* (d. Victor Fleming 1939).

10. See for instance, Spearing 1985, Lerer 1993, Haydock 1994, and Pinti 1998.

11. From "honour corruption villainy holiness," in e. e. cummings (p. 661).

12. Note as well that the recent *The Da Vinci Code* (d. Ron Howard 2006) also begins with an academic public lecture on symbolic repetitions across times and cultures, complete with slides and intercut with shots of a violent murder, one in which the victim uses his own blood and body to reproduce Da Vinci's "Vitruvian Man." See chapter 7 below.

13. I would also note yet a final example of historical differences denied, which depends not on what a director does with the camera or in the editing room but rather on the subjects he chooses to place before his camera. Roberto Rossellini's *The Flowers of St. Francis* (1950) is cast for the most part with young monks from a Franciscan monastery, whose joy and naivety renders inconsequential any difference between them and the original followers of St. Francis. The film's neo-realist cinematography has also been seen as an attempt to reproduce the flattened dimensions of medieval art. As Peter Brunnette argues in an essay anthology included in the DVD package: "Throughout, we see the monks in almost total isolation from any (real) world, functioning, like medieval art, symbolically, as an emblematic community of the possible. The shots are continually flattened to eliminate perspective, thus putting man and nature on the same level and suggesting the two-dimensionality of the highly symbolic space of medieval art, before the conquest of realistic Renaissance perspective, which entails an entirely different kind of worldview. This pictorial flattening creates a kind of minimalist *paysage moralisé* out of the monk's simple community, a stylized, antirealistic locus of genuine Christian kindness and joy" (*Roberto Rossellini's The Flowers of St. Francis*, Criterion Collection DVD, 2005, p.7).

14. For a concise discussion of these categories upon which my discussion relies see Myers, pp. 56–61.

15. For a wide-ranging and entertaining introduction to the phenomenon see Ewen and Ewen (2006).

16. *Beowulf* predicts that even though he has killed the two supernatural embodiments of feuding, feud itself has an uncanny immortality passed down through generations: "Oft seldan haer/ aefter leod-hryre lytel hwile / bon-gar bugeth" (lines 2029b-2031a) and then goes on to imagine a young retainer being goaded into breaking a pledge of peace by taking revenge for the death of his father (lines 2046-2066).

17. See Derrida (1987). The postcard that excites Derrida's imagination is itself an example of a medieval misrecognition — even the postmodern deconstruction of the oral/written binary is sourced as medieval. The illustration in the Bodleian Library MS Ashmole 304 of Matthew of Paris's *Prognostica Socratii Basilei*, which shows Plato dictating to Socrates, is not simply an error of identification but an uncanny anticipation (within a fortune-telling book) of Derrida's own project. Of course movies work in this way as well, displacing or reversing their dependence on a literary source, particularly for the thousands who read novels or histories after seeing filmic adaptations. Jean-Jacques Annaud dubs his film a "palimpsest of Umberto Eco's novel," which thereby positions itself as logically prior to the novel, as something beneath or always already implicit beneath it. This transposition of source and adaptation is repeatedly reflected in paperback book covers that capitalize on films by reproducing shots from the film adaptation of it, encouraging readers to view the book as an adaptation of the film.

18. See Eco's essay "The Frames of Comic Freedom" in Sebeok (1984) and also Theresa Colletti's thoughtful discussion of the distinction between Bakhtin's comedy and Eco's valoration of humor (pp. 139–41).

19. Directors often cite attention to detail in the reproduction of objects, as evidence of a film's historical authenticity. For a nineteenth-century version of this see Kathleen Biddick's (1998, 36–57) intriguing discussion of the campaign of William Morris to prevent restorers of historical buildings from using the copies of Gothic ornaments that his company produced.

Chapter 2

1. The reference is to T.S. Eliot's "The Hollow Men," see in particular Part V:

Between the idea
And the reality
Between the motion
And the act
Falls the Shadow
  For thine is the Kingdom

Between the conception
And the creation
Between the emotion
And the response
Falls the Shadow
  Life is very long

Between the desire
And the spasm
Between the potency
And the existence
Between the essence
And the descent
Falls the Shadow
  For Thine is the Kingdom

2. See Cowie's discussion of Bergman's original play and the discussion in Bragg (pp. 27–36).

3. For an analysis of the forged legend of Kriakutnyi's 1731 flight and its mobilization as Soviet propaganda during the era of *Sputnik*, see Robert Bird's entertaining discussion (pp. 18–22). On the themes of falling and flying in Tarkovsky's films, see Johnson and Petrie (p. 219).

4. See "Ane Ballet of the Fenyit Freir of Tungland" in Dunbar (ed. Kinsley 1979, 161–64).

5. Albert Laffay, "Les grands thèmes de l'écran," *La Revue du Cinéma* 2, no. 12 (1948): 8, quoted in Kracauer (1960, 78). Tarkovsky criticizes the "montage cinema" of Eisenstein on much the same grounds, because it does "not allow the film to continue beyond the edge of the screen" but instead presents riddles with one-word solutions (Tarkovsky 1986, p. 118).

6. I take this to be a clear example of what might be called the ethical component in Tarkovsky's famous notion of "imprinted time." In *Sculpting Time*, he insists "I am interested in the inner, moral qualities essentially inherent in time itself [....] Given any effect, we constantly go back to its sources, its causes — in other words we could be said to be turning time back through conscience. Cause and effect may, in a moral sense, be linked retroactively; and then a person does, as it were, return his past" (pp. 58–59).

7. Nikos Kazantzakis's *The Last Temptation of Christ* was published in 1951; Martin Scorsese's film of the same name was released in 1988.

8. Just as in *Sansho the Bailiff* (d. Mizoguchi 1954), released in the following year, the boat fragments families and hints at the journey that all must take. Mori Ogai upon whose novel this latter film was based has one of the kidnappers leave the children's frantic mother with these parting words of cold comfort indeed: "Any boat you board is the ship of the Buddha, bound for some Other Shore" (qtd. in Andrew and Cavanaugh. p. 55).

9. A fine introduction to the institution of the samurai class is Jansen, ed. For what its author calls "the taming of the samurai," see Ikegami.

10. See Mitsuhiro Yoshimoto's contention: "Instead of forming a simple dichotomy, illusion and reality are often mutually implicated. *Kagemusha* highlights the ambivalent interaction of reality and image by refusing to reduce the relationship of Shingen and the thief to that of original and copy" (p. 350).

11. In Michael Crichton's novel, Chris Hughes is Edward Johnston's graduate student, not his son. The change highlights the genealogical nature of the recovery of the past in the film.

Chapter 3

1. The term is Frederick Jameson's (1991) and refers to the idea that no history exists independently of its expression in textual form. In cinema the term may be used to suggest that no representation of an historical Middle Ages can be independent of earlier film representations.

2. "The whole life of those societies in which modern conditions of production prevail presents itself as an immense accumulation of spectacles. All that once was directly lived has become mere representation" (Debord, p. 12).

3. McHale (1987) maintains that postmodernism is philosophically centered on questions of ontology, as opposed to the epistemological concerns of modernism.

4. In fact John Gardner's approach to the historical Chaucer (that is both the medieval individual and his fictions about the past) could well serve as an epigraph to Helgeland's movie. "We have no choice but to make up Chaucer's life as if his story were a novel, by the play of fancy on the lost world's dust and scrapings. So Chaucer himself made up the

classical age, dressed up young Troilus in crusader's armor and decorated legendary Theseus' Athens with battlemented towers, wide jousting grounds, and sunny English gardens" (p. 3).

5. Rebecca A. Umland and Samuel J. Umland (pp. 94–100) survey reaction to the film and provide a lukewarm defense. Aberth (p. 16) is more categorical: "Will Hollywood never learn?"

6. See, for instance, William Paden's praise of Bergman's *Seventh Seal*: "Bergman's film presents... a case in which Bergman has reconstituted the past more faithfully than available traces gave him any apparent means to do.... Bergman produced an image of the Middle Ages more faithful than he can have known" (p. 288).

7. For a general introduction to some of the issues involved see Patrick Phillips (pp. 161–208).

8. The classic discussion of auteurism is Sergei Eisenstein (1957). A cogent overview of the challenges to and adaptations of the approach is available in Robert Stam (2000, pp. 83–88 and 123–85).

9. Jerry Zucker's credits in film parodies include: *The Kentucky Fried Movie* (1977, codirector and cowriter), *Top Secret* (1984, cowriter and codirector), *Ruthless People* (1986, codirector), *Naked Gun: From the Files of Police Squad* (1988, cowriter), and *Naked Gun: The Smell of Fear* (1991, cowriter). For a systematic analysis of the importance of parody in cinema and in theoretical discussions of film, see Harries (2001).

10. I owe this suggestion to Tom Shippey.

11. The term "interpellation" is Althusser's and is commonly used in film studies to signal the ways in which cultural practices implicate audiences and construct the subject positions from which audiences will view a film. See Stam (2000, p. 134): "Ideology operates through what Althusser calls 'interpellation.' Originally derived from French legislative procedure, the term 'interpellation' evokes the social structures and practices which 'hail' individuals, endowing them with a social identity and constructing them as subjects who unthinkingly accept their role within the system of production relations."

12. Blind Hary in Book VII of the Wallace has the episode occur in 1297 when Wallace was approximately 20 years old. His father and brother are not mentioned among the dead. See *Hary's Wallace*, ed. McDiarmid (pp. 78–123). The changes in the legend were introduced by Randall Wallace's novel, *Braveheart* (1995).

13. It is interesting to note that the "novelization" of the film (which perhaps reflects the original screenplay) has Lancelot 19 years old at the time of the attack of the warlords when his pregnant wife and parents are killed. The film, however, clearly shows him witnessing their immolation as a young boy of 11 or 12.

14. See the engaging discussion of this scene in Jacqueline Jenkins (pp. 84–85) in which Lancelot's hair shaking signifies a "new, specifically American, triumphant freedom."

15. Phallic jokes could almost be called a visual signature of the Zucker brothers' film parodies. In *Naked Gun 2 & ½* the lovemaking scene between Lt. Drebin (Leslie Nielsen) and Jane (Priscilla Presley) climaxes with a comic montage of fifteen phallic jokes, including a missile launch, a foot-long hot dog, and the obligatory reference to Hitchcock of a train entering a tunnel.

16. I have represented the entries as they are in the *Oxford Latin Dictionary* but not in their entirety (Glare, pp. 1363–64).

17. Roman Jakobsen (p. 78) suggested that close-ups are akin to the rhetorical figure of synecdoche and equated the kind of editing technique being employed here (which he calls "superimposed dissolves") with similes. In essence, Zucker's extensive employment of the trope of the burning eye, as we shall see, moves from a rather straightforward simile to a broader, political metaphor. Note too that the trope of the burning eye as synecdoche and metaphor is also employed in Peter Jackson's *Lord of the Rings* trilogy in a more extensive way to image Sauron's disembodied, evil eye. See Jakobsen (1956, 78).

18. The lesson of a charitable love triumphing over selfishness is also the main theme of Zucker's next film, *My Best Friend's Wedding* (producer, 1997). However, we should also note that Malory's Mellyagaunce episode on which the screenplay is loosely based does celebrate a form of patient love: "But nowadayes men can nat love sevennyght but they muste all their desyres. That love may nat endure by reson, for where they bethe sone accorded and hasty, heete sone keelyth. And ryght so fareth love nowadayes, sone hote and sone colde. Thys ys no stabylyté. But the olde love was nat so. For men and women coude love togydirs seven yerys, and no lycoures lustis was betweyxte them, and than was love trouthe and faythefulnes. And so in lyke wyse was used such love in kynge Arthurs dayes" (ed. Vinaver, pp. 1120–21).

19. For a range of critical analyses of the ideologies of the war, see Renson (1993). Perhaps the supreme irony of Arthur's sentiments is their reappearance almost verbatim in George H. Bush's National Security Strategy on September 20, 2002, which assured us, as Arthur did Camelot, that there is "a single sustainable model for national success" that is "right and true for every person in every society" and that "these principles are right and true for all people everywhere."

20. For a discussion of Chaucer's use of this concept and its relationship to literary and social conventions, see Saul (pp. 41–58).

21. One particularly salutary effect of postmodern metafiction is to defamiliarize the prior textualization of historical representation. It is difficult to listen to Helgeland's soundtrack without pondering why the "classical" music of nineteenth-century Germany now seems to us so natural an accompaniment to representations of the Middle Ages.

22. If such a cultural translation from Chaucer's pun to an analogous, modern one is indeed what the screenplay intends, this updating of medieval allegory is cleverly embedded within the film's time scheme. The young Chaucer of the film has, at this point, written only *The Book of the Duchess*. Indeed the whole interview between Jocelyn and William could profitably be compared to Chaucer's earliest dream vision.

23. The reference is, of course, to Paul Strohm's superb *Social Chaucer* (1989).

24. See Derek Pearsall's reflections on Chaucer biographies in *The Life of Chaucer: A Critical Biography* (pp. 1–8). Pearsall emphasizes how bias determines the kind of Chaucer biographers create, from English "snobbery," which presses "the Lancastrian connection," to the American Horatio Alger Chaucer to the general consensus that Chaucer was "a decent sort of fellow." Choosing a "differently prejudiced view," Pearsall dares to imagine Chaucer's life "as that of a time-serving opportunist and placeman, who pictured his own pliability in all that he saw. He might be seen as one who had outlived the idealisms of chivalry and faith but found nothing to fill the vacuum that they left; who exposed the meretriciousness of institutional religion, but retreated into its most inflexible dogma when his humanity was exhausted; who recognized no central social value in law and other forms of contract, but saw only what was hollow and saleable; who made many generous gestures towards women, but returned generally to a conventional misogyny; who viewed life in a spirit of pessimism interspersed with irrepressible hilarity" (p. 8). The Pearsall prejudice has certainly taken hold in contemporary scholarship, and while it is considerably darker than Helgeland's portrait, it is easy to see the same Chaucer in both. In Helgeland's 20-something Chaucer are the seeds of Pearsall's 50-something Chaucer.

25. These portraits have been widely disseminated across a wealth of media. For a concise introduction to the portraits, see Pearsall (pp. 285–305).

26. The notion of fiction as personal revenge is central to the poetics of the *Canterbury Tales* themselves (e.g., "The Reeve's Tale") and to fifteenth-century Chaucerianism. Robert Henryson's *The Testament of Cresseid* revisits Chaucer's *Troilus* to punish the wayward Cresseid with a venereal disease, and the anonymous *Canterbury Interlude* makes Chaucer's Pardoner the butt of fabliau justice once he arrives in Canterbury. In this way Helgeland's Chaucer "quits" the Pardoner with a literary castration. See: Fox, ed., *The Poems of Robert Henryson* (1981) and Bowers, ed., *The Canterbury Tales: Fifteenth Century Continuations and Additions* (1992). On fifteenth-century readers revenging themselves on Chaucer's fictions, see Haydock, "Remaking Chaucer" (1994).

Chapter 4

1. On Trojan narratives as nation-making gestures see Federico, MacDougall, Geary, and Haydock (2006).

2. See Dinshaw: "Now it may well be that these two perspectives on the Middle Ages — seen as a period that produces our modernity and as a period quite separate and different from our own — are conceptually coherent, part of a whole genealogical approach to the modern subject. The demonstration of modern contingency traces the forces that produce us and at the same time suggests that we can be different in the future because we were not always like this" (1998, 200). See also Woods.

3. For me the most cogent discussion of the development of film technologies is Cook (p. 1–27).

4. The romantic projection of nationalism into a medieval past is a definitive feature of Jules Michelet's mid-nineteenth century study of Joan. For Michelet, "Joan created

France, the *Patrie*." As Susan Dunn maintains: "Michelet transformed the monarchist myth of the king as the incarnation of the State into the myth of Jeanne d'Arc as the incarnation of the sovereign French people" (qtd. in Meltzer, p. 226).

5. My alteration of the *fons et origo* formula to *fons et figura* attempts to formulate the diachronic as well as the synchronic nature of movie medievalism's apprehensive past: the source and distant figuration of contemporary institutions, conflicts, characters, and so forth. On *figura*, see Auerbach.

6. While neither author discusses Besson's film, both provide abundant examples of the kind of voracious expropriation I'm alluding to here. For example, Blaetz's book recalls the Boston premiere of Cecil B. DeMille's *Joan the Woman* (1916), where Geraldine Farrar "wrapped herself in the American flag to sing the National Anthem" (55). Astell (p. 80) reminds us that the fictional narrator for Twain's novel is writing down his "personal recollections" in 1492, more than fifty years after the events he describes but exactly coincident with the European discovery of America.

7. I am much indebted here to Meltzer (especially, p. 197). Generally, Meltzer uses Joan as a point of rendezvous to contemplate Western theories of subjectivity up to and including the very denial of the individual in much postmodernist thought.

8. In a provocative essay that even manages to dust off Julian Jaynes's *The Origins of Consciousness in the Breakdown of the Bicameral Mind*, Gwendolyn Morgan judges this scene "evidence of its (the film's) feminist undercurrents" (p. 41). Though Morgan has little sympathy for such "re-creations," which "ignore the fundamental medieval reality of Joan as a woman of unshakable faith in her personal and profound experience of Christianity" (p. 39). Meltzer (pp. 157, 237) compares Joan's voices to Socrates' daemon and also goes on to suggest the connection of Jaynes's theory of the bicameral mind with the nature of Joan's "voices."

9. The classic study of the *topos* is by Magoun. The *topos* is present too in Christine de Pisan's taunt of the English in the Ditié de Jehanne d'Arc, lines 318–20: "You'll have to beat your drums elsewhere if you do not want to taste death like your companions whom the wolves may well devour, for they lie dead in the fields." For the original, see Kennedy and Varty. Translation is quoted from Blumenfeld-Kosinski (p. 258). In Besson's montage the

topos, which is well-established in Anglo-Saxon and Germanic poetry, unsurprisingly associates the wolves with the English.

10. Jules Michelet, *Joan of Arc* (p. 19), notes that contemporary sources compare the eighteen-year-old Joan to a "poor little shepherdess" in her first appearance before the dauphin. This volume seems to have been very influential in Besson's reconstruction of her early life. The first "epoch" of Cecil B. DeMille's *Joan the Woman* (1916) likewise portrays Joan as a shepherdess. See Robin Blaetz, *Visions of the Maid* (pp. 47–64).

11. As Anke Bernau remarks: "The virginal performance is, however, *always* dependent on being watched and *read*, and these acts shape virginity even while virginity also transmits to the viewer types of social knowledge" (p. 104).

12. Incidentally the screenplay includes a scene much later (not included in the cut of the film released in theaters or on the DVD) in which Blackbeard reappears, enters Joan's prison cell, and tries to rape her.

13. In a provocative forthcoming essay, Susan Hayward highlights the flexibility of gender in the Joan myth and traces Joan's camp performance of androgyny in Besson's film: "Small wonder she has to be burnt for playing on the phallic economy and exposing it for what it is.... Jeanne is a myth adrift in culture, and can be taken and remodeled to suit our own desire, either as camp or as lesbian, just as much as she is constantly remodeled to suit political desire and purpose. The powerful message of Besson's film remains, therefore, that in appropriating camp Besson's Jeanne problematizes identity politics; she extends the limited possibilities of the subject and, by circumscribing the overtly simplistic gender divide, gives us a knowing link in which we can all delight." See "Jeanne d'Arc: High Epic Style and Politicising Camp," in *Luc Besson: Filmmaker as Bard*, eds. S. Hayward and P. Powrie (Manchester University Press, forthcoming). My thanks to Professor Hayward for allowing me to see an advance copy of this essay. For me, Joan's queering of the siege engine, her gendered *bricolage* as I've dubbed it, is an enormous example of Joan's "playing on the phallic economy" and exposes the danger that androgyny poses in such an economy. The siege engine too is androgynous; its reversibility exposes the vulnerability of man's feminine side quite literally!

14. In the most intriguing study of the trial documents I have read Karen Sullivan reminds us that the identification of Joan's voices as Sts.

Michael, Catherine and Margaret is confined to the trial itself and to writers who were influenced by what was said at the trial. Sullivan suggests that these specific identifications may have been produced by the judges' questions. Her argument is plausible, so much so in fact that it should prevent us from criticizing Besson for failing to include them in his film. See Sullivan (pp. 21–41). Françoise Metzer suggests that the splitting up and then variously "embodying" what is at first only a single, unidentified voice in the trial transcripts represents Joan's attempt to "placate her captors and thus escape their final agenda" (p. 157n58). Indeed, analysis of this facet of the trial by Sullivan and Meltzer suggests an ambivalent heroine not so far from Besson's, who is neither "a diabolical self-creator" nor "a blessed medium of a transcendent will" (Sullivan, p. 60).

15. Sullivan, *Interrogation* (p. 126) quotes Pierre Maurice warning Joan against "enemies of God transforming themselves sometimes into the appearance of Christ, angels, saints...."

16. The history of Joan of Arc that seems most to have inspired her presentation in the film is the romantic vision of Jules Michelet. See, for instance, his speculations on the mixture of sanctity and bloodlust, so important a characteristic of Besson's Joan: "War, saintliness, two contradictory terms; it seems that saintliness is the very opposite of war, that it implies charity and peace. But how could a young and valiant heart be engaged in warfare without yielding to the bloodthirsty intoxication of combat and victory?" (p. 51).

17. While there is not space here to work out the argument in detail, I believe that Besson's construction of Joan is ultimately a conservative one, indebted to the theology of Saint Josemaria Escrivá and the personal prelature granted to his order of Opus Dei by John Paul II. Besson is rumored to belong to the order, though their secrecy makes it difficult to confirm this. John Aberth (p. 257) claims that Besson is a member (though he doesn't say of what standing) and suggests that scenes such as Joan's tabooed Eucharist and the interrogation of her "Conscience" reflect Besson's "agenda" in this film. Numerous details that Besson invents for Joan seem to derive from the golden legend of Josemaria. For instance, the film's first scene, in which Joan confesses that she stole her father's shoes to give to a poor monk whom she saw walking barefoot, perhaps reprises St. Josemaria's intimations of

love when he saw footprints in the snow made by a barefoot monk. Escrivá's final confirmation of his mission came in Madrid on October 2, 1928, the Feast of the Guardian Angels, when he interpreted the bells of Our Lady of the Angels as a personal calling to do Opus Dei. Likewise, the young Joan hears church bells calling her name, "Jeanne, Jeanne." Guardian Angels went on to play a crucial role in Josemaria's theology, just as they do in the personal spirituality Besson invents for Joan. A crucial part of Josemaria's teachings concerns his meditations on simple wooden crosses, like the one repeatedly highlighted in the film. For example, his *vademecum, El Camino*, or *The Way* exhorts: "When you see a wooden Cross, alone, uncared for, and of no value ... and without its Crucified, don't forget that that Cross is your Cross: the Cross of each day, the hidden Cross, without splendor or consolation ..., the Cross which is awaiting the Crucified it lacks: and that Crucified must be you" (Point 178).The cross as a call to martyrdom is plainly evoked in *The Messenger* when, during the rape of Catherine, her crude wooden cross falls to the ground, and the camera follows its fall, pointing its significance. Joan later retrieves this cross and it is her most prized possession, the only thing she asks Cauchon to return to her after her capture. When it is not returned she uses her chains to scratch a makeshift cross on the stonewall of her cell — a painful gesture that connects her own suffering to Christ's sacrifice. This would also seem to explain the odd syllogism that the Conscience figure represents: If her Conscience is necessarily Joan herself, and if Conscience is also Christ, then Joan is Christ. As Josemaria explains in one of his meditations: "to carry the cross is to identify oneself with Christ, to be Christ, and therefore to be the son (sic) of God." Perhaps the most crucial connection is the founder's conflation of patriotism and faith. Point 525 of *The Way* begins: "To be 'Catholic' means to love your country and to be second to none in that love." Certainly Joan's unification of faith and patriotism qualifies as this severe form of Catholicism. Obviously, Opus Dei, with its regime of mandatory weekly confession, its championing of a stern "examination of conscience," and its trust in uncompromising Guardian Angels bears a strong resemblance to Joan's hectoring but finally merciful confessor in *The Messenger*. As a warrior actively participating in the violence and complexity of the real world, as a famous figure of lay celibacy and lay sanctity, and as a nationalistic martyr to a patriotic cause, Joan of Arc makes an ideal representative of the order's philosophy and the charisma of its worldly chrism. One of Josemaria's most controversial exhortations: "Let us bless pain. Love pain. Sanctify pain ... Glorify pain." certainly appears to be advice well and seriously taken by Besson, as well as by Mel Gibson in his *Braveheart* and *Passion of the Christ*.

18. Incidentally, concerning Morgan's point ("Modern Mystics, Medieval Saints") about the "rational atheism" of equating Christ with conscience, John Paul II explicitly justifies the connection of conscience with Christ in quoting from the papal encyclical *Gaudium et spes*: "Conscience is the most secret core and sanctuary of man (sic), where he finds himself alone with God, whose voice can be heard in his innermost being" (p. 140). Members of Opus Dei agree to follow a "plan of life," known in English as "the norms." Among the requirements is "a daily examination of conscience." See Allen, *Opus Dei* (p. 30).

19. Ron Maxwell has been engaged in a Joan of Arc project for more than a decade, beset by problems in obtaining funding. His review, "*The Messenger:* Dumbed Down Dame, Is It Poetic License to Kill?", criticizes the lack of historical fidelity in Besson's film. Maxwell's indignation is palpable, though it perhaps derives at least in part from his own frustrations. His screenplay, a portion of which was presented at "Getting Medieval on the Movies" (a conference organized by Richard Burt at the University of Florida in September, 2005), seems to confuse historical truth with melodrama. One does hope to see this film get made (and to see the Mighty Aphrodite Mira Sorvino as the Maid), but one also fails to see how Maxwell's melodrama is a lens any less convex than Besson's postmodernism.

20. Crusading rhetoric and ambitions are a well-documented part of Joan's calling, from the early "Letter aux Anglais" through her heresy trial transcripts. Christine de Pisan particularly emphasizes this point in *Le Ditié de Jehanne d'Arc*. See Fraioli (p. 119): "The greatest validation of the French offensive, however, comes from the prospect of a crusade and the attainment of universal peace. In the *Lettre*, the promise that Paris will be retaken is presented as the will of God, occurring in order that the French proceed to the more grandiose responsibility of preserving the faith. For Christine, this casts even the reconquest of Paris as part of the crusade phenom-enon, since Christian unity is a prerequisite for confronting the Saracens."

21. I have greatly benefited from the comments of Richard Burt and Thomas Shippey on earlier versions of this chapter. My sincerest thanks to them both.

Chapter 5

1. As this book was being readied for submission to the publisher I came upon Arthur Lindley's superb essay "Once, Present and Future Kings: *Kingdom of Heaven* and the Multitemporality of Medieval Film." Lindley (pp. 17–20) records many of the same reactions I discuss below. His work on what he calls the "multitemporality" of medieval film (see the series of his essays he references [p. 28n12]) clearly has interesting parallels with my use of the time-image.

2. One could cite many examples of this kind of discourse, perhaps the most salient is Daniel Robinson's piece in *Commentary* (July-August 2005), which champions recent interpretations of the Crusades by Cambridge historians and quite plainly connects modern failures to defend the Crusades with the failing strategies of intervention in the Middle East: "When Westerners today condemn the Crusades, they send a coded message both to Israel and to the Muslim world. The message says that just as these Westerners, and especially the Christians among them, are not ready to defend their own ancestors, so they are unprepared to lift a finger to defend the Jewish state, still less to defend the invasion and occupation of Iraq [....] The Crusades are an organic part of Western history. They are also a *casus belli*, and will remain so for as long as its suits the Islamists. On the cultural front of that war, one side has gone disastrously far in the direction of unilateral disarmament."

3. For a good example of this, see the rabble-rousing, bestselling book by Robert Spencer. His discussion of *Kingdom of Heaven* (p. 171–74) cites the negative reactions to the film by Crusade scholars like Jonathan Riley-Smith and Jonathan Philips. Each chapter in this book contains balloon comparisons, showing how Christ is better than Mahammed.

4. My notion of the paracinema is obviously indebted to Gérard Genette's (1997) work on the "paratext." It is also inspired by Richard Burt's (2007) thoughtful application of

Genette's concept to movie medievalism in the recent volume of *Exemplaria* 19.2 (2007) on which we served together as "co-guest editors."

5. By "remediation" here I understand something like a *mise-en-abyme* of representations that radiate outward from the kernel of the "real" event and which filter and construct our perception of history. See Bolter and Grusin (pp. 146–59). Indeed, a dominant theme of this chapter is that the reactions of academics to *Kingdom of Heaven* were informed by their politics and that these reactions are themselves remediated (taken into and transformed) in a variety of ways in successive versions of the film.

6. The distinction being made here is similar to that between "intrinsic" and "imposed" allegory.

7. This is perhaps most easily seen in the deployment in the West of the terms "crusade" and "jihad." The use of the term "crusade" to characterize Western interventions in the Middle East has been widely criticized by liberals and conservatives alike. While "jihad" is routinely employed by all sides in current conflicts, though obviously for different reasons, to denote a fundamental continuity between medieval and modern Holy Wars. As Ganim points out in *Medievalism and Orientalism*, the term "medieval" has come to serve as a chronotope in which the past is quite literally *an other* country, reflected in "negative rhetorical implications, from 'medieval justice' to the 'medieval' social conditions and practices in, most revealingly, Islamic states" (p. 4). Westerners can on occasion "get medieval," while Islamic fundamentalists are imagined to be "still medieval." For a conservative, polemical view of the essential unity of Islam over the course of its history since the times of the Prophet Muhammed, see Spencer; for an almost equally polemical argument about the ideology of Holy War being alive and well in the contemporary West, see Tariq Ali. A more disinterested, though already dated, popular account of the analogies between medieval crusades and modern wars in the Gulf is that by Karen Armstrong.

8. Walter Scott's *Tales of the Crusaders* is comprised of *Ivanhoe*, *The Betrothed*, and *The Talisman*. See also Steven Runciman, *A History of the Crusades*, as well as Terry Jones, *Chaucer's Knight* and his four-part documentary, *The Crusades* (1995), produced by the BBC.

9. Quoted in Bob Thompson, "Hollywood on Crusade," *Washington Post*, May 1, 2005. In its hyperbolic anti-medievalism Riley-Smith's condemnation recalls Twain's judgment on Scott's nineteenth-century namesake: "Sir Walter had so large a hand in making Southern character [...] that he is in great measure responsible for the (Civil) war" (qtd. in Hayden, p. 538).

10. See, for instance, Phillips, *The Fourth Crusade and the Sack of Constantinople*; Carole Hillenbrand, *The Crusades: Islamic Perspectives*; Jonathan Riley-Smith, *The Crusades: A History*; and Riley-Smith, ed., *The Oxford History of the Crusades*. Phillips was much more balanced in his evaluation of the film, calling the battle scenes "visually stunning" but rankling a bit at Scott's pre-preview lecture that highlighted the research undertaken for the film (on which see below). Hillenbrand in an interview given to the BBC is reported as having said that "film represents an attempt to grapple with serious issues" and finds nothing amiss in its depiction of mutual respect and cooperation between Muslims and Franks — a particular point of contention for Riley-Smith. For Philips's remarks, see Thompson, "Hollywood on Crusade"; for those of Hillenbrand, see Jonathan Marcus, "A Small Matter of Crusader History."

11. The Old Dominion essay is available online in "The National Review" under the title "Jihad Crusaders: What an Osama bin Laden Means by 'Crusade.'"

12. As Riley-Smith goes on to explain: "They felt that they had beaten the crusaders comprehensively.... But as they began to take an interest in the historical parallels between contemporary and medieval Christian-Muslim interaction, they were confronted with Western rhetoric portraying contemporary empire builders as quasi-crusaders returning to complete the work their ancestors had begun.... This struck a chord in Arab nationalism."

13. See especially Said, *Orientalism* and *Culture and Imperialism*. While Said's basic point about the mutual implication of imperialism and representation is unassailable, his credentials as a scholar have been devastatingly questioned by many. See, for instance, Bernard Lewis (p. 99–118).

14. Sir Edmund Allenby is reported to have said upon entering Jerusalem in 1917: "Today the wars of the Crusaders are completed." General Henri Gouraud, kicking Saladin's tomb in 1920 Damascus was even more provocative in calling forth a very potent ghost: "Awake, Saladin, we have returned." Also see the widely reproduced *Punch* cartoon

of Allenby dressed as Richard I gazing down upon Jerusalem from a mountaintop.

15. The *National Review* soon after Bush's speech ran a cover depicting Bush in a crusader's tunic. In its parody of the *Punch* cartoon's parody of Allenby (see previous note) the illustration demonstrates an appreciation for what Richard Burt would call the "schlock" of medievalism; Middle Eastern reactions to the speech were more in line with the "shock" variety of medievalism — on which see Kathleen Biddick's definition of medievalism as "an abiding historical trauma" (p. 3).

16. Pope Urban II George Bush II is not, but both leaders exaggerated the evidence in calling their crusades. While Bush ultimately drew back from the connotations of his remarks, the identification of the Taliban and al-Qaeda with the "medieval" only intensified. See Holsinger (2007).

17. Or so he dubs them in the article entitled "Religious Warriors: Reinterpreting the Crusades" (1995). For Riley-Smith the most recent proper historical analogy to the Crusades is not contemporary wars in the Gulf but rather liberation theology and its role in struggles for liberation in Latin America.

18. An interesting footnote to the prediction that the film would fuel Islamic hatred comes from a report by the journalist Robert Fisk who watched it in Beirut, Lebanon: "After Balian has surrendered Jerusalem, Saladin enters the city and finds a crucifix lying on the floor of a church, knocked off during the three-day siege. And he carefully picks up the cross and places it reverently back on the altar. At this point the audience rose to their feet and clapped and shouted their appreciation. They loved the gesture of honour. They wanted Islam to be merciful as well as strong. And they roared their approval above the soundtrack of the film."

19. Hillenbrand questions the veracity of this story on the basis that Usama claims in other places that he does not understand the language of the Franks. This may be overscrupulous, deep and abiding friendships do grow between people who don't understand one another's language. One who doesn't speak Spanish, for instance, can quickly learn the meaning of *mi amigo* or *mi hermanito* without being able to follow a conversation or read a page of Spanish.

20. Of course, the model for the film as well as the actual location of many of its scenes is the formerly Muslim Spain and Morocco (also used in *Gladiator*). The *convivenzia*

depicted in the film found its most impressive and lasting expression in the Spanish Middle Ages. See María Rosa Menocal's fascinating reconstruction of the intellectual culture of Al-Andalus in *The Ornament of the World*.

21. See the comments of Amin Maalouf, author of *The Crusades through Arab Eyes*, who reminded all: "It does not do any good to distort history, even if you believe you are distorting it in a good way. Cruelty was not on one side but on all" (qtd. in Edwardes).

22. For a synopsis of the legal case, see Waxman.

23. Reston makes the intellectual patronage of his own view of period abundantly clear when he says in an interview with Sharon Waxman: "I suppose there is a legal argument that he (i.e., Monahan) had it in mind all along, that they knew about Balian of Ibelin, that he got it from somewhere else, reading 1950s Cambridge, England, stodgy old histories. But I don't think so." One suspects that Reston would like to say that what was stolen from him is his attitude toward his materials, but of course that's impossible since his attitude is largely that of Steven Runciman's "1950s Cambridge, England, stodgy old history."

24. In *The Talisman* (p. 29), Sir Kenneth responds to his adversary's boasts about the speed and agility of his Arabian stallion with a droll conundrum to the effect that his horse has galloped across a great lake without ever getting his hooves wet.

25. Many reviewers were struck by Bloom's frailty, noting that Russell Crowe was the first to be offered the part. But the casting perhaps also reflects the film's cinematic tradition. Bloom's characterization descends from Peter O'Toole's portrayal of Lawrence of Arabia in David Lean's 1962 Academy Award winning masterpiece. See Allen, *The Medievalism of Lawrence of Arabia*.

26. The character is based on the real figure Imad ad-Din, secretary to Nur ad-Din and later to Saladin, he was also a perhaps too eloquent poet and historian. For a short biography and selections from his works, see Gabrielli. Imad is erroneously listed in the credits to the theatrical release and the first DVD as Nasir, a mistake duly recorded and corrected in the "Director's Cut."

27. In an extended scene in the film, Balian uses his engineering know-how to dig a well and irrigate Ibelin. Sibylla tells him that "you have been given a desert and it seems you will build a New Jerusalem here." Seeing Balian

primarily as an engineer, both in war and in peace, puts a particularly American face and an American spin on wars as the leading edge of humanitarian and technological advancements in the Middle East.

28. Interestingly, the Jerusalem set was built in two parts, its nether side doubling as Balian's castle at Ibelin.

29. See Ganim's chapter "The Middle Ages as Genre," (pp. 17–56), which suggests medieval romance as a kind of master-discourse which ultimately absorbs medieval studies itself, which "first imagines the Middle Ages as a romance, and then gradually becomes a species of romance itself" (18). See further Heng's superb *Empire of Magic: Medieval Romance and the Politics of Cultural Fantasy*. The work of Ganim and Heng first appeared in the ground-breaking anthology edited by Jeffrey Jerome Cohen, *The Postcolonial Middle Ages*.

30. See Gablik and Foucault (1982). These images are also widely available on the internet.

31. See Mitchell's discussion of the role of the imagetext in modern theoretical debates in the introduction to *Picture Theory* (pp. 1–10), and more generally the evolution of his thinking about the "imagetext" from *Iconology: Image, Text, Ideology* (1986) through *Pictorial Theory* to *What Do Pictures Want?* (2005), especially the first chapter: "Vital Signs/ Cloning Terror" (pp. 5–27).

32. Indeed, it is in his interactions with Balian that Saladin appears in his most generous and courtly light. For descriptions of their negotiations, see Edbury as well as Gabrielli (pp. 87–254).

33. The trope is as old as modern medieval studies. Ganim notes J. M. Kemble's nineteenth-century comparisons between Anglo-Saxon and modern villages in India: "Where the English were in the Middle Ages, so was India today" (p. 8).

34. These remarks are quoted in the EG from an interview given by Monahan in which he responded to Reston's charges.

35. Massoud no doubt refers to the 1963 film *Saladin* by Youssef Chahine.

36. See especially the "Introduction" to *Black Skin/White Masks* by Homi K. Bhabha (1986, pp. 110–12). I am particularly dependent here on Bhabha's chapter "Interrogating Identity" in *The Location of Culture* (1994, pp. 57–93).

37. From the biography of Saladin written by Bahá al-Din Ibn Shaddâd (1145–1234).

38. For a discussion of the *memento mori* theme in Bergman and Besson, see chapters 2 and 4.

39. A direct quotation of the two shots in Bergman's *Seventh Seal*, discussed in chapter 2.

40. The director's cut also brings back the subplot of Sibylla's child, completely cut from the theatrical release, who also suffers from leprosy. When he begins to show signs of the disease she euthanizes him.

Chapter 6

1. Incidentally, many elements of the film commonly sourced as stemming directly from historical scholarship had already been translated to popular culture in Arthurian fiction well before Francioni's screenplay. Parke Godwin's *Firelord* (1980) depicts Arthur as half-Pict in order to ease his uniting of the native peoples in defense against the Saxons. The Guinevere of Kim Headlee's *Dawnflight* (1999) is a Pictish warrior princess. And perhaps most importantly, Diana L. Paxson's *The Hallowed Isle* series (1999, 2000) draws heavily upon the Sarmatian theory of Arthurian origins.

2. Note that in the *King Arthur* video game the Picts themselves employ this strategy of felling trees to entrap Arthur and Lancelot.

3. "All around them, the interconnected vines shot up with precision and speed, creating a webbed blockade that prevented the knights from exiting the forest in several directions" (Thompson 2004, 118).

4. Note too the same use of unheroic crossbows to kill three of Ridley Scott's seven "samurai" in the scene early in *Kingdom of Heaven* mentioned above.

5. I do not mean here to suggest that the Saxons and Christians are consciously in league in the film, merely that from their separate agendas both work toward the subjugation of the native Britons. All non–Roman groups in the film (the Picts, Sarmatians, and Saxons) treat the Catholic Church with unmitigated contempt.

6. Tom Shippey (2000, 134–38) treats the question of Manichaeism in Tolkien with much more finesse than I have done here, chiefly as a conflict in Tolkien himself between the doctrinally correct Boethian conception of the nonexistence of evil and his own observations of a world at war. "Tolkien was a more orthodox Christian than Lewis, and less tolerant of anything like heresy. Nevertheless, his education, his faith, and the circumstances of his time, all set up what seemed to be a

deep-seeded contradiction between Boethian and Manichaean opinions, between authority and experience, between evil as an absence ("the Shadow") and evil as a force ("the Dark Power"). In *The Lord of the Rings* this contradiction drives much of the plot" (134–35).

7. Quite recently a film (*The Pathfinder* d. Nispel 2007), indebted but in many ways superior to *King Arthur*, has adapted most of the Manichean elements discussed above to a conflict between native American Indians and Viking raiders. Its hero is also hybrid (a Viking reared by the Indians) and its villains larger than life ethnic cleansers against whom the natural world itself seems to conspire. Half of the Vikings die when they fall through the ice, while the rest plunge to their doom during an avalanche.

8. Again *The Pathfinder* has its Vikings express identical sentiments.

9. In *Braveheart* a different strategy of genetic engineering is pursued by the Norman-descended Edward I who says of the Scots, "if we can't wipe them out, we'll breed them out," and in pursuit of this goal he revives the fanciful custom of *ius prima noctis*. (Randall) Wallace, the film's screenwriter, turns this bit of genetic engineering around by having William Wallace father Edward III, thereby installing a bastard Scot upon the English throne more than two centuries before the ascension of James I of England and VI of Scotland.

10. A recent low-budget, independent film made in Puerto Rico, *Tainos: La Ultima Tribu* (2005) offers interesting points of comparison. Its premise relies upon a recent study finding that 62 percent of Puerto Ricans had some Taino strands in their DNA. This pre–Columbian tribe is definitively "medieval," traditionally believed to have been wiped out by disease when Columbus stopped here on his second voyage to the New World in 1493. The cast of characters embodies the contradictions inherent in *puertorriqueñidad*. The heroine, Sara (Christie Miro), is an anthropology student who recruits five friends to go with her on a trip to examine the Taino petroglyphs in the remote Mora Caves of Comerío. Sara adored her late grandfather but did not believe his contention that the Tainos were alive and well, living still in the interior of the island. Yabey, played by Josue Reyes, has a Taino name and leads a double life as a college student and as the heir apparent of the tribe's chief. His major nemesis is Harold (Danny Frat-

icelli), an alcoholic paramilitary control freak, apparently trained by the United States Army. Harold and his two late arriving comrades-in-arms are gun-crazed bullies, rapists, and murderers of children. Clearly they represent the American military presence in Puerto Rico, but the satire is made even more biting by the fact that these three loose cannons in fatigues and "Army" tee-shirts are themselves Puerto Rican. Sara is a lonely young woman, cut off from her past by the death of her mother and beloved grandfather. In doing archaeological work on the Tainos, she hopes to establish a connection with the past of her country and gain a deeper sense of her own cultural identity. The son of the chieftain of this last tribe of Tainos is "Yabey" whose apparent participation in the modern world is only a ruse, a lifeline to the outside world that permits the continued existence of a vital separateness. Sara ultimately marries Yabey, thereby providing the tribe with the required new genetic material that will prevent the disastrous results of inbreeding. The Manichean conflict here resides within Puerto Ricans themselves, between the occult preserve of a pure Taino heritage and the degradations of military base colonialism. Such genetic and genealogical fables of identity bespeak a longing to bridge the gaps of Puerto Rico's fractured past and to attach *puertorriqueñidad* to its imagined source in Taino culture, a source that the film supposes relatively undiluted by the post–Columbian influence, a genetic and cultural purity located somewhere in the heart of Puerto Rico.

Chapter 7

1. See Holsinger, *Neomedievalism, Neoconservatism, and the War on Terror* (1997): 37–84.

2. The image recalls medieval and early modern illustrations of the battle between good and evil taking place between an angel and a demon over a single human being.

3. Interestingly, Žižek's title (*The Plague of Fantasies*) is a quotation from Petrarch's *Secretum.*

4. For *Holy Blood, Holy Grail*, see Baigent, et. al. (1983); for *Templar Revelation*, see Picknett and Prince (1997).

5. See Žižek's *The Puppet and the Dwarf: The Perverse Core of Christianity* (2003).

Works Cited

Aberth, John. *A Knight at the Movies: Medieval History on Film*. New York: Routledge, 2003.

Ackroyd, Peter. *Albion: The Origins of the English Imagination*. New York: Anchor Books, 2002.

_____. *Chatterton*. London: Penguin Books, 1993.

Agamben, Giorgio. *States of Exception*. Trans. Kevin Attell. Chicago: University of Chicago Press, 2005.

Ali, Tariq. *The Clash of Fundamentalisms: Crusades, Jihad and Modernity*. London: Verso, 2002.

Allen, John L., Jr. *Opus Dei: An Objective Look behind the Myths and Reality of the Most Controversial Force in the Catholic Church*. New York: Doubleday, 2005.

Allen, M.D. *The Medievalism of Lawrence of Arabia*. University Park: Pennsylvania State University Press, 1991.

Andrew, Dudley, and Carole Cavanaugh. *Sansho Dayu*. London: British Film Institute Publishing, 2000.

Armstrong, Karen. *Holy War: The Crusades and Their Impact on Today's World*. New York: Doubleday, 1991.

Aronstein, Susan. *Hollywood Knights: Arthurian Cinema and the Politics of Nostalgia*. New York: Palgrave, 2005.

_____, and Nancy Coiner. "Twice Knightly: Democratizing the Middle Ages for Middle-Class America." *Medievalism in North America, Studies in Medievalism* 6 (1994): 212–31.

Astell, Ann W. *Joan of Arc and Sacrificial Authorship*. Notre Dame, IN: University of Notre Dame Press, 2003.

Auerbach, Erich. *Scenes from the Drama of European Literature*. Minneapolis: University of Minnesota Press, 1984.

Augustine, Saint. *City of God*. Vols. 8, 14, 24. Eds. Gerald G. Walsh, et al. New York: Fathers of the Church, 1950, 1952, 1954.

_____. *De civitate dei*. Ed. Bernardus Dombat and Alphonsus Kalb, 2 vols. *Corpus Christianorum, Series Latina*, 47, 48. Turnhout: Brepolis, 1955.

_____. *On Christian Doctrine*. Trans. D.W. Robertson, Jr. Indianapolis: Bobbs Merrill, 1958.

Baigent, Michael, Richard Leigh, and Henry Lincoln. *Holy Blood, Holy Grail*. New York: Dell, 1983.

Bakhtin, M. M. *The Dialogic Imagination: Four Essays*. Trans. Caryl Emerson and Michael Holquist. Austin: University of Texas Press, 1981.

_____. *Rabelais and His World*. Trans. Hélene Iswolsky. Bloomington: Indiana University Press, 1984. Original Russian copyright 1965, original English translation copyright 1968, Massachusetts Institute of Technology.

Baudrillard, Jean. *Simulacra and Simulation*. Trans. Sheila Faria Glaser. Ann Arbor: University of Michigan Press, 1994.

Baudry, Jean-Louis. "Ideological Effects of the Basic Cinema Apparatus." In *Narrative, Apparatus, Ideology: A Film Theory Reader*. Ed. Philip Rosen, 286–98. New York: Columbia University Press, 1986.

Benjamin, Walter. *Illuminations*. Ed. Hannah Arendt. Trans. Harry Zohn. New York: Schocken Books, 1968.

Benson, Larry D., ed. Revised by Edward D. Forster. *King Arthur's Death: The Middle English Stanzaic Morte Arthur and Alliterative Morte Arthur*. Kalamazoo, MI: Medieval Institute Publications, 1994.

Bergman, Ingmar. *Images: My Life in Film*. Trans. Marianne Ruuth. New York: Arcade Publishing, 1990.

Bernau, Anke. "Girls on Film: Medieval Virginity in the Cinema." In *The Medieval Hero on the Screen: Representations from Beowulf to Buffy*. Eds. Martha W. Driver and Sid Ray, 94–114. Jefferson, NC: McFarland, 2004.

Besson, Luc. *Images from* Joan of Arc. Paris: Gaumont, 1999.

Bhabha, Homi K. "Introduction." In *Black Skin/White Masks*. London: Pluto, 1986.

_____. *The Location of Culture*. London: Routledge, 1994.

Biddick, Kathleen. *The Shock of Medievalism*. Durham, NC: Duke University Press, 1998.

Bird, Robert. *Andrei Rublev*. London: British Film Institute Publishing, 2004.

Birkin, Andrew, and Luc Besson. *The Messenger: The Story of Joan of Arc*. Screenplay. http://www.hundland.com/scripts/The Messenger.txt.

Blaetz, Robin. *Visions of the Maid: Joan of Arc in American Film and Culture*. Charlottesville: University Press of Virginia, 2001.

Bolter, Jay David, and Richard Grusin. *Remediation: Understanding New Media*. Cambridge: MIT Press, 2000.

Boorman, John. *Adventures of a Suburban Boy*. London: Faber and Faber, 2004.

Bordwell, David. *Narration in the Fiction Film*. Madison: University of Wisconsin Press, 1985.

_____, Janet Staiger, and Kristin Thompson. *The Classic Hollywood Cinema: Film Style and Mode of Production to 1960*. New York: Columbia University Press, 1985.

Bowers, John M., ed. *The Canterbury Tales: Fifteenth Century Continuations and Additions*. Kalamazoo, MI: Medieval Institute Publications, 1992.

Bowie, Malcolm. *Lacan*. Cambridge, MA: Harvard University Press, 1993.

Bragg, Melvin. *The Seventh Seal/ Det Sjunde Inseglet*. London: British Film Institute Publishing, 1993.

Brewer, Derek, ed. *Chaucer: The Critical Heritage (1385–1837)*. Vol. 1. London: Routledge & Kegan Paul, 1978.

Burgoyne, Robert. "Memory, History and Digital Imagery in Contemporary Film." In *Memory and Popular Film*. Ed. Paul Grainge, 220–36. Manchester: Manchester University Press, 2003.

Burrow, J. A. *The Ages of Man: A Study in Medieval Writing and Thought*. Oxford: Oxford University Press, 1988.

Burt, Richard. "Getting Schmedieval: Of Manuscript and Film Prologues, Paratexts, and Parodies." Ed. R. A. Shoaf, guest eds. Richard Burt and Nickolas Haydock. *Exemplaria* 19.2 (2007): 1–22.

Carnes, Mark C., ed. *Past Imperfect: History According to the Movies*. New York: Henry Holt, 1995.

Cavalli-Sforza, Luigi Luca. *Genes, Peoples, and Languages*. Trans. Mark Seielstad. Berkeley: University Press of California, 2000.

Cavell, Stanley. *The World Viewed: Reflections on the Ontology of Cinema*. New York: Viking Press, 1971.

Chadwick, Elizabeth. *First Knight*. London: BoxTree, 1995.

Chaucer, Geoffrey. *The Riverside Chaucer*. Ed. Larry D. Benson. Boston: Houghton Mifflin, 1987.

Cohen, Jeffrey Jerome, ed. *The Postcolonial Middle Ages*. New York: Palgrave, 2000.

Coletti, Theresa. *Naming the Rose: Eco, Medieval Signs and Modern Theory*. Ithaca, NY: Cornell University Press, 1988.

Cook, David A. *A History of Narrative Film*. 4th ed. New York: Norton, 2004.

Cowie, Peter. *Ingmar Bergman*. London: Martin Secker & Warburg, 1982.

Crichton, Michael. *The Thirteenth Warrior* (original title *Eaters of the Dead*). New York: Ballantine, 1976.

_____. *Timeline*. New York: Knopf, 1999.

cummings, e.e. *Complete Poems: 1913–1962*. New York: Harcourt Brace Jovanovich, 1972.

Debord, Guy. *The Society of the Spectacle.* Trans. Donald Nicholson-Smith. New York: Zone Books, 1994.

Deleuze, Gilles. *Cinema 1: The Movement-Image.* Trans. Hugh Tomlinson and Barbara Habberjam. Minneapolis: University of Minnesota Press, 1986.

———. *Cinema 2: The Time-Image.* Trans. Hugh Tomlinson and Robert Galeta. Minneapolis: University of Minnesota Press, 1989.

———. *The Logic of Sense.* Trans. Mark Lester. New York: Columbia University Press, 1990.

de Pisan, Christine. *Christine de Pisan: Le Ditié de Jehanne d'Arc.* Eds. Angus J. Kennedy and Kenneth Varty. Oxford: Society for the Study of Medieval Languages and Literatures, 1977.

———. *The Selected Writings of Christine de Pizan.* Ed. Renate Blumenfeld-Kosinski. New York: Norton, 1997.

Derrida, Jacques. *The Postcard: From Socrates to Freud and Beyond.* Trans. Alan Bass. Chicago: University of Chicago Press, 1987.

Dinshaw, Carolyn. "Getting Medieval: *Pulp Fiction*, Gawain, Foucault." In *The Book and the Body.* Eds. Dolores Warwick Frese and Katherine O'Brien O'Keeffe, 116–63. Notre Dame, IN: University of Notre Dame Press, 1997.

———. *Getting Medieval: Sexualities and Communities, Pre- and Postmodern.* Durham, NC: Duke University Press, 1999.

Eco, Umberto. *Faith in Fakes: Travels in Hyperreality.* Trans. William Weaver. London: Vintage, 1998.

———. *Foucault's Pendulum.* Trans. William Weaver. New York: Harcourt, Brace, Jovanovich, 1989.

———. *The Name of the Rose.* Trans. William Weaver. New York: Harcourt, Brace, Jovanovich, 1983.

———. *The Open Work.* Trans. Anna Cancogni. Cambridge, MA: Harvard University Press, 1989.

Edbury, Peter W. *The Conquest of Jerusalem and the Third Crusade.* Burlington, VT: Ashgate, 1998.

Edwardes, Charlotte. "Ridley Scott's New Crusades Film 'Panders to Osama bin Laden.'" *Telegraph,* January 18, 2004.

Eisenstein, Sergei. *Film Form and Film Sense.* Cleveland: Meridian, 1957.

Eliot, T.S. *Collected Poems, 1909–1962.* New York: Harcourt, Brace and World, 1970.

Ellis, Steve. "Popular Chaucer." *Studies in Medievalism* 9 (1997): 26–43.

Escrivá, Josemaria. *The Way.* New York: Image, 2006.

Ewen, Elizabeth, and Stuart Ewen. *Typecasting: On the Arts and Sciences of Human Inequality, A History of the Dominant Ideas.* New York: Seven Stories Press, 2006.

Fanon, Frantz. *Black Skin, White Masks.* Trans. Constance Farrington. New York: Grove Press, 1991.

Fay, Elizabeth A. *Romantic Medievalism: History and the Romantic Literary Ideal.* New York: Palgrave Macmillan, 2002.

Federico, Sylvia. *New Troy: Fantasies of Empire in the Late Middle Ages* Minneapolis: University of Minnesota Press, 2003.

Finke, Laurie A., and Martin B. Shichtman. *King Arthur and the Myth of History.* Gainesville: University Press of Florida, 2004.

Fisk, Robert. "*Kingdom of Heaven*: Why Ridley Scott's Story of the Crusades Struck Such a Chord in a Lebanese Cinema." *The Independent,* June 20, 2005.

Flaxman, Gregory, ed. *The Brain Is the Screen: Deleuze and the Philosophy of Cinema.* Minneapolis: University of Minnesota Press, 2000.

Fox, Denton, ed. *The Poems of Robert Henryson.* Oxford: Clarendon Press, 1981.

Foucault, Michel. *This Is Not a Pipe.* Trans. James Harkness. Berkeley: University of California Press, 1982.

Fraioli, Deborah A. *Joan of Arc: The Early Debate.* Rochester, NY: Boydell Press, 2000.

Frantzen, Allen J. *Desire for Origins: New Language, Old English and Teaching the Tradition.* New Brunswick, NJ: Rutgers University Press, 1990.

Franzioni, David. Interview of David Franzioni with John Matthews. *Arthuriana* 14.3 (2004): 115–20.

Freud, Sigmund. *Civilization and Its Discontents.* Trans. James Strachey. New York: Norton, 1961.

_____. *The Freud Reader.* Ed. Peter Gay. New York: Norton, 1989.

_____. "The Uncanny." In *Norton Anthology of Theory and Criticism.* Ed. Vincent B. Leitch, 929–51. New York: Norton, 2001.

Friedberg, Anne. *The Virtual Window: From Alberti to Microsoft.* Cambridge, MA: MIT Press, 2006.

Gablik, Suzi. *Magritte.* New York: Thames and Hudson, 1985.

Gabrielli, Francesco. *Arab Historians of the Crusades.* Trans. E.J. Costello. Berkeley: University of California Press, 1957.

Ganim, John. *Medievalism and Orientalism: Three Essays on Literature, Architecture and Cultural Identity.* New York: Palgrave Macmillan, 2005.

Gardner, John. *Grendel.* New York: Knopf, 1971.

_____. *The Life and Times of Geoffrey Chaucer.* New York: Vintage Books, 1977.

Geary, Patrick J. *The Myth of Nations: The Medieval Origins of Europe.* Princeton, NJ: Princeton University Press, 2002.

Genette, Gérard. *Paratexts: Thresholds of Interpretation.* Trans. Jane E. Lewin and Richard Macksey. Cambridge: Cambridge University Press, 1997.

Geoffrey of Monmouth. *History of the Kings of Britain.* Trans. Lewis Thorpe. New York: Penguin Books, 1966.

Gerald of Wales. *Journey through Wales and the Description of Wales.* Trans. Lewis Thorpe. New York: Penguin, 1978.

Glare, P.G.W. *Oxford Latin Dictionary.* Oxford: Clarendon Press, 1976.

Harries, Dan. *Film Parody.* London: British Film Institute Publishing, 2001.

Harty, Kevin J., ed. *Cinema Arthuriana: Twenty Essays.* Jefferson, NC: McFarland, 2002.

_____, ed. *King Arthur on Film: New Essays on Arthurian Cinema.* Jefferson, NC: McFarland, 1999a.

_____. *The Reel Middle Ages: American, Western and Eastern European, Middle Eastern and Asian Films about Medieval Europe.* Jefferson, NC: McFarland, 1999b.

_____. "Review of *King Arthur.*" *Arthuriana* 14.3 (2004): 121–23.

Hayden, John, ed. *Walter Scott: The Critical Heritage.* New York: Routledge, 1995.

Haydock, Nickolas. "Remaking Chaucer: Influence and Interpretation in Late Medieval Poetry." Ph.D. dissertation, University of Iowa, 1994.

_____. "Treasonous Founders and Pious Seducers: Aeneas, Gawain, and Aporetic Romance." In *Sir Gawain and the Green Knight and the Classical Tradition: Essays on the Ancient Antecedents.* Ed. E. L. Risden. Jefferson, NC: McFarland, 2006.

Hayward, Susan. "Jeanne d'Arc: High Epic Style and Politicising Camp." In *Luc Besson: Filmmaker as Bard.* Eds. S. Hayward and P. Powrie. Manchester: Manchester University Press, forthcoming.

Heng, Geraldine. *Empire of Magic: Medieval Romance and the Politics of Cultural Fantasy.* New York: Columbia University Press, 2005.

Higham, N.J. *King Arthur: Myth-Making and History.* London: Routledge, 2002.

Hillenbrand, Carole. *The Crusades: Islamic Perspectives.* New York: Routledge, 1999.

Hofstadter, Richard. *The Paranoid Style in American Politics and Other Essays.* Cambridge, MA: Harvard University Press, 1952.

Holsinger, Bruce. *The Premodern Condition: Medievalism and the Making of Theory.* Chicago: University of Chicago Press, 2005.

Hutcheon, Linda. *A Poetics of Postmodernism: History, Theory, Fiction.* New York: Routledge, 1998.

_____. *The Politics of Postmodernism.* New York: Routledge, 1989.

Ikegami, Eiko. *The Taming of the Samurai: Honorific Individualism and the Making of Modern Japan.* Cambridge, MA: Harvard University Press, 1995.

Jackson, Kenneth Hurlstone. *Language and History in Early Britain.* Edinburgh: Edinburgh University Press, 1953.

Jakobsen, Roman. "Two Aspects of Language and Two Types of Aphasic Disturbances." In *Fundamentals of Language.* Eds. Roman Jakobsen and Morris Halle. The Hague: Mouton, 1956.

Jameson, Fredric. *Postmodernism, or the Cultural Logic of Late Capitalism.* Durham, NC: Duke University Press, 1991.

Jansen, Marius B., ed. *Warrior Rule in Japan.*

Cambridge: Cambridge University Press, 1995.

Jenkins, Henry. *Convergence Culture: Where Old and New Media Collide.* New York: New York University Press, 2006.

Jenkins, Jacqueline. "First Knights and Common Men: Masculinity in American Arthurian Film." In *King Arthur on Film.* Ed. Kevin J. Harty, 81–95. Jefferson, NC: McFarland, 1999a.

Jewers, Caroline. 2007. "Mission Historical, or '[T]here were a hell of a lot of knights': Ethnicity and Alterity in Jerry Bruckheimer's *King Arthur.*" In *Race, Class, and Gender in 'Medieval' Cinema.* Eds. Lynn T. Ramey and Tyson Pugh, 91–106. New York: Palgrave Macmillan, 2007.

Jones, Terry. *Chaucer's Knight: A Portrait of a Medieval Mercenary.* Baton Rouge: Louisiana State University Press, 1980.

Jung, C.G. *Four Archetypes: Mother, Rebirth, Spirit, Trickster.* Trans. R.F.C. Hull. Princeton, NJ: Princeton University Press, 1959, 1969.

Keathley, Christian. *Cinephilia and History, or the Wind in the Trees.* Bloomington: Indiana University Press, 2006.

Keen, Maurice. *Chivalry.* New Haven, CT: Yale University Press, 1984.

Kinsley, James, ed. *The Poems of William Dunbar.* Oxford: Clarendon Press, 1979.

Kracauer, Siegfried. *From Caligari to Hitler: A Psychological History of the German Film.* Princeton, NJ: Princeton University Press, 1947, 2004.

_____. *Theory of Film: The Redemption of Physical Reality.* London: Oxford University Press, 1960.

Landsberg, Alison. "Prosthetic Memory: *Total Recall* and *Blade Runner.*" In *Cyberspace/Cyberbodies/Cyberpunk: Cultures of Technological Embodiment.* Eds. Mike Featherstone and Roger Burrows, 175–89. London: Sage, 1995.

Landy, Marcia. 1996. *Cinematic Uses of the Past.* Minneapolis: University of Minnesota Press, 1996.

_____, ed. *The Historical Film: History and Memory in Media.* New Brunswick, NJ: Rutgers University Press, 2001.

Lerer, Seth. *Chaucer and His Readers: Imagining the Author in Late-Medieval England.*

Princeton, NJ: Princeton University Press, 1993.

Levi-Strauss, Claude. *The Savage Mind.* Chicago: University of Chicago Press, 1966.

Lewis, Bernard. *Islam and the West.* Oxford: Oxford University Press, 1994.

Lindley, Arthur. "Once, Present and Future Kings: *Kingdom of Heaven* and the Multitemporality of Medieval Film." In *Race, Class and Gender in 'Medieval' Cinema.* Eds. Lynn T. Ramey and Tyson Pugh, 15–30. New York: Palgrave Macmillan, 2007.

Littleton, C. Scott. "Some Possible Arthurian Themes in Japanese Mythology and Folklore." *Journal of Folklore Research* 20 (1983): 67–82.

_____. "Yamato-Takeru: An 'Arthurian' Hero in Japanese Tradition." *Asian Folklore Studies* 54 (1995): 259–74.

_____, and Linda A. Malcor. *From Scythia to Camelot: A Radical Reassessment of the Legends of King Arthur, the Knights of the Round Table and the Holy Grail.* New York: Routledge, 1994.

Lupack, Alan. Review of *King Arthur. Arthuriana* 14.3 (2004): 123–25.

Lyotard, Jean-François. *The Postmodern Condition: A Report on Knowledge.* Trans. Geoff Bennington and Brian Masumi. Minneapolis: University of Minnesota Press, 1984.

Maalouf, Amin. *The Crusades through Arab Eyes.* Trans. Jon Rothschild. New York: Schocken Books, 1984.

MacDonald Fraser, George. *The Hollywood History of the World: From* One Million Years B.C. *to* Apocalypse Now. New York: Fawcett Columbine, 1988.

MacDougall, Hugh A. *Racial Myth in English History: Trojans, Teutons, and Anglo-Saxons.* Hanover, NH: University Press of New England, 1982.

Magoun, Francis P. "The Theme of the Beasts of Battle." *Neuphilologische Mitteilungen* 56 (1955): 81–90.

Malory, Sir Thomas. *Le Morte Darthur.* Ed. Steven H.A. Shepherd. New York: Norton, 2004.

Manovich, Lev. "What Is Digital Cinema?" In *The Digital Dialectic: New Essays on New Media.* Ed. Peter Lunenfeld.

Cambridge, MA: Harvard University Press, 2000.

Marcus, Jonathan. "A Small Matter of Crusader History." http://news.bbc.co.uk/2/hi/middle_east/4544173.stm.

Matthews, David O. "Speaking to Chaucer: The Poet and the Nineteenth Century Academy." *Studies in Medievalism* 9 (1997): 5–25.

Matthews, Jack. *The Battle of Brazil.* New York: Crown Publishing, 1987.

Maxwell, Ron. "The Messenger: Dumbed Down Dame, Is It Poetic License to Kill?" http://www.ronmaxwell.com.

McDiarmid, Matthew P., ed. *Hary's Wallace.* Edinburgh: William Blackwood, 1969.

McHale, Brian. *Postmodernist Fiction.* London: Methuen, 1987.

Meltzer, Françoise. *For Fear of the Fire: Joan of Arc and the Limits of Subjectivity.* Chicago: University of Chicago Press, 2001.

Menocal, María Rosa. *The Ornament of the World: How Muslims, Jews, and Christians Created a Culture of Tolerance in Medieval Spain.* Boston: Little Brown, 2002.

Metz, Christian. *The Imaginary Signifier: Psychoanalysis and the Cinema.* Trans. Celia Britton, Annwyl Williams, Ben Brewster, and Alfred Guzzetti. Bloomington: Indiana University Press, 1982.

Michelet, Jules. *Joan of Arc by Jules Michelet.* Trans. Albert Guérard. Ann Arbor: University of Michigan Press, 1957.

Mitchell, W.J.T. *Iconology: Image, Text, Ideology.* Chicago: University of Chicago Press, 1986.

_____. *Picture Theory.* Chicago: University of Chicago Press, 1994.

_____. *What Do Pictures Want?: The Lives and Loves of Images.* Chicago: University of Chicago Press, 2005.

Morgan, Gwendolyn. "Modern Mystics, Medieval Saints." In *Studies in Medievalism 12: Film and Fiction: Reviewing the Middle Ages.* Eds. Tom Shippey and Martin Arnold, 39–55. Cambridge: D. S. Brewer, 2002.

Mulvey, Laura. "Visual Pleasure and Narrative Cinema." *Screen* 16. 3 (1975): 6–18.

_____. *Visual and Other Pleasures.* London: Macmillan, 1989.

Myers, Tony. *Slavoj Žižek.* London: Routledge, 2003.

Paden, William D. "Reconstructing the Middle Ages: The Monk's Sermon in *The Seventh Seal.*" In *Medievalism in the Modern World: Essays in Honour of Leslie J. Workman.* Eds. Richard Utz and Tom Shippey, 287–306. Turnhout, Belgium: Brepolis, 1998.

Pearsall, Derek. *The Life of Chaucer: A Critical Biography.* Oxford: Blackwell, 1992.

Phillips, Jonathan. *The Fourth Crusade and the Sack of Constantinople.* New York: Penguin Books, 2004.

Phillips, Patrick. "The Film Spectator." In *An Introduction to Film Studies.* Ed. Jill Nelmes, 129–208. New York: Routledge, 1999.

_____. "Genre, Star and Auteur — Critical Approaches to Hollywood Cinema." In *An Introduction to Film Studies.* Ed. Jill Nelmes, 129–208. New York: Routledge, 1999.

Picknett, Lynn, and Clive Prince. *The Templar Revelation: Secret Guardians of the True Identity of Christ.* New York: Simon and Schuster, 1997.

Pinti, Daniel J., ed. *Writing after Chaucer: Essential Readings in Chaucer and the Fifteenth Century.* New York: Garland, 1998.

Prince, Steven. *The Warrior's Camera: The Cinema of Akira Kurosawa.* Princeton, NJ: Princeton University Press, 1991.

Ramey, Lynn T., and Tyson Pugh, eds. *Race, Class and Gender in "Medieval" Cinema.* New York: Palgrave Macmillan, 2007.

Reid, Howard. *Arthur the Dragon King: The Barbaric Roots of Britain's Greatest Legend.* London: Headline, 2001.

Renson, Stanley A., ed. *The Political Psychology of the Gulf War: Leaders, Publics, and the Process of the Conflict.* Pittsburgh: University of Pittsburgh Press, 1993.

Reston, Jr., James. *Warriors of God: Richard the Lionheart and Saladin in the Third Crusade.* New York: Doubleday, 2001.

Riley-Smith, Jonathan. *The Crusades: A History.* New Haven, CT: Yale University Press, 1987, 2005.

_____. "Jihad Crusaders: What an Osama bin Laden Means by 'Crusade.'" *The National Review.* http://nationalreview.com/comment/riley-smith200401050839.asp

_____, ed. *The Oxford History of the Crusades.* Oxford: Oxford University Press, 1995.

_____. "Religious Warriors: Reinterpreting the Crusades." *The Economist*, December 23, 1995. Also at http://grailwerk.com/docs/economistarticle.html.

Rodowick, D.N. *Gilles Deleuze's Time Machine*. Durham, NC: Duke University Press, 1997.

Rollins, Peter C. *Hollywood as Historian: American Film in a Cultural Context*. Lexington: University Press of Kentucky, 1983.

Rose, Margaret. "Post-Modern Pastiche." *British Journal of Aesthetics* 31.1 (1991): 26–38.

Rosen, Philip. *Change Mummified: Cinema, Historicity, Theory*. Minneapolis: University of Minnesota Press, 2001.

Rosenstone, Robert A. *History on Film/Film on History*. New York: Pearson Longman, 2006.

_____, ed. *Revisioning History: Film and the Construction of a New Past*. Princeton, NJ: Princeton University Press, 1995a.

_____. *Visions of the Past: The Challenge of Film to our Idea of History*. Cambridge, MA: Harvard University Press, 1995b.

Runciman, Steven. *A History of the Crusades*. 3 vols. Cambridge: Cambridge University Press, 1951–1953.

Sackville-West, Vita. *Saint Joan of Arc*. New York: Grove Press, 1936.

Said, Edward W. *Culture and Imperialism*. New York: Vintage Books, 1994.

_____. *Orientalism*. New York: Vintage Books, 1979.

Sanello, Frank. *Reel v. Real: How Hollywood Turns Fact into Fiction*. New York: Taylor Trade Publishing, 2003.

Saul, Nigel. "Chaucer and Gentility." In *Chaucer's England: Literature in Historical Context*. Ed. Barbara A. Hanawalt. Minneapolis: University of Minnesota Press, 1992.

Scott, James. *Domination and the Arts of Resistance: Hidden Transcripts*. New Haven, CT: Yale University Press, 1990.

Scott, Sir Walter. *The Talisman*. Doylestown, PA: Wildside Press. Reprint of the 1832 edition.

Sebeok, Thomas, ed. *Carnival!. Approaches to Semiotics*. New York: Mouton, 1984.

Shippey, Tom. "Fuqua's *King Arthur*: More Mythmaking in America." *Exemplaria* 19.2 (2007): 310–26.

_____. *J.R.R. Tolkien: Author of the Century*. London: HarperCollins, 2000.

Shutters, Lynn. "Vikings through the Eyes of an Arab Ethnographer: Constructions of the Other in *The Thirteenth Warrior*." In *Race, Class, and Gender in Medieval Cinema*. Eds. Lynn T. Ramsey and Tyson Pugh, 75–90. New York: Palgrave Macmillan, 2007.

Spearing, A.C. *Medieval to Renaissance in English Poetry*. Cambridge: Cambridge University Press, 1985.

Spencer, Robert. *The Politically Incorrect Guide to Islam*. Washington, DC: Regnery Publishing, 2005.

Stam, Robert. *Film Theory: An Introduction*. Oxford: Blackwell, 2000.

Stewart, Mary. *The Merlin Trilogy*. New York: Eos, 2004.

Strohm, Paul. *Social Chaucer*. Cambridge, MA: Harvard University Press, 1989.

Sullivan, Karen. *The Interrogation of Joan of Arc*. Minneapolis: University of Minnesota Press, 1999.

Sykes, Bryan. *Saxons, Vikings, and Celts: The Genetic Roots of Britain and Ireland*. New York: Norton, 2006.

_____, *The Seven Daughters of Eve: The Science That Reveals Our Genetic Ancestry*. New York: Norton, 2001.

Tarkovsky, Andrei. *Sculpting in Time: Reflections on the Cinema*. Trans. Kitty Hunter-Blair. Austin: University of Texas Press, 1986.

Thompson, Bob. "Hollywood on Crusade." *Washington Post*, May 1, 2005.

Thompson, Frank. *King Arthur*. New York: Hyperion, 2004.

Tolkien, J.R.R. "*Beowulf*: The Monsters and the Critics" (1936). Reprinted in *Interpretations of Beowulf: A Critical Anthology*. Ed. R.D. Fulk, 14–44. Bloomington: University of Indiana Press, 1991.

Toplin, Robert Brent. *Reel History: In Defense of Hollywood*. Lawrence: University Press of Kansas, 2002.

Twain, Mark. *The Personal Recollections of Joan of Arc*. Mineola, NY: Dover Publications, 2002.

Umland, Rebecca A., and Samuel J. Umland.

The Use of Arthurian Legend in Hollywood Film: From Connecticut Yankees to Fisher Kings. London: Greenwood Press, 1996.

Vinaver, Eugene, ed. *The Works of Sir Thomas Malory.* 3 vols. Oxford: Clarendon Press, 1947.

Wallace, Randall. *Braveheart.* New York: Simon and Schuster, 1995.

Waxman, Sharon. "Historical Epic Is Focus of a Copyright Dispute." *Los Angeles Times,* March 29, 2005.

Wells, H.G. *The Time Machine.* New York: Dover Publications, 1995.

Weston, Jessie. *From Ritual to Romance.* New York: Cosimo Publishing, 1920, 2005.

Williams, Raymond. *Keywords: A Vocabulary of Culture and Society.* New York: Oxford University Press, 1985.

Wojtyla, Karol (Pope John Paul II). *Sign of Contradiction.* New York: The Seabury Press, 1979.

Woods, William F. "Authenticating Realism in Medieval Film." In *The Medieval Hero on Screen: Representations from Beowulf to Buffy.* Eds. Martha W. Driver and Sid Ray, 38–51. Jefferson, NC: McFarland, 2004.

Wyke, Maria. *Projecting the Past: Ancient Rome, Cinema and History.* New York: Routledge, 1997.

Yoshimoto, Mitsuhiro. *Kurosawa.* Durham, NC: Duke University Press, 2000.

Žižek, Slavoj., ed. *The Fright of Real Tears: Krzystof Kieslowski between Theory and Post-theory.* London: British Film Institute Publications, 2001.

_____. *How to Read Lacan.* New York: Norton, 2006.

_____. *Looking Awry: An Introduction to Jacques Lacan through Popular Culture.* Cambridge, MA: MIT Press, 1991.

_____. *The Plague of Fantasies.* London: Verso, 1998.

_____. *The Puppet and the Dwarf: The Perverse Core of Christianity.* Cambridge, MA: MIT Press, 2003.

_____. *The Sublime Object of Ideology.* London: Verso, 1989.

_____. *The Ticklish Subject: The Absent Centre of Political Ontology.* New York: Verso, 1999.

Index